Rainbow Loom Fun: A Beginner's Guide to Rainbow Loom with Beautiful and Easy to Follow Patterns Included

Disclaimer

The contents of this guide were drafted based on extensive research and testing of rainbow loom projects. Although every effort has been made to ensure that this guide is as accurate and proper as possible, the writer and publisher of this guide cannot guarantee that every aspect of this publication can work as desired.

The writer and publisher of the guide cannot be held liable for any concerns or liabilities that may come about as a result of misusing the data listed in this guide.

This guide has not been endorsed or approved of by any entities involved with the production, usage or resale of rainbow loom-related products.

Summary

This book is all about the world of rainbow loom fashion and how you can use it to your advantage. This covers information on how the rainbow loom works and the types of materials that you will need in order to complete any kind of loom project. You will also learn about how to prepare a basic bracelet. Instructions on how to work with other design options are included in this guide as well.

You will also learn about what you should be doing when preparing to make something on your own. There are also a few questions and answers that will be covered later on in the book. The goal of this book is to help you learn how to make things with the rainbow loom so you can be empowered to come up with your own special designs.

Table of Contents

Disclaimer 2

Summary 3

Introduction 5

What is the Rainbow Loom? 8

   What makes it special? 10

Materials to Use 13

   Standard Base 13

   Hook 15

   Bands 17

   C-Clips 18

Preparation Tips 21

Making a Basic Bracelet 25

Great Styles to Play With 34

   Single Band Bracelet 34

   Squared Single 37

   Rainbow Pattern 39

   Fishtail 40

   Railroad 43

   Diamond 45

Frequently Asked Questions 47

Conclusion 51

Back cover description for the book 52

Introduction

Are you interested in making your very own bracelets or necklaces? These are great fashion accessories in their own right but sometimes they can mean a whole lot more if you can make these things on your own. Today you can use a unique product called a rainbow loom to create all sorts of amazingly varied and beautiful fashion accessories.

This guide will provide you with plenty of details on how to create different types of fun-looking and vibrant bracelets, necklaces and other items. You will learn about just what it is about a rainbow loom that makes it effective and useful. You will see that the concept of the rainbow loom is very easy to work with.

This guide will also help you learn about the materials that you will need to make your rainbow loom project all the more effective. These include many great materials that are easy to arrange and set up with care. You will learn about how to use these materials so it will not be too hard for you to create something amazing.

The traditional routines and steps that you will utilize when working with a rainbow loom are also covered in this guide. You will even learn about some attractive design options that you can use on your own right now. Each design choice is clearly designed and features some simple steps that can quickly be followed.

This is a great guide to explore if you are looking to create your own special arts and crafts items. The rainbow loom will allow you to create all sorts of fun things that you can wear anywhere. The only limit there is with regards to creating some fun things comes from your personal imagination.

CAUTION!

While the materials that are used in the process of creating great things with your rainbow loom are safe and easy to handle, you might want to watch for how you are going to use some of the utensils. These utensils can be dangerous to some people if not used properly as people can easily hurt themselves by poking at things too hard. Also, if you are a parent then you must make sure you supervise your children as they work with it. This is to ensure that they will know what to do without being at risk of harm.

If children are going to use this then it helps to make sure they are old enough. This is for those who are eight years of age or older as the bands that you will use can be interpreted as choking hazards.

Do not keep any of the materials used in this guide around pets. While the bands are non-toxic, they are indigestible, thus meaning that it can be a challenge for the pet to handle such a material after swallowing it.

Also, the bands that will be used around a loom will create a good deal of force as they will be under tension. While it's true that these bands will not shoot off if the process for creating something is handled the right way, you must still be cautious as rubber bands that are placed under a good deal of tension might create a good deal of force.

What is the Rainbow Loom?

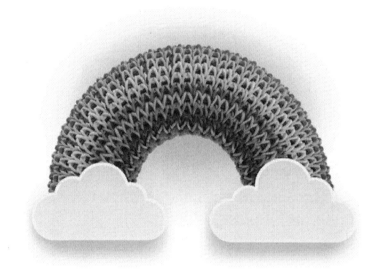

The rainbow loom is a special type of plastic loom that can be used to create bracelets, charms and other fun fashion accessories on your own. This loom was originally created in 2011 by Cheong Choon Ng. He created the concept of the rainbow loom after noticing his children creating bracelets with rubber bands.

This cause him to develop a unique system that entails the use of a special rack that features a series of pushpin-like materials. These are materials that bands can be strung along to get separate bands to link and connect with each other.

The Rainbow Loom product that he created with his children was designed to make it very easy for people to create different types of bracelets and other accessories. The product has become amazingly successful in that it has sold more than eight million units around the world as well as about forty million packets of rubber bands that can be used with the loom. It has become so popular that some competitors have come about and tried to create their own copies of the product, risking the potential for patent infringement in doing so.

What makes it special?

The concept of the rainbow loom is a simple product. It is one that makes it to where you can easily get different fashion accessories created by just using a simple plastic loom. You just have to get some bands that are specifically made for it together and then string them around the loom.

However, there is more to this than what meets the eye. The biggest advantage that comes from using the rainbow loom is that it is a product that makes it very easy for people to create all of these items. What used to take a long time to create is now easy to build thanks in part to this unique material.

Today you can quickly gather different bands together and string them around in many forms and patterns to create an extensive variety of fun products. These are easy to create and can provide you with anything that you want to create. You can choose whatever colors and patterns you want to stick with while playing with the rainbow loom.

In fact, you might be amazed at the extensive variety of colors for you to choose from while you are creating your own rainbow loom materials. You can choose from different options that will provide you with some entertaining looks that are different from what you might expect to find in some spots.

What's more is that the designs can be so unique that you could sell or trade these bracelets and other items to different people. You can create your own options with your specific special color and pattern themes and then sell them to others if desired.

It is clear that the rainbow loom is a big hit among people these days. The fact that you can do anything you want with it just makes it all the more amazing.

It should not cost too much to get rainbow loom items either. A typical rainbow loom starter kit can cost about $15 to get. You can also buy a good number of bands for less than five dollars on average. You could even get close to two thousand of these bands for that amount of money.

If you prepare whatever you want to do for your desires then you can see that it will be very easy for you to create some unique items with the use of your loom. You can use the loom to quickly create some attractive and handsome features that you know will be attractive and ideal to hold.

Materials to Use

It is not too difficult for you to get the materials that you need ready for use when getting some great rainbow loom items created. Here's a quick look at what you need to get in order to create stuff on your own with a rainbow loom.

Standard Base

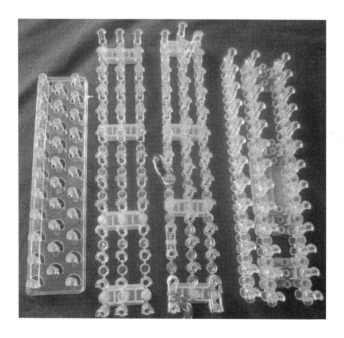

A standard base will be required at the start of the loom process. You can use a standard base to string your bands around.

This base will typically be made with three columns of pegs. These will extend outward in a vertical position and provide you with more than enough coverage for whatever it is you want to work with.

The base will have a series of pegs all around it to ensure that the bands will be strung out as required.

You will notice that there are a few dark-colored items strung around a typical base. These dark items that are found at the bottom parts of a base are typically used with the intention of holding it together. You can also take them apart to help you remove the bands from the loom when you are done. You should be careful when getting the base to work for you though so you don't put yourself at risk of having a hard time trying to get your base to work for you.

The picture that you see above should give you a good idea as to what to expect out of such a base. You might also notice here that there are a few openings around the bottom parts of some of these looms. These openings are designed to allow you to connect several looms to each other, thus giving you the option to create much larger works of art.

This should be sized to make it very easy for you to get the bands that you have ready and capable of being strung up quite well. However, the other materials that you will have to use can be important just as well.

Hook

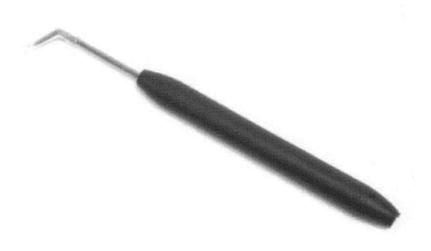

The hook that you will be using in the rainbow loom process can really make a difference in terms of how well your project is going to run. The hook is a material that will help you to string the bands around all around the body of the loom. It is a handheld item that is typically small and should not be too hard to use and manage.

A traditional loom hook will be needed in the process. A loom hook is an item that has a small curved tip at the end. The curved tip will stick right into the band and can help you string out the band to get it up to another peg or through another band.

It should not be too hard for you to find a good hook here. However, you should still be very careful when getting your hook to work for you. You must handle it properly and avoid holding it in a manner that makes it to where you could easily poke someone with it. Some hooks are designed with points that are deep and can hurt anyone. In fact, if you are going to allow kids to make their own rainbow loom products then it helps to watch and see how they use their hooks to ensure that no one will get hurt by anything in the process.

You can also choose to work with a small crochet hook if you are interested. This smaller type of hook can be designed with a better point that is a little deeper and slimmer in its size. It may be harder for anyone to hurt themselves with such a hook but it is still critical for you to watch for how any child who uses this works with the hook so you will not be at risk of injuries in some way.

Bands

You will clearly need some bands at this stage in the process. After all, you need to have plenty of bands to work with if you're going to get a good series of bracelets and other items set up through the loom.

The bands that are used in the rainbow loom are typically a little smaller in size than a traditional rubber bad like what you'd find wrapped around a newspaper or something else that needs to be rolled up. However, the bands that a rainbow loom typically uses will be much stronger than what you'd get out of traditional rubber bands.

Rainbow loom bands are known to be dense. That is, they are packed in well to the point where the potential for something to break apart will be rather minimal. This should make for something that is effective and useful for your needs.

In fact, these bands are available in a massive variety of colors. You can choose to get a standard bag that has an assortment of various colors or you can go along with individual bands that have just one color. Whatever it is you want to get, you can rest assured that it will be very easy for you to get some good bands ready for whatever it is you want to craft.

C-Clips

A circlip, or C-clip as it is also known, is a popular type of clip that can be used to fasten different materials. It is a metal ring that has a C-shaped body to it. The open ends will allow you to snap items in place and work within a machined groove to allow it to rotate without moving far too much.

These clips can help you out with fastening whatever you want to use. You will use it to secure the entire set to where both ends will be fully connected. This can easily help you finish the job after you are done creating something.

You should make sure the clips are attached and secured with care no matter what you want to get out of the setup. This should be done to give you a little more help with anything that you want to establish and create with ease.

These are all materials that can be very easy to use when getting different types of bracelets, necklaces and other items created with care. It's not too hard to get them all together and to have them work.

In fact, it can be very easy for you to get all of these different types of materials from a traditional arts and crafts store. Places like AC Moore and Michael's can easily provide you with more than enough options to choose from. Of course, there is a countless number of online retailers out there right now that can provide you with some good items to have.

Preparation Tips

If you are going to create your very own bracelets or other items with your rainbow loom then you need to follow a few sensible tips. These are good tips that can help you get the most out of your project.

Keep all of your bands organized.
You need to get every single band for your loom organized the right way. That is, you have to do a whole lot more than just get all your bands stored in a simple case. You have to get them all divided up as well as possible.

A simple carrying case that has plenty of compartments will always be worthwhile. A carrying case can come with such things as a individual spaces for different colors plus sections for C-rings and other materials that you might use. This can really do well for your needs so it will not be too hard for you to stay organized and prepared for when you're looking to get a great project up and running.

You can easily buy a carrying case at any arts and crafts store. Some rainbow loom products will come with their own cases with individual dividers.

Check every band that you use first.

While it is true that the bands you can use in your rainbow loom project can be very effective and useful, they may still be susceptible to tears and other threats. These tears can be bothersome and can cause a band to snap apart.

You need to be certain that your bands are sturdy and will not break apart all that easily. You must watch to see how your bands are designed and make sure you check each option for tears, cuts, holes or other things that might get in the way.

These bands are sturdy but there's always that potential that one or two bands might not have been made properly during the manufacturing process. After all, millions of of these bands can technically be made within one factory in a single day.

Work with a large flat surface.

Always prepare your loom projects on a flat surface that has more than enough space. A good kitchen table or desk can be a great spot to work with.

You could technically work on the floor if you wanted to as well. However, some floors may be designed with carpeted materials that may be a little too soft. The floor must be flat and clean if you're actually going to work on that surface.

Choose the colors that you want before starting.

Think about how you're going to design your necklace or bracelet or other item before you start. You need to be certain that you've got more than enough bands in the colors that you want to work with.

On a related note, think about the number of bands that you will have to use. This is to keep you from running out.

Don't be afraid to have a few extra bands just in case. It is better to have some bands that are left over than it is to run out. (Having some extra bands can also help in the event that a band or two breaks for any reason.)

Make sure you finish your project before going on to a new one.

As good of an idea as it can be to work on many projects, you work on just one project at a time. This is to ensure that you can actually finish off whatever you want to do. If you work on far too many projects at once then you will lose track of what you are doing.

With all of these points in mind, it is time to take a look at what you can do in order to get your project to run the right way. Let's take a look at a basic routine that you can use right now.

Making a Basic Bracelet

The following section is devoted to showing you how to work with a basic bracelet. This is the most common type of project that you can utilize and is a good way for you to start with the process of using the loom.

This routine can work with pretty much any color you want. This is just going to help you understand how to work with the basics that come with creating your very own bracelet.

1. **Gather the materials that are needed for the bracelet.**

   Refer to the appropriate part of this guide to see what you need to get. Don't forget to prepare your plans for getting a bracelet ready although this chapter is devoted to just a basic bracelet.

2. **Lay out the bands on the loom in an appropriate manner.**

The process for laying out the bands should be easy to figure out. You'll have to add each band on diagonal points.

Specifically, you will have to start by placing the a band on the lowest hook on the middle part of the loom. You then have to place the other end of that band on the lowest hook on the left part. You should keep the bands close to each other to make it a little easier for you to get your bracelets created.

Make sure the middle part of the loom is the lowest to you. That is, the middle part should be organized to where the spot will be a little more accessible and easier to handle.

3. **Lay bands on top of each other in a zig-zag position around the two columns on the loom.**

As you will see in the picture shown above, you need to place the second band over the end of the first band. You can then get the third band to go over the second band, the fourth over the third and so on.

You will have to get the hook to help you out in this case. A good hook will help you to stretch the bands over the right way. This is important as your fingers will probably be far too big for you to handle the small pegs and bands on your own.

Be sure to repeat the process all the way along the loom. Remember, the newest band that you place on the loom must be above the last band that you prepared.

4. Use the hook to loop the bands.

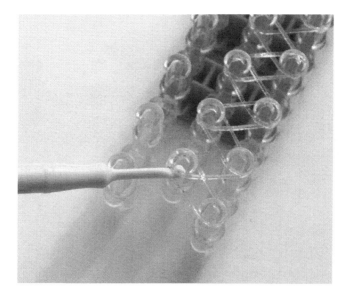

This step will help you loop the bands over each other. This will help you get the bracelet to have a good look and to also keep the bands from being stuck together and far too hard to manage.

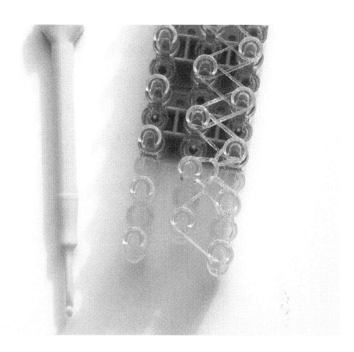

You'll have to turn the loom around so its arrows will face you. Insert the hook under the band that you placed between the first middle peg and the second right peg. Pull the band up and over so it will be on top of the second right peg. (Note: These instructions are valid provided that you flipped over the loom.)

Notice the light green band on the picture you see below. It has been stretched out well to where it will go onto that peg.

After this, go to the second right peg and and grab the band that is attached to the second middle peg. Insert the hook and grab that band to pull it up and over so it will be on the second middle peg. That is, it will not be on the right peg anymore. The bright pink and in the picture you see above is an example of how this will work.

The picture that you see above you should give you an idea of how the bands are to be stretched after a bit of time. Notice how the bands are going to be connected with each other. Always go after the band that is under the one that you have looped. Do this for the entire loom.

5. **Finish off the top part of the loop and get a C-clip to secure it.**

After you are finished with the last step, you need to watch for the last band that was on the end near the arrow that you started at. You will have to take off that last band. It should be easy to take off with the hook as the rest of the bracelet will have been tightly wound up.

A C-clip should be added onto this part of the band. The clip must handle both sides of the band. This clip will be responsible for getting you to secure whatever you've got.

6. Remove the band from the loom and secure it.

After the C-clip is added, you can always remove the band from the loom. The band should be removed carefully with the C-clip being the thing that you hold onto during the process.

The strand should be removed carefully. This is to ensure that the bands will not snap apart or wear out in some way.

After this, use the C-clip to string the other end of the strand with the one you are holding onto. You might have to ring the entire band around itself in order to make this work.

After you do this, you should have a fully completed wristband. This should not be too hard for you to handle provided that it is all maintained the right way.

Great Styles to Play With

You can easily create one of many different types of band styles that can be fun to have. These popular band styles are good options to choose from in that you can opt to play with any style and prepare a band that is designed to be capable of creating some impressive colors.

With all this in mind, let's take a look at a few simple choices to go along with when finding something to play with. These are all good choices that are enticing and interesting for you to hold.

Single Band Bracelet

This is a basic style that can work with as many colors as you want to work with. This is designed with a series of basic lines and will be easy for all to play around with.

1. Start by choosing the specific colors that you want to work with on your band. Make sure you think of a good pattern at the start.
2. Add the first color onto the bottom part of the loom.
3. After this, add a different color onto the next part. That is, it will go over the first band and move from the lowest side peg to the second middle peg.
4. Add a third color or repeat the second color.
5. Repeat the color pattern that you have chosen until you get to the end part of the loom.
6. Flip over the loom and then use the hook to string the bands over each other as mentioned earlier.
7. Add the C-clip to the end.
8. Take it all apart and then ring the C-clip around the last open band at the other end.

Squared Single

This option features a slight design that utilizes a series of smaller color points that will be scattered around the body of the band. This will work best if you stick with something that features just two colors. This is to create a secure setup that is not going to be too hard to handle.

1. Lay out two bands of one color at the bottom pegs on the sides of the loom. Make sure they cover the first two pegs on each side.
2. Take a second color band and add it over the top ends of those two pegs. Stretch it out to go to the third pegs on each side. This should create a rectangle-like shape.

3. Keep repeating this process until you get to the end of the loom.
4. Stretch the ends of the bands that are on the sides over one another.
5. Take the bands that were stretched in rectangular shapes and then string one line over the side pegs that they are next to.
6. Secure the C-clip at the far end of the band.

Rainbow Pattern

This is a pattern that will feature a rainbow color. Specifically, it will have the rainbow colors on one half of the band and a white color on the other half. This is designed to give you a more vibrant look that is a little more detailed and attractive, thus giving you a quality look that is set quite well.

1. Start with a series of white bands. Try and get about halfway through the loom with these white bands.
2. Start working about halfway through with different bands that are colored like a rainbow. Arrange the colors in their proper order and try to use the same number of bands for each color at this point.
3. Work with the band in a traditional process until you get to the very end.
4. Tie up the bracelet by stretching the bands as needed in order to create a longer design.
5. Close it off with the C-clip as needed.

Fishtail

The fishtail is designed to where the bands that you are using are connected a little closer to one another. The band appears to be much denser than what you've normally got to work with.

1. Take one band, twist it around to create two different holes and then string them around the first two pegs on a side.
2. Take a band of another color and then place it over that first band.
3. Take a band of the original color and then go over the second band.

4. Stretch the lower band by removing it from the bottom peg and then move it to go about halfway in between the pegs.
5. Stretch the top part of that lower band over and move it into the middle.
6. Push the entire material down and then add another band over it.
7. Stretch the second band over the mix in the same way that you did in steps 4 and 5.
8. Push down to then add another band over it. Repeat the process once again. As the process goes along, you will be adding more strands over time to allow the band to go as long as desired.
9. Keep on adding more bands and stretching them over for as long as you want.

You can do this to create a small bracelet or a larger necklace. You can even organize the colors to create some special effects. These include rainbow effects like what you see with the picture above.

10. Add a C-clip to connect the open ends of the project near the loom after you are done.
11. Tie that clip up to the opposite end of the strand to finish the job.

Be sure to watch for how well you set this up and make sure you use an appropriate number of bands based on how long you want this to be. You can always stick with a standard total that features about twenty to thirty bands at a time but you can go with even more of them if you want to really create something extensive and big in its size.

Railroad

The railroad style is one that features a series of bands that are connected by one extensive series of links. That is, it might come with two standard bands that are connected with all of these different features to create a great setup that is easy to use.

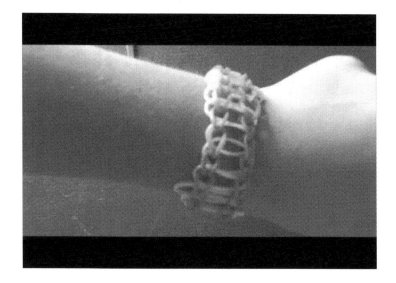

1. Take one color and then stretch it from the bottom middle ring to the bottom ring on a side.
2. Add rings of the same color around the side pegs, finishing it all off at the top of the middle column.
3. Repeat the same but with the other side of the loom. This should work to where the same color is used on

all pegs except the ones in the center column outside of the top and bottom spots.

4. Take bands of another color and then add them going parallel from one side to the next.

5. String one band of the color that is used on the borders and place it onto the end spot of the middle column. Make sure the band is strung around to where it will wrap around that one peg twice.

6. Take the bands at the bottom and stretch them over around the adjacent side pegs.

7. Repeat the process of stretching out the bands throughout the entire body of the setup.

8. After the entire set is done, add a C-clip on one end and then tie it up around the opposite end to finish the bracelet.

Diamond

The diamond pattern features a design where the colors or other features are designed to be a little closer or in depth with each other. However, this pattern works with a setup that is controlled with a series of diamond-shaped weavings.

1. String bands of one color on the end.
2. Take bands of another color over the others and go to the second middle peg. This should create a diamond-shaped look with one color on top of the other.

3. Continue to repeat the same pattern throughout the entire loom. You can use different colors if you want but try and stick with two colors to use throughout the setup if possible.

4. Use the hook to string the bands over each other. Go from a middle peg to one of the side to start.

5. Stretch the first color that was used around to where the bands in that color will meet up in the middle of the band.

6. Add a C-clip to one end and then tie it up around the end.

All of these choices for your use can really be sensible and helpful for the requirements that you might have when trying to create some nice bands for your desires. You can use these options to create some amazing styles that are fashionable and attractive for you to hold.

Frequently Asked Questions

You should be certain when getting your rainbow loom project handled that you are doing it all the right way. There are a few commonplace questions that deserve to be asked beforehand so you can be certain that you are getting it all to work to your demands.

What should I do in the event that one of the bands in my setup breaks apart?
You will typically have to build a new project if one band ends up breaking apart. This is due to the rather intricate nature of the bracelet and the fact that all the bands are carefully strung together. Fortunately, it will not take that much time for you to get the new band set up.

How many colors can I use in my items?
You can use as many colors as you wish. Most people tend to stick with just two colors at a time, what with it being so easy to facilitate. However, you can stick with

multiple colors at a time if you prefer to head in that route.

Is there a way how I can go after with taking a traditional bracelet design and extend it to work with a full necklace design? That is, can I make it a whole lot longer than what it looks like in the instructions featured here?

You can make these bracelets a little longer by allowing for a band to be extended onto a second separate loom. This can be perfect to handle because the loom is designed to where there is a bit of an opening at the top that allows it to connect with the first one. You can make something as long as you want but it will take a little longer for you to get it ready.

Can these bracelets fit onto anyone's wrist?

It should be rather easy for you to get a bracelet to go over your wrist with ease. You might have to be careful though as there is a potential for your bracelet to break apart of someone's wrist is far too big. Make sure you don't stretch these out far too much so you will not be at risk of breaking anything off.

If you ever need help with figuring out if someone can actually wear a band then try to measure that person's wrist. If the person's wrist appears to be very large, say about more than seven inches from one end to the next when taking a flexible ruler and strapping it over, then you might want to stick with a few extra bands.

How many bands am I supposed to be using when getting my bracelets made up?

You should probably use about 25 or so bands on average. Of course, the total number that you will actually use will vary based on how intricate the band you will be using is.

This total number will also vary based on how big the bracelet is. The 25 total is primarily going to work if you are sticking with something that is capable of fitting over an average person's wrist.

There's lots of different types of rainbow loom products that are available but they don't have that rainbow loom name to them. Are these still okay to use?

While you could technically work with one of those, it is best to stick with something that actually has the rainbow loom brand on it. The problem with these alternate options is that they are made of inferior materials that are based heavily on what some people might think is appropriate. In addition, some of the bands made by other companies might not be as strong.

You are better off sticking with the actual rainbow loom brand. This is to provide you with a little more control over the loom experience.

Can I use a plastic kind of hook or do I have to stick with a metal hook?

You can go with a plastic hook if you want but you need to be certain that you've got to get a metal hook to work for you. The materials that come with a metal hook tend to be thin and easier for you to handle. If you stick with a plastic option then you'll probably end up having something that is too thick and might be a challenge to string around the materials you want to work with.

Conclusion

The rainbow loom is one of the greatest inventions in the world of accessories in the past few years. It makes it to where you can quickly and easily create your own amazing fashion accessories at home. You can practically create any type of accessory that you want and make it into something that is truly your own as long as you use the right steps for doing so.

We hope that this guide has helped you understand everything you need to know about how to handle a great rainbow loom project. Remember that it can take a bit of practice for you to create things but once you get the hang of it, it will not be all that hard for you to come up with some unique and thrilling options that will look great on anyone.

This guide has all the options that you could ever utilize and enjoy having when it comes to creating great wristbands and other items. We suggest that you start working with the projects seen here and then go on to working with some other options based on your preference. If you start out small and then go forward with some more unique design choices then you will discover after a while that you can really create some unique stuff if you just put your mind to it.

Thanks for reading and have fun with creating some of the best types of bands around!

Back cover description for the book

If you are looking for a way to create different rainbow loom bracelets and necklaces then this will be the perfect guide for you to check out. This is a great guide that will list information on how you can work with the rainbow loom.

You can learn about how to create different items by using the right materials. There are full details on the materials to use in the process plus a series of steps on how to make different patterns in this guide. These include a few of the most common patterns that you can stick with.

The points that are listed in this guide will help you to get the most out of whatever you've got to create. Be sure to check out this guide when looking for ways to get more out of the great world of rainbow loom projects.

Manufactured by Amazon.ca
Bolton, ON

17801643R00165

Made in the USA
Charleston, SC
01 March 2013

Dee

Lunch with Fellini, Dinner with Fidel

An Illustrated Personal Voyage
From the Cold War to the Arab Spring

Deeno Stuyler,

Cover by Laura McDonald

All photos by the author except where indicated.

Books by Deena Stryker

The Two Hundred Days of '81/2' (as Deena Boyer)
Cuba 1964: When the Revolution was Young
Une autre Europe, un Autre Monde (France)
A Taoist Politics: The Case for Sacredness
America Revealed to a Honey-Colored World (forthcoming)
Lovers and Others: Short Stories and Vignettes (forthcoming)

Website and blog: www.Otherjones.com

TABLE OF CONTENTS

Preface   4

Part One: Teen Expat

I Early Comings and Goings   7
II First Flight   20
III Spirit's Way   35
IV Love's Tears   42
V Last Tethers   56
VI New Druthers   66
VII Fact and Fantasy   78

Part Two: Raulinko, Regina and Me

VIII Fantasy and Reality   112
IX Fatherland   126
X Italian Interlude   139
XI Eastern Detour   145
XII Childfest   153
XIII Regina's Land   168
XIV Exoticism in Europe   187

Part three: My Left Brain

XV Home Again With Goulash Communism   195
XVI Time In Our Lives   205
XVII In The Belly Of The Beast   217
XVIII Thrashing Around   227
XIX Passing Go   236
XX Europe Personal and Political   249
XXI Last Fling in a Not-so-Douce France   262
XXII God, Otherness and Politics   273
XXIII God the New Science and Politics   280
XXIV America Revisited   290
XXV: Our Lives in the World   301

4

Whenever I drive along the Schuylkill River in Philadelphia, admiring the wide green banks and old stone bridges that evoke the Moldau River in Prague, I think of the game of Monopoly. I wonder whether Kelly Drive existed when I was an adolescent, and if it did, whether one has to Pass Go many times in order to discover beauty obscured by childhood wounds.

I've always been very sure of my feelings and beliefs, knowing why I did even the most unusual things, such as spending most of my life in a series of foreign countries. As the decades passed, my decisions put me increasingly in the path of history, and if there was a link between my idea of home and a rejection of nationalism, I was unaware of it.

For six years before rediscovering my birthplace, I lived in a little town on the Côte d'Azur, finding serenity in an ancient wisdom that retrospectively provided a reassuring view of a life that emotion and reason had run by turns. Suddenly at the turn of the millennium, my comforting rug was almost pulled out from under me, as I found myself living with my mother for the first time since adolescence. But as I cared for her, several family secrets were revealed to me, my parents' behavior came into focus, and I received a request for forgiveness from an unexpected quarter. The back story of my unusual life unfolded just as the America I had largely avoided was coming to a crisis of historic proportions.

My story enfolds a succession of oceans, planes, trains, faces that faded even as I imagined them fading, impersonal quays in a city I knew too well, or was leaving with a superstitious prayer for return. At ten years interval there was a departure by steamship for postwar Europe, then a return by plane at the height of the Cold War. After a twenty-four year absence, a return from behind the Iron Curtain with two children; and after ten more years - and again at a twenty-four year interval - a second arrival in France where I would remain for an incredible nineteen years before finally being at home in the place where I was born.

How many transitions mark the stages of this journey, separating them like ribbons around packages of letters, into long tears or marveling laughter! A life which, from the height of my twenty-five years, seemed to belong to someone else, but which I now recognize as having been tenaciously mine. In what follows, I shall try to trace its currents, winds and tides, aware that until the voyage is over, certainty can at any moment give way to revision.

Part I: Teen Expat

Chapter I - Early Comings and Goings

[Sedate on a Sled]

How did it happen that a fourteen year-old girl from a middle class Jewish family in Philadelphia embarked on a life of travel and adventure, starting in war torn Holland, Germany, and France?

In the summer of 1964, I stood on the outskirts of Havana beside broken railroad tracks embedded in rubbery asphalt with the father of the child I did not know I was carrying. As I idly tried to imagine how a train could ride these rails, an electric engine appeared pulling a series of very old cars and slowly came to a halt.

I could not believe that what I was seeing was real. My lover and I boarded the high steps, and the seats of plaited, varnished straw with copper handles that had to be there appeared as if by magic. I recognized the windows with small handles that one presses between thumb and forefinger to raise, the upper part painted green against

the sun. At the end of the car was the copper water tap fitted into the wall over a small basin.

It was from a railroad car exactly like this one that my father had disappeared almost completely from my life when I was three years old. As I waited on that dusty train for him to return from the restroom, I must have stared at the water tap for a long time - or perhaps I was thirsty and my mother left her seat to fetch me a drink in a pointed paper cup like the ones I now saw hanging from the holder. I feared to take my eyes off the raised edge of the basin, lest it not be there when I looked back, marveling that mind could bypass time accumulated to reveal one perfectly intact image.

Sitting in the dusty train with the man I had loved after seven years of superficial relations, I was moved beyond words. I tried to tell him what this scene meant to me, but he did not know how it felt to be the child of divorced parents, any more than I could imagine how it had felt for him, at the same age in Warsaw, to answer the phone for his mother and hear Nazi threats.

A few months after my father's disappearance, I awoke in the double bed that I shared with my mother to find her sobbing: "Why are you crying?" I asked. "I'm crying because I have no more husband", she whined. Then, in the sententious tone that would become her hallmark: "But you mustn't cry, for he'll always be your father." I obeyed, learning only in middle-age that I had been expected to console her, denying my own grief - and the need to protect myself.

My parents were an oddly-assorted couple who never should have married. The known, maternal side of my father's family, the Kadzans, harked back to a hussar, an actress, and a Count's overseer on an estate near the Romanian border of Hungary. His father's side originated near the Austrian border, and it was a mystery how my grandparents could have met. As for my mother's family, it brought together Belarus and Ukrainian merchants, the former inclined to tragedy, the latter to making things work. The entrepreneurial family was noisy, the other quiet. My mother was a jealous older sibling and her mother's nemesis. My father had five sisters and was spoiled. My maternal grandfather, Jacob Oxman, thought that once married

these two would grow up together. Both died without having done so.

[With May]

During the depression, my mother May gave up studying journalism to become a secretary. Her future husband, Howard had left home and school at fourteen, gone to work as a copyboy and become a journalist who had trouble keeping a job. Now I know from watching old movies on TCM that in those days journalists frequented nightclubs and other glamorous places. May probably enjoyed that, before I came, all the while determined to regain the security she had known as a child. Howard, on the other hand, loved improvisation, and had a knack for securing what he wanted. May was a control freak while Howard was a spendthrift.

Though both would turn out to be basically monogamous in their successive marriages, when I was three May precipitated the divorce by feigning retaliation when Howard dallied. They spent a weekend in Atlantic City trying to patch things up, but when May asked Howard how much spending money he would need, he knew

it was useless. I sat next to him on the train back to Philadelphia. At one point he said he was going to the bathroom. I waited in vain for him to return, staring at the copper water spigot at the end of the car, until my mother came and told me he'd got off. This incident transformed an active toddler into a quiet child who needed a tonic to eat and was allergic to lies. By the time I was four my parents had divorced, and my mother joked that I grinned like a monkey. It never occurred to her that this was an attempt to deny adversity.

A clue as to how the introverted child turned into an adult traveling on various passports to forbidden places lies in a recently discovered photo showing a feisty, happy three year-old, belly flopping on a sled. It is in complete contrast to the pendant that had been given to me for my album that shows the kind of person I was expected to be: seated primly, feet on the ground. I first began to think independently when at around four, noticing the absence of a chimney for Santa Claus to come down in Jake's house, I realized that Santa didn't exist. Having discovered that I didn't have to believe everything I was told, it soon occured to me that I could refuse to obey. However, I shunned violence: the first time a playmate hit me, I ran crying to our black maid, whose round resilient forms suggested power. She admonished: "When someone hits you, you hit back." I took her advice, but would prefer words to fists. By the time I was five, my life's set of building blocks was in place: a need for quiet, coupled with intolerance of pessimism and control. Energy which could have been spent frolicking was devoted to analysis and resistance. When my red hair and model's figure turned into assets, I did not capitalize on them. May had not taught me to flirt.

On a gray day in 1947, I stood on the deck of the SS Westerdam, in the port of Hoboken, New Jersey, as my mother's face receded into the distance. There had been a long and tedious customs ceremony, a baggage ceremony, a ticket ceremony; the coming aboard of other passengers and their clutches of relatives, who like us were photographed and re-photographed in different combinations, and finally, the interminable raising of the gangplank. At last the ship set sail with a shudder, and I discovered the

extraordinarily gentle but powerful throbbing of the motors. Thrilled for the first time in my life, I turned to tell my father that tea was being served right there, by a waiter all dressed in white, with impeccable white gloves, as the deck rocked gently on the expanse of gray water on this surprisingly mild December afternoon.

[Goodbyes in Hoboken, December 1947]

"And all you care about is tea?" my father retorted, emphasizing the last word. Turning to my stepmother Bette, who was already feeling seasick, and switching to the theatrical tone they used together, he decreed that I was without heart. Alas, I didn't know how to deal with irony; I knew only head-on battles, hysterics, screams. Mute with shock, I failed to point out that I was only exhibiting the inner strength I'd had to develop to endure the woman he had fled. For years I had wanted to live with my father because I thought we were alike. How could he expect me to cry when my wish was being fulfilled? Perhaps he was remembering the defiance with which May left him, seeing me in her image. On a second level, though he knew May had made me unhappy, perhaps he felt the need to unnerve me, precisely because I was her child, a fact he would confess with rage years later.

This was the first in a long series of misunderstandings between me and the world. But there is a deeper explanation for the nonchalance that many people would criticize; by liberating me from a mother who was as harmful as any illness, my departure for

Europe threw a line to the belly-flopped girl on the sled, ensuring that from then on, curiosity would win out over anxiety and fear.

[On the SS Westerdam]

Another picture in my first photo album shows me standing on the deck of the SS Westerdam looking at least eighteen, leaning backwards into the wind, eyes closed, hands trustingly in coat pockets. The dreamy smile suggests the way I would confront life, open to what it brought but often accused of living in a world of my own. Having been transformed from a happy child into a somber one rejected by both parents, I created my own space, blind to the pitfalls of certain realities because they represented an indispensable elsewhere.

After my parents separated, Howard's visits had been too rare to make up for May's lack of warmth. Then the war came, and he was drafted. His last visit before being sent overseas took place indoors on a cold and rainy afternoon. I sat on a straight-back chair near the front windows, Howard folded his 6'4" frame into my grandfather Jake's armchair, and with that gentle patience that

charmed all women, taught me to knit the way his mother did, with the wool intricately wrapped around the fingers of the left hand.

War accorded perfectly with the dramatic atmosphere that reigned in Jake and Rose's home, insinuating itself into the space that already separated me from that Rinso-White world. Years later, during one of the few times May talked about herself, she told me that when she was about three, Rose had reacted to her misbehavior by screaming that she wished her child had never been born. Now, discovering her early pictures, I realize she must have been a mischievous child and a flirtatious teen-ager. It's easy to imagine her being the apple of her father's eye, and Rose being jealous. No wonder that, forced to endlessly affirm her existence in the face of a mother's curse, May would maintain a lifelong determination that her needs come first. On her death-bed she confessed how, as a child she had firmly believed Jake should have married her.

As I remember Jake, he is almost bald, his nose scarred by pock marks acquired during his childhood in Odessa - or was it already Kishinev? In a family portrait taken shortly after they arrived on Ellis Island, he's an earnest ten year old looking out at the world over big feet. Father and sons drove milk wagons, then set up small candy stores. In the family album, Jake is more slender than when I knew him, but shows the steadfast Ukrainian kindness that was so different from Rose's somber Bela Russian ethos.

Jake provided generously for his family with a bar-restaurant in old Philadelphia. He watched over the roast beef, kosher sausages and sauerkraut, stuffing bagels with lox, or darting out from behind the cash register to help a waiter, without losing a beat or a smile. From time to time, he downed a small glass of Bourbon, and at all times, he put up with Rose. (Rose held sway over the communicating bar, and rare was the client who crossed her!) I was taken to this place of exotic delights for an ice cream after my tonsillectomy; but for the child who continued to see in her dreams the round face, white beanie and blinding headlight of the surgeon, it was its charms were overshadowed by the resigned gait of horses drawing the city's last wagons.

Divorce was rare, and hence dramatic. But the strident sounds of my mother's family were aggravated by political tensions. For Rose and Jake, who had escaped the Russian pogroms, America was everything, while May's subscription to the left-wing *New Masses* caused the FBI to ransack her bookcase on behalf of the *House un-American Activities Committee*. This did not deter her from taking me to a rally for Roosevelt's Vice-Presidential nominee Henry Wallace, during the 1940 election campaign. Distributing leaflets in the great hall, I was part of a reassuring wave whose vibrations would recur at other, similar moments.

[Rose and Jake]

The seeds of those emotions had been sown a few months earlier, on the summer evening that marked the end of my childhood. We were sitting on the cement stairs beside Jake's house which, as in many Philadelphia neighborhoods, led to a wide back driveway that served as playground and access to the basement and garage. The sky had an eerie greenish hue as the day ended. With a heavy step, Jake came out of the house where he had been listening to the news. I can still hear the unfamiliar tone of his voice, low and grave, as he said: "There will be war." I now realize that he was probably

reacting to the French debacle of June, 1940, and wondered how there could be war when we had such a great president. Roosevelt's energetic, smiling portrait sat on the side table next to Jake's chair, and Rose spoke of him with emphatic reverence.

Tensions with Rose eventually escalated to the point where May and I went to live with May's sister Rachel and her husband Walter, who allowed us to occupy the two-rooms and bath on the third floor of their new house. Rachel taught me to wash dishes to perfection, ensuring that I never forgot - and creating a life-long conviction that there were more important things to do. One day I would have a husband who put dirty pot lids back in the closet, and couldn't believe this was happening to me. Husbands would be a recurring theme in my life, as would less formal relationships, but my children and the wider world were ultimately what counted most.

Between first and sixth grade, May and I moved several times between Rose's and Rachel's. I went in and out of the same schools, left and found again the same friends according to the needs of the two high-strung women who alternated as my caretakers. I had inherited the Oxman family's myopia, and by the time I was seven it was 'galloping'. To limit reading outside of school and avoid electric light, I was ordered to bed as soon as I had finished the dishes, with only the radio to keep me company in the dark. Notwithstanding three years of this regime, I accumulated five degrees of myopia, a good astigmatism and a slight strabismus which some people later found attractive. But also, an ability to be alone, and hence to reflect.

For my seventh birthday, instead of the bicycle I wanted, I was given a piano; luckily, with hands unusually big for a girl, practicing was almost never a chore. On Sunday morning, after serving pancakes, Jake would settle in his armchair to listen. During the periods of my life with piano and those without, I would remember how he praised my light touch. Another solitary pursuit was a puzzle of South America: seeing how its eastern coast seemed to nestle into the western coast of Africa, it occurred to me that the two continents might once have been joined. But in a family where learning was revered, no particular attention was paid to my intelligence.

When May got a new job visiting soldiers' dependents all over the state, leaving me at the mercy of the Oxman women's temper. I insisted on moving to the home of my paternal grandparents Regina and Morris, where I had spent happy weekends and holidays. Rose's door was always bolted; Regina's I discovered, was always open, and a few blocks away, her sisters always seemed to be talking about, making, or serving pastries.

Life at Regina's was also centered on the making and enjoying of food. The oven was located next to, rather than beneath the burners, a precursor of the wall oven whose advent was probably delayed by the war. It was often lit, especially on Fridays, when Regina made bread and pastry. The ivory-painted metal table in the middle of the kitchen was transformed into a work surface by folding back the ironed-thin tablecloth, and lunch was taken on the covered part during a suddenly decreed halt. (Regina probably had a pre-diabetic sugar curve, as I do, since she died of diabetes.) I watched her freckled, wrinkled hands, sunburned from working in her small garden, knead bread, pour marble cake, shape apple strudel, and layer my favorite noodles with apricot jam - too many tasks for her to teach me these skills! I did however help my grandfather Morris fill out the arrears cards for his low-income insurance clients on the round mahogany dining-room table, and perhaps this suggested that numbers and letters counted more than flour and eggs.

Right after their wedding, in 1902, Morris had decided that his bride would make the 500 mile trip from Eastern Hungary to Trieste by train, while he hitchhiked to elude Emperor Franz-Joseph's recruiters. The trip from the town with the almost unpronounceable name of Nyreghasza, to the Mediterranean port which is now in Italy, took Regina through the capital of what was still the Dual Monarchy, and this was the only time she saw Budapest. When I finally walked in her steps, I regretted that the only thing she remembered of that journey was being "oh so seasick".

Love disposed me well toward everything Regina did, but when I accompanied her to Temple, the purpose and meaning of

prayers remained as elusive as algebraic formulae. Luckily, her live and let live attitude saved me from faking belief, and since neither the existence nor the non-existence of God could be proven, I concluded it was pretentious of anyone to claim certainty in the matter.

[Morris and Regina]

Unlike May, Rachel and Rose, Regina never indulged in hysterics. I helped her with the housework because I loved her, and somehow I knew how to cope with Morris' stubbornness. Regina was all the gentleness I knew during my childhood, and I was happy not to look or behave like the women 'on the other side'. To Regina I owe my black eyebrows that met in the middle before I started tweezing them, while it was Morris who gave me my red hair. Recently I learned that Regina had been rather frigid, notwithstanding - or because of? - having six children, and that Morris the taciturn had been a ladies' man. Although Regina was probably not responsible for my loving all the good things in life, nothing can alter my feelings for her.

[With Regina, 1937]

The war Jake had foreseen became a reality in Regina's home when the Hungarian government allied itself with Nazi Germany. (My father would later point out to anyone not privileged to be Hungarian that fascism had actually been invented by its ruler, Admiral Horthy.) Although Hungary had been as anti-Semitic as any place in Europe, the Jews were more or less let alone until 1944, when most of them were wiped out. Cousins and friends who left in time found their way to Regina's table set with paprika colored China teacups and fresh strudel. I could not grasp the meaning of their conversations (in contrast to the Oxman's ever somber intonations, the Kadzan's did not expose children to tragedy), but I sensed that the people from 'over there', who filled the air with a heavy silence, were no different from us.

At Regina's I discovered poetry and sensuality, curled up in a wicker chair on the front porch with a thick slice of rye bread and butter, a sheet of summer rain almost close enough to touch, or picking flowers in the incredibly varied back garden. Alas, after a few months I became seriously ill, and my mother decided I should no longer stay there. The war was over and with a new job, May rented a two room apartment in center city, where I was enrolled in Girls' High, Philadelphia's answer to gifted females. Now that I no

longer needed to be looked after, May spent most of her free time with the man she was dating. I signed up for a dance class, and was chosen to be the teacher's partner, since I was tall and had a good sense of rhythm. Soon I had a partner my age, with whom I went to Philadelphia Orchestra concerts at the Dell, a natural dating venue for Jewish teenagers raised on recordings of the classical repertoire.

The army had realized that Howard would be more useful as a correspondent for Yank Magazine, than on K.P., where his lack of martial talents often landed him. He ended up wandering around Europe on his own, and when he accompanied the French General Leclerc into Paris, his lowly rank of corporal was embellished by the French Croix de Guerre. I cut out his stories as they appeared, and vented my frustrations in long letters typed on May's big Remington, acquiring the haphazard fingering that would lead to my becoming a writer instead of a secretary. As if in anticipation of that development, when the future Queen Elizabeth turned eighteen, I won third prize in an essay contest for suggesting that nations should learn from one another.

During Howard's service, Bette, the woman he had divorced my mother for, would sometimes take me to lunch. I understood that they loved each other passionately, having previously ignored the existence of such feelings. As soon as the war was over Bette joined Howard in Paris, and the following year, they both got jobs on *Stars and Stripes*, the Army newspaper whose European edition was published in Germany. Suddenly, they announced they were coming to fetch me. I had just tasted my first kiss, when on December 13, 1947, the three of us sailed from Hoboken on the Dutch ship SS Westerdam bound for Rotterdam.

Chapter II - First Flight

Everyone remembers their first kiss, and I have often re-experienced that unique, lifting sensation. Yet at the time, the attraction of a foreign land, coupled with the desire to leave my unhappy world was greater.

The lure of an unknown place echoed the partiality I felt for Howard's family, more closely identified with their European origins than May's. But foreign names and places were also familiar to me from *The Book of Knowledge*, where May showed me words in French, and from literary heroes that reflected her internationalist fervor. One of my favorites was Ping, a Chinese fishing duck, always last to board the master's boat. One day the boat left without him, and he fell asleep among the reeds. The next day, a fishing family caught him and held him captive under a basket. Luckily, a compassionate child returned him to the water, where, from afar, he saw "the houseboat which was his home." Last on board as always, he received the usual tap on the back, understanding that it was the price of safety.

Unlike Ping, I've always managed to catch the trains and planes that punctuated my life, however I preferred insecurity to the safety of home. Not for me the life of *Ferdinand the Bull*, who eschewed the arena to sit under a tree smelling flowers, although I do share his stubbornness. The fact that both these early heroes were males probably contributed to my weaknesses invariably being denied – by men.

After ten days at sea, the sturdy little ship Westerdam reached Holland. From our vantage point on deck, Rotterdam was a carpet of ruins. In ludicrous contrast to the desolate scene, a passenger asked my father to let me wear a fur coat through customs so he could avoid paying duty. The lone figure we saw huddled on the quay turned out to be my great-uncle Pal, a brother of Regina's who had become the dean of foreign correspondents in Amsterdam. We barely became acquainted over dinner in a newly reopened restaurant, but I

would turn to my Dutch uncle twenty-four years later under even more unusual circumstances.

On the night train to Paris, I marveled at the wood-paneled Wagon Lits' velvet upholstery, and thick, impeccably ironed linen sheets. Upon arriving in Paris, I commented that, just as I had read, the Eiffel Tower looked like an oil rig, provoking Howard's indignant condemnation. Every time we emerged from the hotel into the raw cold of the city of light. I whined, hunkered down in a woolen coat. After a few days, Bette remembered the thick sheepskin Howard had worn during his wartime peregrinations; they bought a huge amount of stiff black corduroy, and announced they would make sure I was never cold again.

On New Years morning we arrived in the little Hessian village of Pfungstadt, Germany, the home of *Stars and Stripes*. The couple who were house-sitting, plus another women, were asleep in the master bed. As with the fur coat, there was neither condemnation nor approval. Within days, a local tailor had produced a long, gored coat so heavy that it gave me back problems for the rest of my life.

It soon became clear that Bette's wishes were paramount, but I never knew how to behave as the third person in a trio. During that winter in the unpaved, muddy village, I was at loose ends. I read *Kristin Lavrensdatter* and listened to Howard's favorite artists, the new French popular singer, Edith Piaf, and Lili Pons singing *Bachianas Brasileiras*,. A German musician gave me lessons on the grand piano in the officers' club, a French friend tried to build on the few months of French I'd had at Girls' High, and Howard judged nil the book review he had suggested I do for the paper. Since it was impossible for my father to be wrong about anything, I knew I would never be a writer.

Notwithstanding my lack of promise, I was to continue my education in Paris, the schools for army dependents being even more mediocre than those at home. Howard probably wanted the best for me, but we never discussed what that was. On Easter weekend, he entrusted me to the conductor of the *Orient-Express*, and scribbled an address on a scrap of paper, which I was to hand to a taxi driver at the end of the line in Paris. He had arranged for me to board with the

family of a young woman who had been his sister Shirley's pen pal before the war, and whom he'd looked up at the liberation.

A rose tinted sun was rising in the deserted Paris streets that Sunday morning as I stepped out of the Gare de l'Est. Traffic being almost nonexistent, my taxi soon arrived at the address on rue La Bruyère, where I was dumped unceremoniously on the sidewalk with my belongings. Unaware that I had just been introduced to French politesse, I dragged my bags through the carriage door. The silence of what turned out to be a hydraulic elevator seemed ominous. On the third floor, I rang at the Doctors Mounier. The door was opened by a smiling young woman with fat rosy cheeks and long curly hair who had obviously just fallen out of bed. Evelyn worked in the archives of a scientific research institute and spoke good English, having been active in the resistance. She showed me to a small room with a black and white marble fireplace, an Empire bed and matching secretaire. Everything was going to be all right!

We deposited my bags, passed the bathroom, mysteriously devoid of toilet, and entered an enormous kitchen, in the middle of which stood a big table covered with faded oil-cloth. Evelyn served me tea in a bowl that held two large cups, cut a thick slice of bread, opened a jar of preserves and explained that rationed sugar and butter were reserved for homemade deserts. Never having drunk tea for breakfast, I decided I might as well have it unsweetened, missing only the butter on the bread that reminded me of Regina's.

Marching back along the unlit corridor, we entered a room darkened by rose-colored velvet curtains. I was not prepared for the sight of Evelyn's mother, a tiny, incredibly thin woman with enormous dark eyes, short dark hair and slurred speech. Later I learned that she took frequent doses of morphine to relieve a painful hip. Her husband soon appeared from the adjoining room, as round as his wife was thin, and as voluble as she was quiet.

A decisive adjustment occurred at that first meeting with my hosts: in a leap of faith that was also a definitive commitment to reason, I put down my uneasiness. Their adult children would joke about their strangeness, but I was grateful for their kindness. I considered all but normal their incessant ramblings, and spent

precious hours in the shadows of the 'little drawing room' where *Madame le docteur* Mounier slept on a rose colored velvet couch surrounded by worn leather-bound books and silver knickknacks.

Although she had been one of the first women admitted to the Paris Faculty of Medicine, I gradually realized that she and her doctor husband now subsisted mainly on memories. They were passionate about literature, and introduced me to Musset and Courteline, Molière and Pierre Louys, Colette and Gide, not to mention Jerome K. Jerome, whose name I never heard again after leaving their home. During frugal meals they told anecdotes about French battles, ancient history punctuated by Latin quotes, and quips by famous authors or musicians from prewar Parisian life. I took piano lessons on a grand Erard, at times playing four hands with Mme Mounier, a passionate and well-trained musician. No one mentioned the fact that when confronted with the German's final solution, Dr. Mounier had converted to Judaism to share his wife's fate.

Since heating gas was rationed, baths were limited to one a week. Scrupulous, I waited until the following Sunday to lock myself in for what was to be a voluptuous cleansing. Evelyn had instructed me to open the window while I filled the tub, since the gas heater leaked; but not having smelled the slightest odor of gas when I washed at the basin, and desperate for warmth in the poorly heated apartment, I ignored her warning. When the tub was full to the brim with steaming water I gingerly stepped in. Soon I was blissfully, totally immersed. But when I stood up to wash, my head felt strangely light. I barely managed to put one foot over the edge of the tub. When I came to, I was in bed, the worried faces of the entire Mounier family hovering over me. They had broken down the door when the maid in the adjacent kitchen heard me fall. As I listened to my hosts proffer words of relief and encouragement, I realized that under the blankets, I was naked. The Mouniers' composure had been refined over centuries of European diplomacy, but I, suddenly had to treat the fact that complete strangers had handled my naked body as the most banal thing in the world! At that moment, I learned to meet the most embarrassing situations with apparent equanimity. The fact

that I had almost been asphyxiated by a gas heater while trying to take my first Paris bath was never mentioned again.

Life was slowly returning to normal in postwar France. Soon rationing would be over, and cars were beginning to appear on the streets. But having assumed there were only two kinds of government, fascist and democratic, I now discovered that the world was a lot more complicated. In France, there were many parties, from extreme right to extreme left, and no matter what government was in power on any given day, it was in turmoil, trying to control the communists and socialists, who formed a majority in Parliament, while holding on to France's Asian Empire, where communists and socialists were leading the fight for independence. My hosts, still recovering from the events of the recent past, left me in ignorance of what was in fact the start of the Cold War.

During that first year in Paris I rose like a patient from a long illness, drinking in the beauty of my surroundings. Each small facet of my new world was beautiful, even if it was very old and crumbling on all sides. This foreign land illuminated my past, drawing into focus what had until then been only a suspicion: in my childhood world, personal anxieties had been magnified by inelegant surroundings and my mother's lack of grace and graciousness. Rides on Philadelphia's number ten trolley through dilapidated neighborhoods and industrial wastelands to Saturday classes at the Greek Revival Art Museum had prevented me from knowing that besides paintings and sculptures, humans could also create cityscapes that would elevate and inspire. In Paris, even the cracked window frames were beautiful, and every day from the platform of the 68 bus I could contemplate the garden of the Louvre. I bought into beauty the way others buy into religion. Swimming in beauty, drunk with beauty, I was touched by the grace that religion had failed to provide.

How could I not want to belong to this world? My French was coming along so well that after a few months Evelyn did the raspberry whenever I lapsed into English. However, in order to be admitted into the French school system in the fall, I had to make up two years of Latin. After attending the Alliance Francaise in the

morning, then lunching frugally in the Mounier's blue painted dining room with sculpted wall cornices, I crossed the city again to the Place de la Sorbonne, climbed up to a garret, and waged a losing battle against a dead tongue with the help of an old, very ugly, and very formal teacher.

During summer vacation in Pfungstadt, a scene reminiscent of the one on the Westerdam occurred. When I innocently referred to Paris as 'home', Howard exploded: "Home! But you've only been there three months!" Rendered incautious by my newfound happiness, and wanting to say that home was where I felt right, I answered flippantly that it was where I hung my hat, adding another charge to the case my father was building against me. I had been expected to acknowledge the home he had given me, however far it was from where I hung my hat.

It would be many years before I could allow Howard's rebukes to slide over me like water off the back of a duck. As new evidence about my childhood appears, I realize that because I did not 'belong' emotionally to my parents, the place they inhabited was not necessarily 'home'. The constant change of surroundings in a childhood marked with family strife made me at home with myself. (It's probably because writing is a way of being alone without being lonely that writers are not much fun to be with. They move through life in aloneness, and like it that way.)

[First painting]

On his next visit to Paris Howard retaliated for my seemingly blasé attitude by taking me to a very chic restaurant, ordering oysters, and offering me one. Sensing this was a setup, I opened my mouth warily, and in fact, the oyster refused to go down. Stiffening his great frame, my father fixed me with round, hard eyes and commanded: "Swallow!" I didn't eat oysters again for forty years.

Howard and Bette came to Paris several times a year. Very much the hard-edged journalist, Bette was also fanatical about the way she looked, wearing stunning clothes and heavy make-up. Setting off to shop and tour the galleries they would say: "There's a great concert at the Salle Pleyel" - or the Salle Gaveau - give me some money and tell me where to meet them for dinner. I would take a taxi, buy fifty francs worth of chocolates (always chocolates), and an orchestra seat, returning on foot for the pleasure of finding my way, turning right or left without knowing what I would see, but certain I would never be lost. Years later, living in New York, I realized that one of the reassuring things about European cities was that you couldn't walk for more than a few minutes without coming to a monument, or at least a distinctive square or plaza, and that very differently from modern cities, which can extend for miles without an identifying feature, the ubiquitous landmarks of continental capitals make visitors feel at home. In Paris, I soon had a favorite time of day, discovered as I strolled in the soft spring air on the Boulevard de la Madeleine gently lit by a late afternoon sun. That particular light continued to occupy a special place in my personal gallery even after Bette pronounced a watercolor rendition I bought to be kitsch - a term which I sensed was pejorative.

At that time, I wanted to be an early childhood teacher, and one day in a large bookstore I came upon a thick scholarly volume that appeared to cover the question completely. Although my French was still rudimentary, I spent many months ploughing through it, in the first of many intellectual challenges.

During the 1949 Easter vacation in Pfungstadt I became more aware of the wider world. France, the U.S. and Great Britain had been drafting a new statute of occupation for their three zones of postwar Germany, and they were discussing the future of the coal-

rich, largely German border region of the Sarre, where tensions had been rising. (France and Germany had fought three wars in a century and the Sarre had been a French protectorate before and right after the war.) What was shaping up as America's attitude toward the rest of the world would be expressed in a report that crossed my State Department desk thirty years later. It lamented: "To think we used to run that place..." In 1949 America did run Europe, but it didn't occur to the people involved that they could be affected by European realities, even when the dramatic Berlin Air Lift that marked the beginning of the Cold War was going on.

During that Easter vacation, as usual I traveled between France and Germany in second class on the night train, since there were few voyagers and I didn't mind stretching out on the large upholstered seats. On the way back to Paris, knowing the train would cross the Saar border around midnight, I waited before lying down. Very much the international traveler, I handed my passport to the controller while continuing to read a magazine.

"Where is your tripartite pass?"

Looking up I answered: "I'm sorry but I don't know what you mean".

"You know very well that to transit the Saar you have to have a tripartite pass", the man articulated in heavily accented English, as though hearing it clearly would make a difference.

Thinking there must be a mistake, I answered calmly: "I came through here about ten days ago, I didn't have a pass, and nobody asked me for one."

"It's up to you to be informed!" the man answered curtly. "Come with me."

Struggling off the train in my sheepskin coat, dragging my heavy suitcase, I was led to a wooden building on the quay. Several people sat waiting beside a coal-fired stove under the watchful eye of an armed guard. Soon it was my turn to face the officer, now seated behind a great desk in the next room. He reiterated his request for a pass, and I reiterated my response.

"You know", he said threateningly, "I could put you in jail."

"Maybe so", I answered, "but I would ask you to first call my father, who works for *Stars and Stripes*."

"Your father!" he exclaimed, frantically searching for my birth-date in the passport he'd confiscated. Looking at the picture, then at me, he asked incredulously: "You're only fifteen?"

His surprise must have been partly due to the fact that I didn't cry, as my French classmates did at the slightest failure. "This time, I'll let you through; but next time you'd better have your tripartite pass!" Fifteen years later, a guard at a neighboring frontier would wonder why I grinned when a similar incident occured with my first-born. But in subsequent travels to and from Germany in those postwar years, I was never asked for the tripartite pass again. America did run the place.

For the moment, I had to get back on the train before it left. It was one o'clock in the morning, my knees were shaking and my suitcase seemed heavier than ever. As I emerged from the shack onto the platform, the train started to move. I pictured myself spending the night at the frontier, without sleep, a concern always foremost in my mind. Then miraculously, the train stopped. Terrified it would move again, I clambered up the nearest steps, hindered by my heavy coat. As I clumsily lifted my suitcase onto the platform, I twisted my ankle. Though it was cold, I was perspiring. Crashing into the first compartment, which luckily was empty, I sat trembling for several minutes. Then, covering myself with my coat, I stretched out on the upholstered seat and fell asleep.

I woke up at dawn, trembling again, but this time from the cold. On the opposite seat, a young man in uniform slept soundly. As I peered at him he opened one eye and exclaimed: "Good God, what's going on?" Feeling the cold radiator, he went to look for the conductor, and soon came back with two cups of tea. The heat was not working, and I spent the rest of the trip in shipwreck-type conversation with the young man, who was a French aviator and a gentleman. (In those days in France only upper middle class men were admitted to OTS…) When we finally arrived in Paris, he asked if he could write to me. Not wanting to seem impolite, I gave him my address. A few weeks later a package arrived containing a copy

of Balzac's *The Lily in the Valley*. Although Howard had congratulated me on my handling of the tripartite incident, he ordered me to return the book and asked Evelyn to put me in touch with people my age.

My American education level had placed me with students younger than myself, but now, in addition to wonderful youth concerts, and singing Bach's *Magnificat* in Evelyn's glee club, I was enrolled in a youth camping group. Howard remarked that the organization might be a communist front, but didn't veto the idea. Actually it was a communist organization, all political parties being legal. Trips were planned at weekly meetings in a 'People's House' on the left bank. I knew the Russians had been our allies during the war, and appreciated the warmth and sincerity of these young students and workers who were curious about life in the United States. The blond-haired boy I had noticed at the first meeting asked me if I'd like to sit in on an English class given by the *Knowledge Society* at the Sorbonne.

I'm not sure the classes helped my French, but I enjoyed being with Jacques. Soon we began to meet at the St. Geneviève library to do our homework together; then at metro stations to explore different neighborhoods. Jacques was several years ahead of me at Henri IV, a prestigious high school just across the Place du Pantheon from the library. One day, after bucking wind and cold for several hours, we took refuge in a warm, cozy café, where we drank grog and watched the card players. Letting the warmth sink in, silently, we held hands.

My love for Jacques was like new snow on which not even a bird had set foot; happiness struck at my throat like blinding sun on a white plain. Prescient, I suspected we had met too soon, and since we were not masters of our lives, we would be separated, my life determined by having loved at fifteen instead of twenty.

I came and went freely, the Mouniers merely enquired about my day as part of the ritual of 'politesse'. One night Jacques and I drifted as far as the Porte des Lilas where a neighborhood movie was showing *The Children of Paradise*. Jacques wanted me to see it, and when it was over, the last metro having gone, we walked as far as we

could together. As my lone footsteps echoed on the deserted streets, fear was merely a counterpoint to the harmony of the dimly lit scene, a particular night stillness scarcely ruffled by an occasional purring automobile.

One Sunday in May, Jacques and I took the suburban train to Bourg-la-Reine and wandered among villas overhung with wisteria and bougainvillea. It was warm, as only a Paris spring warmth that will not last can be. After about an hour we penetrated an unkempt area of the Parc de Sceau through a breech in the wall and stretched out under a tree. As I talked, I raised myself on one elbow for a closer look at Jacques' face. He had thick eyebrows and long hair that made him look a bit wild, but his large brown eyes were deeply intelligent. A straight nose and generous lips gave him an open, gentle and - although the word was unknown to me - sensuous expression. When he kissed me I felt perfect happiness. His arms holding my body gently to his, I tasted the tepid sun, the color and smell of new leaves. Jacques seemed to have no other need than to kiss me softly from time to time.

One day at the library we noticed a young couple flirting at the next table. A week or so later Jacques failed to appear for our English class. As the minutes passed, I knew something was wrong. I walked up the hill to the library, hoping to find him cramming for the Baccalaureat exams. I scanned the area where we usually sat. His old leather bag was on a table next to the young woman we'd seen flirting. I asked her whether Jacques was sitting there. She answered that he'd gone to look up something in the dictionary. I found him waiting for me, and suddenly felt off-balance. He scarcely said hello, but opening a big Larousse, pointed to the word 'separation'. Stunned, I said I would return the books he'd lent me the next day, and left. At the corner of Boulevard St. Michel and Rue des Ecoles I went into a café and phoned the Mouniers to say I would be late for dinner. It was almost dark. As I walked along the Seine, which had never seemed so beautiful, a deep well formed inside me which I knew would for a long time be filled with melted snow.

Resigned to beginning my adult life with love's place in my heart already taken, I lived until summer vacation in a comatose

state, papered over with everyday gestures and words. But like a recently discovered hero, Alfred de Musset's *Perdican*, I was convinced love lost was preferable to the loveless life I had known as a child. Wondering whether my being an American had anything to do with Jacques' sudden rejection, the need to be in charge of my life grew stronger.

Following this episode, Howard determined that I should have 'appropriate' company of my age. I met with the Baronne d'Ambert, a mother of five, with a view to boarding with her family in September. This tall, forty-year old woman with a prominent nose impressed me with her bobbed hair, long painted nails, jewels, and mischievous hazel eyes. It was my first encounter with nobility, and I did not quite know what to make of it. A few days later I drove with Howard and Bette in a brand new Citroen 15 to the Basque coast, and after a short vacation, took the train from Biarritz to Cherbourg, where, with no more hesitation than if I were taking the metro, I embarked on the Queen Elizabeth bound for New York.

I had been away for almost two years, yet my maternal relatives were more interested in the novelty of television than in my tales from abroad. At Morris' and Regina's there was no television, and on one typically hot Philadelphia summer day, as I sat on the three quarters bed in the back bedroom where I had been dangerously ill a few years earlier, Morris, very thin and naked to the waist, told me that he had to pray a lot because he was going to die soon. He said he was glad that although I lived in Paris and traveled on big ocean liners, I still dressed in cotton skirts and blouses like the ones Regina had sewn for me. His words were prescient: though I would soon be a fashion model, I would always prefer comfort to fashion.

In that summer's upside-down world, I felt like an exile. Pining for my adopted country even kept my lovesickness at bay. When at last I stood on the deck of the *Ile de France* in early September, I felt my life was back on track. I had been assigned to a cabin occupied by three born-again Christian women who, having never left their southern homes, were on their way to Bethlehem.

Upon hearing my destination, they got down on hands and knees and asked the Lord to look after me in the city of perdition. Within an hour I had changed cabins.

Back in Paris, I was unaware of leaving a world of intellectual endeavor and resistance for the royalist right. With most of my new family still at the country chateau, for a few days I shared the apartment with the older son, whose lycee started on the same day as mine. The maid treated us deferentially, and one evening Jean asked a friend to wait in the living room because I had come to the dinner table in my bathrobe. I learned that Madame always had a lover, and that when Monsieur, taciturn but chivalresque, found the steak tough, he praised the taste.

I was registered at the neighborhood lycee appropriately named after Moliere a court comedian. On Sunday afternoons the oldest d'Ambert daughter was allowed to mix with common folk as long as they were foreigners, and the two of us went dancing at the Cité Universitaire. Several partners of various nationalities had already propositioned me when I met René, the son of a deceased general who was eleven years my senior and told me that lovemaking was the most beautiful thing in the world.

In my ever logical way, I decided that if I could not have love, at least I could have sex. A few months later, during summer vacation, Bette questioned me casually and revealed to Howard that I had made love. At once his worldly attitude crumbled: he thrashed me and sent me back to my mother. The fear that hostilities might break out in Europe as a reaction to the Korean war, America's first new postwar cause, gave a political veneer to his decision. The little ship on which I traveled flew a Panamanian flag, but mockingly called itself Europa.

It may seem strange, but I did not hold Bette's behavior against her. I was convinced there must be things I didn't know that explained her attitude. As for my mother May, she was hardly delighted to have me back, and made only the slightest effort to convince me to go to college. Feeling completely out of my element, I desired only to be back in France. I've wondered, from time to time, how my life would have played out had I gone to Penn State in

Scranton and married my childhood sweetheart, but none of the scenarios were convincing. When my French lover, hoping to make up for being the poor cousin of a wealthy family by marrying an American, wrote asking for my hand, untypically May consulted my father. He roundly insulted her for even thinking of allowing me to marry instead of going to college, and she, out of spite, gave her consent. In December, 1950, I sailed back to France with a dowry consisting of a set of Community Chest tableware and a quilt, hardly enough to meet the expectations of a tax inspector who counted every centime.

War had meant collaboration or resistance, black market or denunciations. In postwar France, people got by using the "systeme d" (for "se debrouiller" = "to manage"). For the d'Amberts and Mouniers, this had meant taking in a foreign boarder. For me, after the ocean liners and the chateau, it meant getting married in a black long-sleeved woolen dress that would serve on other occasions, then setting off in a 10 year old Hotchkiss convertible while holding the roof down with a freezing hand, for a honeymoon of sorts in the sunny south. I would never forget waking from an uncomfortable nap along the way to a display of olive trees, their silver boughs undulating in the wonderfully soft night air. We shared my mother-in-law's modest flat for a few days, during which, between trips to a pebbly beach, she taught me to iron shirts and mend socks.

Back in Paris, Jean and I took possession of a sixth-floor walkup consisting of a large room and a kitchen, with a Turkish toilet on the landing. A few months later, a doctor friend of Jean's induced an abortion with which I coped alone. The decision had been mine as well as his, given the lack of prospects for better housing. I did not agonize over it, but feared dying or being caught.

When my husband brandished his army revolver over some trivial matter, I remained outwardly calm. But one day he decided that although we lived in one room, we had to have traditional tableware for guests. When I pointed out that the lid to the soup bowl that had been delivered was darker than the rest of the service, he slapped me hard enough to knock my glasses off. I feigned a mild reaction, but knew I had to leave him. With his unsuspecting

blessing, I signed up at a modeling school. A few months later, I got my first job, rented a room from an old woman on rue des Martyrs, astonished my husband by announcing that I was leaving him, and moved out before he had time to react.

A few days later, at a 14th of July street dance, I met a shy young Catalonian refugee who hoped to emigrate to Canada to raise horses. He gave me the pleasure I had not known with my experienced husband, and we were together until the following spring when he left. I was very fond of Enrique, and knew he would have taken good care of me. But being taken care of was not how my life was meant to be.

Chapter III - Spirit's Way

I preferred uncertainty in rainy Paris to being taken care of in the Canadian cold. But when I failed to obtain working papers by the end of my first month on the job, I was let go by each fashion house that hired me. For a while I worked as a receptionist for Gilbert de Rothschild. One day his partner, Budd Schulberg, ran into my father, who was an old friend, and was astonished to learn that we were not speaking. I hoped Howard would get in touch, but did not seek him out. Not long after, thanks to a Russian immigrant with connections, I obtained a work permit and was hired for Marc Bohan's first collection, in which I wore the bridal gown. I had a job, a lodging of sorts, and, after Enrique's departure, a new boy friend who was a medical student.

At twenty, I knew that my life would have to be invented piece by piece, but I still hadn't deciphered the old world social code. Several months and another abortion later, I realized there was a line which a middle class student could not cross. I took it as just one more problem, but was in distress. Dimly aware that my emotional needs were draining my energy, I tried paralegal studies, but had to accept the evidence: memorizing dry texts was not for me. I decided to study Russian, but because I had not completed my baccalaureate I had to take an exam to get into the School of Oriental Languages, the faculty where Russian was taught. I force-fed myself a second language, and later would be glad it was Spanish. After months of indifference, I was in a sort of rage to live - yet still with an empty feeling as soon as I stopped being very busy.

At one point Howard sent a friend to see me. I told him I was incapable of making plans, had no idea what I wanted to do, couldn't even imagine wanting to do anything in particular. It seems incredible now, but at that time my only goal was to learn to play the piano reasonably well. I wanted to read, go to the theater, be able to listen to music in a home I did not yet have. Since it was the low season for fashion, I looked to another kind of modeling while studying for my entrance exam.

Posing at the famous art school, *La Grande Chaumiere* was no more embarrassing than being discovered unconscious while trying to take a bath. Soon I no longer felt a raised arm, and I liked having my two feet firmly planted on the ground, in contrast to the fatigue of a fashion fitting in high heels. As for models 'getting into trouble', when I undressed and stepped onto the dais, I left 'Deena' on the dressing room stool with her clothes and became 'the model'. I liked the atmosphere of quiet concentration, the silence as everyone worked, the smell of paint, the people coming to look, quietly, with a handshake here and there, night falling, and finally, breaking the silence, the word "Rest". During the break I was myself again, covered and mixing with the others. The young men had no ulterior motives: they simply admired a good-looking girl.

Having realized I could do this, I sought out the well-known artist Segonzac. A tiny old woman with glasses opened the door on the top floor of an old building on rue Bonaparte: "You're a model? I don't know if he has time to see you. Come in."

[Modeling, 1953]

A dark, narrow, crowded hall, a large room covered with linoleum, paintings stacked against the walls, near the window a table with an enormous typewriter. The woman went toward a door at the back and called out in a grand-mother's voice:

"It's a model."

Segonzac appeared, the grandmother's spouse. "Monsieur Jos sent you from the Grande Chaumiere? May I look at you?"

He disappeared. I undressed in an alcove in the hall. "Take off your glasses", the grandmother advised. She called him, he came and looked at me from afar. "Very beautiful, unusual - I'm going to work with you. Here, my child, for the subway," handing me 200 Francs, enough for half a dozen rides. I almost refused, but realized he would be offended. Alas, I never did pose for Segonzac, perhaps because I couldn't be reached at the left bank hotel where I lived.

After several months working at the art school, I had saved enough to take a Christmas vacation. I wanted to ski, and chose the resort of Cortina d'Ampezzo, since I'd never been to Italy. (Killing two birds with one stone had become my standard modus operandi.) After half an hour on an easy slope I fell and twisted my ankle. A very sweet young man who had struck up a conversation on the way up helped me back to the boarding house. A doctor bandaged my ankle and ordered bed rest. The young man brought me fruit and flowers, stayed to keep me company, and learned to make love. He and his more sophisticated cousin took turns sacrificing sport to a different pleasure, and that's when I discovered that casual lovemaking can be perfectly charming when carried out in a spirit of respectful complicity.

I managed to get into the School of Oriental Languages, notwithstanding my rudimentary Spanish, and my failure, at the oral, to know that Baku, in Azerbaijan, was where the Russians got their oil. At the annual 'Langues O' dance, I met Leo Boyer, an alumnus who had grown up in China. He was hardly taller than me, but an excellent partner, with the green eyes and blond hair that would be my damnation for years to come. We danced all evening, then made love all night.

Leo had not been as lucky as Ping, the Chinese duck of my childhood. His father had engineered railroads for Chang Kai Chek, then for Mao, and been killed by the Japanese during the war. Leo's mother consoled herself by marrying a banker, but when the family returned to France in 1950, Leo was unable to transfer his law credits from Shanghai University to the Sorbonne. He got a degree from the School of Oriental Languages, hoping to become a diplomat; but just at that moment, relations with Communist China broke down, and the French Foreign Ministry stopped recruiting Sinologists. At twenty-seven, he was more or less estranged from his family and unemployed. The day after the ball, he moved into my hotel room on rue Mazarine, where I had installed a rented piano. The cabinet de toilette doubled as kitchen, Leo was an excellent cook, and a former student at the Paris Conservatory gave me piano lessons.

While taking Russian classes, I modeled at Lanvin's, but Leo and I didn't mix with the fashion crowd: among our wannabe friends was a sculptor who admired my large peasant feet. Leo looked endlessly for a job, while I fell fatally behind in a Tolstoi text that consisted mainly of footnotes. The one thing I retained from those classes because I saw it demonstrated in the successive languages I did learn, was that spoken languages change according to the law of least effort. (Whenever I proffer this knowledge, I feel slightly superior.)

Leo was convinced that politics was a hopelessly dirty business. As for me, I had never been able to get past the messy appearance of French newspapers. The screaming headlines, like the bandwagon aspect of American politics, echoed the aggressive family atmosphere of my childhood. I wanted to understand rather than judge, and although we noted the incessant changes of government, it was not until I began reading *The Economist*, many years later, that I would make sense of French politics.

Then as now, I didn't hanker after high fashion clothes, content when I managed to acquire a trinket that met my artistic standards. My favorite author was Colette, whose earthy hedonism, together with Leo's typically oriental less-is-more technique in love-

making, brought a new awareness of nature to a mind hitherto obsessed with man-made beauty.

Though nights with Leo were sublime, days were difficult: the housing crisis forced us to live in more or less squalid hotels at the day rate, only to be evicted after a few weeks so owners would not have to charge us the cheaper monthly rate required by law One year, I counted nine moves, and that was probably when moving became something that I did at the drop of the hat which was home. Luckily, with no children to make demands on our resources, we didn't have to live in the slums, where the Catholic priest known familiarly as Abbey Pierre was already at work, trying to shame successive governments into building low-rent housing. Key money would still be common in the eighties, when France was the third economic power in the world. And even now, there's an outcry every winter when tramps die in the cold, and poor families resort to squatting unoccupied office buildings.

[With Leo]

Although Leo was intelligent, charming and creative, and I loved his gentleness, making ends meet was a constant challenge. He would pretend to have a job, only to confess at the end of the month

that he'd lied. I gradually became aware that he had a serious drinking problem, yet after living together for two years, we gave in to the weight of convention and May's prodding, and got married.

Hoping Leo would eventually start leading a normal life, I left fashion modeling, where the pay was minimal, to go onstage in a cabaret. I used my body because my mind needed to feel it was in control. My first job was in Montmartre, near the Jules Ferry lycee where I had been a student in a white smock. At night, under soft lights, the tablecloths glowed orange, giving an impression of luxury and desire. The wall coverings looked like velvet, and the girls on the stage were priestesses of vice and lust. But during afternoon rehearsals the clubroom was lit by a solitary bulb called the witness, that left the back of the room dark; the curtains were tired and dirty, and once-white pads covered plain wooden tables. For the ashen-skinned dancers in pants and jacket, rehearsals seemed to go on forever, yet I preferred the numbers danced in street clothes, accompanied by the piano, to the real show, with its illusion of perfection.

Though it may seem incongruous, I again began to take an interest in the larger world. Going to bed in the wee hours, I spent my afternoons reading the new weekly *L'Express*. Powers of observation that had found an outlet in poetry, now turned to ideas. Leo's passivity inspired me to write an article for *Elle* that was probably too far in advance of women's lib to be accepted. It ended like this:

There will always be women for whom it will be a profession to keep house. Why should all of us have to do it?

As for children, is it not absurd to think their mother will blow their noses better than someone else? It's difficult to accept that most men can choose their professions, while

women, just as intelligent and sensitive, are forced to peel vegetables and wash clothes.

Men will protest: "What's a home without a woman?" My answer: "It's too late now, women are educated, and since eating whets the appetite, they'll be ever more determined to work and share your interests, even if that's not their only reason for living. If a woman's life has to stop at twenty-five because she has children, we might as well live in the Dark Ages!"

Leo, was not so much a liberated husband, as one who preferred to stay at home, sheltered from competition, and after almost four years, Leo was still not working. Though determined not to be tied down, I had always wanted children, and feared Leo could never be a responsible father.

While playing in a light comedy, I met Ludovico, an Italian architect who suggested I could find work as a model in Rome. I decided to take up his invitation, if only to see how Leo would get along without me. That move momentarily interrupted the transition from sensations to ideas, and from right brain to left. But hadn't Lin Yu Tang, Leo's favorite author, stressed *The Importance of Being*?

Chapter IV - Love's Tears

If my life were a story, the next part could start like this:

The spring rains had set in; yet undoubtedly, spring was late. Darkening afternoon sky was closing in on the long chasm of the Corso, as Selena turned the car from the wide-open Piazza del Popolo into its slow-moving traffic. The car limped to a stop behind a bus, as other thoughts gently forced their way through the gateway of their irrelevancy to her dawdling mind.

The same image as in preceding years had come and gone, punctual yet fleeting, as though apologizing for existing when it knew its creator was not interested in reaching out to take hold of it, examine it and find out what it meant. As Selena's gaze turned from the broad green back of a bus to encompass the film title on the Metropolitan cinema, she wondered vaguely why the image had returned now, a month or more after the appointed time.

It was an image in three colors: gray, rust and purple, immobilized over the years by sunlight to become the canonical representation of her arrival in Rome.

It was the very gentle stopping of a train along a shaded platform, a gray-haired figure, a bouquet of violets so big that it was several seconds before her eyes registered their extraordinarily deep purple color. The sun-splashed plaza in front of the station,

bounded in the distance by low buildings brought its vast proportions into her comfort zone.

Yearly, with the end of the first week in February, that image would flash upon the screen of her mind, and Selena would experience the pleasure of replacing the number of years she had been in Rome with a larger number. Even when she considered leaving, she noted her continued presence there with satisfaction.

Selena smiled, realizing that anniversary thoughts had caused her to relinquish domination of the thoroughfare. As the little Fiat unerringly rounded the tomb of Augustus, outmaneuvering the other cars and busses, it occurred to her that each anniversary of her stay in a foreign country added a brick to the monument being there represented.

During the first years of Selena's stay in Paris, she had experienced the joy of being somewhere few Americans called home; and as the years accumulated, being there for longer than most. As her ties with France wove an illusion of permanence, exhilaration turned to triumph at having remained in one city, in one country, because it was her choice to do so.

Her arrival in Rome on that sunny Saturday in February had been planned as a long visit, and she would return to Paris thinking it was still her home. But within three months she had detached herself from the first city

she had loved, and begun to grow new, if
again temporary roots.

Ludovico's vague gesture toward the deserted piazza had ended in a dismissive wave toward a Fiat 600. "The other car is too big to use in the city. This little one is more practical." The toy-like conveyance was spacious inside, my luggage fit neatly into place, and somehow, Ludovico's tone was not boastful. I decided to withhold judgment as I carefully, almost reverently, laid the bouquet of violets on the back seat.

We left my things with the hotel porter in an informal curbside transfer, and drove to a brightly lit restaurant on a narrow dark-walled street. My memories of that luncheon are of plain white tablecloths and a silver wine flask whose consumption would be under-estimated by the smiling, sad faced host bending over to talk to Ludovico.

"I want to show you the city", Ludovico said as we folded back into the tiny car. "It's Saturday, and I don't have to go to the office."

"What about your wife?"

"She's quite good at taking care of herself."

I noted the nonchalance, as with the size of the car.

The sun had vanished on this rare gray day and yet, as we drove up and down innumerable hills - "This is Villa Medicis, the French Academy", twisting streets suddenly breaking into wide spaces - "There's the Temple of Venus, and up there, on the left, the Circus Maximus" - my eyes, used to the soft grays of Paris, experienced an overload of color. Red, orange and an almost black green against the cloudy sky seemed invasive.

A week later, I wondered how I could have lived for ten years in a setting all in gray. The right colors for a cityscape were sun on dark green pines and cypresses under a hard blue sky; infinite variations of brown, terra di Siena or Umbria - earthy red, yellow and orange, warm images even in the short, sharp days of February.

Ludovico took me sightseeing while I waited for an interview at a fashion house. After about a week, my fascination with this man who was gay without a trace of vulgarity, learned without pretension, turned to tenderness. Only then did Ludovico show his own feelings.

We had driven to Santa Marinella, ostensibly for a swim. He ushered me into a plainly furnished apartment on the beach, obviously a family getaway. His hands were damp as he touched my shoulder. Then, with a helpless gesture, he opened a closet and rummaged through a pile of sheets, tossing two onto a large bed, all the while looking more absent-minded than seductive. His desire finally broke through the disorder, gentle, clumsy yet all the more real.

This man whom I found myself loving after a few weeks of courtship was a lover of fine buildings, painting, literature, women and food, in that order. He was anything but handsome, his hair a sandy, balding grey at forty-three, green eyes behind glasses always slipping onto his nose, a rather slight, gauche figure who was as absent-minded as he looked. His appearance was so dowdy that I had failed to noticed a sensuous mouth. He admired the French poet Paul Valéry who indulged his senses without allowing them to dominate his head: *Mr. Teste* was his model.

Ludovico confessed that he hated the thought of me taking the modeling job, for we would have less time to see each other. Much later, I realized that as an independent woman, I could have more easily been part of his circle, and thus share more of his life, however, this would have exposed him to competition. In the event, I lived a solitary life, a replay of the time when my eyes had to hide from the light.

Ludovico had booked me at the fashionable Hotel de Ville, at the top of the Spanish steps. After a few weeks he asked his partner Giorgio to let me move into a penthouse he owned near the station. We furnished the studio with a few chests from Ludovico's old Etruscan farmhouse, a new bed with a hand-made woolen mattress, a Swedish teak table whose oval-triangular shape I've never seen since, chairs that were to become modern classics, a thick glass purple-black pitcher-shaped vase, and a large reproduction of a

Matisse which I have to this day. Ludovico decided that the bed and drapes would be blue, with yellow or red pillows. Stunned I realized they exactly reproduced the "blue ball, red ball, yellow ball" of a childhood book.

Except for two penthouses, the building consisted entirely of offices, yet there never seemed to be anyone around. The concierge, a shy provincial woman, came to clean, and cooked real tomato sauce (*il sugo*), complete with carrot and flat parsley, in the tiny kitchen. She also turned out to be a careful seamstress, and I enjoyed designing dresses.

And that was how, at twenty-three, I found myself (found myself!) the mistress of a prominent Roman, reading, painting and enjoying good food and wine (though it was not until twenty years later that was I able to drink wine as though it was water). I could spend hours working on a painting, but knew it was less creativity than problem solving. For a change of pace, I read Bertrand Russell's *History of Western Philosophy,* seated at the egg-shaped teak table during and after lunch. Though I did not fully understand what I read at the time, my favorites remain the Stoics, the Epicureans, Heraclitus and Parmenides. I saw Ludovico several times a week, usually for lunch, except when his wife was on vacation, or when he traveled. He helped me understand Greek philosophy, and I was happy that he identified with just those ideas which I found most attractive.

On rare occasions, we dined together, usually at an outdoor terrace in some old city plaza. One occasion was etched in poetry:

THE MUSICIAN

His background
Two dark facades
Of gray stone
- A baroque palace -
His projectors
Two lanterns

At the door of a restaurant.

He seems frail, just a shadow
And his eyes, very close
Are like two little black stones
Pointed, like his entire face.
He has an absent look
As though beyond
A great suffering
That left him empty
With only his body present.

Even his music seems
To come from afar
As if his soul doesn't know
His hand on the guitar.
Old gray clothes hang hollow
And a large round sleeve
Strums the wood
Of a white, round guitar.

He suffers holding out the cup
He first says "thank you"
Then he waits, and you know
That with his absent look
He wants to melt into the stone
As if this were a dream he's in.

Rome is embodied for me in the lightness of the air, the heat that assails the body on a summer's day, like a hot dry glove and the ocean breeze that cools the evening hours. The parasol pines and cypresses - dark green against a deep blue sky - and the ochre buildings that had shocked me so upon my arrival, now warmed my soul; joyfully baroque monuments which, as in Paris, punctuated the

landscape, were rendered more protective by the hills. And the ruins assembled in the Roman Forum were like figures lost in time

As for Ludovico, the word that comes to mind is equanimity, but that leaves out the deep happiness I experienced by his side. Twenty-three years older than me, he replaced the father who had never shown any warmth, complemented me or indulged me in small ways. But awareness of its psychological dimension took away nothing from my passion. Nourished physically and emotionally, my feelings for Ludovico could only grow. How could I not have wished he would divorce and live with me? Although he could have no more children, I could see myself spending the rest of my life with him, and knew he would not throw away the beautiful thing we shared. But Ludovico had a ten year old son, and could not throw away his wife, who had done nothing to displease him.

What more can I say about the quality of our relationship? Recall deserts us even when it comes to our foundational memories. It's not that Ludovico has been even partially obliterated by the other men I've loved, but rather that now, seen as too old for men I would like to share with, what strikes me most about that situation is how incredibly young I was, in the sense of having all that time ahead of me.

Giorgio, always laughing, though he would soon die of cancer, had transformed one of the ancient Saracen Towers that dot the Amalfi coast south of Naples into a stunning, yet nonchalant vacation home. The images of the times we spent there are fixed forever: The steep stairway of natural stones that led from the road down the side of the Apennine foothills, the parched earth punctuated by prickly pear trees and brightly colored flowers; the relentless heat; the deep purple table service in which we were served seafood and pasta meals by Antonio, a silent, gentle, mustached man who came from the nearby village to make the house live; the hundred more flower-lined steps leading to the pontoon, and immersion in the clear, tonic, life giving sea. It was here that the Mediterranean achieved a place in my life equaled by no other.

[Favorite flowers, 1957]

Ludovico introduced me to Stendhal's four categories of love: passionate, liking, physical and vain. He said our love was the second type, liking love. Later I realized that the complicity, confidence and consideration that make casual lovemaking possible, are a subset of the love for which one has a taste, as for food. Our relationship spilled over into the first and third, both of us being allergic to the fourth, which would have made of me a possession. Still it was a situation of inequality. By now men have adjusted to the idea of women having a profession, but in the fifties (before Sputnik!), if a woman wasn't on a professional track, her life was organized around and in function of the men in it.

But I was not Ludovico's plaything; he taught as others breathe, giving structure to my instinctive quest for knowledge and beauty. Indifferent to Italy's Catholic culture, he had remained with the ancient and embraced the modern: Marcus Aurelius, Braque, Michaud, Valery - and Dylan Thomas. He showed me Giotto's frescos in Assisi, introduced me to the Etruscans - and to Beckett. But although he encouraged me to write, and even, to write every day, we both knew I had to think about the future.

My academic credentials did not qualify me for the university in Rome, and although my life was (and would remain)

more interesting than any curriculum, I felt I should be able to do something other than secretarial work or modeling. As I tried to solve a nuts and bolts problem which Ludovico could not imagine being real, my relationship with him took on a state of urgency. With his love of abstract contemplation and the conviction flowing from it that all things eventually come right, encouragements went over my head. I remember a conversation we had some time after we were no longer lovers, over lunch on the sunny Piazza Santa Maria in Trastevere, its large fountain playing a few feet from our table, still with the aura of our early days. I could not understand what he was trying to tell me then. In fact, he had also expressed it in a letter:

> *I know it's not easy, but I have great confidence in you, in your intelligence, your common sense, your feelings, your honesty and especially your will power. You have to try and see everything objectively, as in a play. You should remain off stage, in an orchestra seat, watching carefully, being critical, meanwhile preparing the speech you too will perhaps make when the time comes.*

Alas, Ludovico's wisdom was unable to penetrate a mind bogged down in a sense of urgency. Later, as things gradually came together for me, I realized that a Stoic and a Taoist, like Leo's Lin Yu Tang, had much in common. But at the time, obsessed with putting an end to suffering, I had not yet acquired the Taoist's awareness that suffering always comes to an end.

Knowing that my relationship with Ludovico had no future, I returned to Paris and tried once again to live with Leo, but as he fell into his old dependency, the fever with which I awaited the daily express letter that arrived from Rome overnight, made both of us realize we could not make this relationship work again, and after a month or two I returned to Rome.

It seems incredible that mail could have been so rapid as to sustain an extremely dense relationship almost as well as the telephone today. I think of how few letters now maintain the threads of intimacy with my children and surviving relatives, compared to the obscenely high telephone bills we countenanced in our need for instantaneous yet perhaps more superficial communication, before electronic connections changed our lives. Those days are more than gone, they are obliterated, as the brutality of 'progress' spells itself out.

About two months ago, I retrieved from a storage box a light green folder, took the letters from their envelopes, opened and dated them, arranging them in their alternating chronological order. Now when I open the bulky folder to carefully turn the pages, trying to decipher Ludovico's impossible handwriting - a task compounded when he wrote on airmail paper which did not broke, over time, being used on both sides – I return to that other dimension of time: intimate time, the time of our lives.

In the summer of 1958, the editor of an American interior design magazine came to do a story on Ludovico's house, and although New York was not, as Ludovico imagined, a village like Rome, it turned out that the editor knew Howard. Ludovico invited me to a dinner for her, so that she could in all innocence tell him she had met me by chance. As he had foreseen, my father immediately invited me to visit him in New York. We stayed up 'til the wee hours in his East End bachelor flat, telling each other what we had done, thought and felt for the past seven years. He was the first to remark on my ability to get other people to do things. I had said casually:

"We've got to change that light bulb, even if your ceiling is ten feet high."

Looking down at me from his 6'4" he queried: "Who's we?"

But beyond a casual complicity with the father who had all but ignored me, America was still an alien universe. Only when something reminded me of Europe did I feel at home. Uncharacteristically protective, Howard tried to persuade Ludovico to leave his wife for me, in a letter that was all the more bourgeois that his own life was not. Although the letter failed to have the

desired result, it made it all the more difficult for Ludovico to imagine that Howard was not a real father. However he did understand how I felt in my birthplace:

> *You're in a country that doesn't suit you, surrounded by an environment of family and friends which is far from your way of thinking and living. And every day you seek a ray of light to penetrate this environment that's no longer yours. You perceive the infinite vibrations society emits, but find in them no interior resonance. It's really a question of tuning. Your receiver is tuned to a different wavelength, so you have to look for a transmitter that suits yours, your spirit. For now, the noise of the transmission covers those you're trying to hear, emitting somewhere in a minor key.*

A few months after I returned again to Rome and my impossible love, Ludovico decided to build a second apartment house in Paris, and sent me to look for a building lot. This was no longer 'my' city, but a hostile environment. The first hotel had no vacancy. Although I no longer asked to be billed by the month, the refusal shot out as though I had been asking for charity. Encountering the same tone at the next three hotels, and the same hostility from the telephone lady in a St. Germain café, I mused that it was time for Kindness Week.

The gentle grayness of the city I had loved so, coming from Philadelphia, now seemed a mournful prison. All those gray cars huddled together between so many gray buildings! The Paris grays failed to mask the Roman colors seared onto the screen of my mind, and places whose charm had increased happiness or exalted pain left me indifferent. On the quays the tempo had quickened, and Notre-

Dame appeared behind the metallic outline of a dredge. A dredge! The usual students, lovers and book sellers seemed incongruous.

True to the season, the leaves were yellow, but they were no longer "Pale lamps, hallucinating like an August sun". The August sun was something else! A burning hand grabbing you at noon as you stepped onto the streets of Rome that were a giant oven until, as if by appointment, the cool sea breeze brought relief, skimming pastel dresses among rose-colored parasols and violet flowers, as evening fell on Via Veneto....

Aside from esthetic considerations, I could not countenance the tired intellectuals of St. Germain des Près, with their existentialist or snob rule. This was a village in the worst sense of the word, where people had nothing more interesting to say than a factory worker undergoing slow death by alcohol. I wondered whether writers only seemed intelligent when they wrote.

During those weeks, monuments disappearing in the mist on a foggy day epitomized a city that now scarcely existed for me. I knew I would never again experience the Paris of 1948: the smells, the tepid sun on a quiet street frequented by one or two timid cars, as I came out of the Alliance Française, or Jules Ferry. Must we always have new places to love?

October, 1957

I know that immobility will always escape me, yet I have no wish to remain in one place, pretending to find peace in sameness. It is easier to be alone with oneself when one is leaving or arriving, than when one is sedentary. Departures are an occupation like any other. When you travel, you're free to think; arriving in a place you don't know - or scarcely - there's always something either very beautiful or very ugly; you take in the colors, the shapes, you think, you think a lot, the machine revs up, reaches cruising speed,

you're someone who lives the world from outside.

Is detachment possible otherwise?

Ludovico would say: "You know this is not a life."

I knew, but cutting myself off from him would not be better. I would appear more available, but still be unavailable inside. Notwithstanding friends, theaters, previews, movie clubs, bookstores, notwithstanding work, there would always be a void. And so, I tortured myself between my four walls, alone at a restaurant, alone with the villagers (sic), alone with Landa, Giorgio's friend, or with the French partner, and, for better or for worse, alone when I wrote to my love, whether a real letter which I mailed 'express', or a diary that he might read some day. I knew that if a wet blanket lays over love long enough, it dies, and I mourned it even while it lived.

Ludovico sincerely wanted me to become my own person. Not because I was a burden to him, as was the case with Howard, but because like me, he believed independence of mind to be the greatest good. And while I knew the difference material circumstances could make, Ludovico was certain of my right to the compensations of intelligence.

Eventually, from hints dropped by acquaintances, I became aware that his wife had a lover, and that he did not want to know. This did not change my feelings for him, for I realized that, like intellectual and moral issues, love cannot be bargained, calculated, or reasoned away. The ties that bound me to this man were weaving the cloth of my life. We may think we cannot live without the person we love, but if we're fortunate, he remains with us always.

The only time I saw Ludovico use capitals was when he wrote: "Our LOVE is in your hands. If it seems too heavy to bear, put it down gently, but if you think you still need it, that when all is said and done it brings you more happiness than pain, then keep it tenderly and kindly, for it is a delicate thing, and now you know how much I care for you, my qualities and defects. To love each other,

two persons must be near each other. When they are apart, the thread, taut at both ends, frays and becomes fragile. One must watch over love attentively, but if it resists these pressures, it is of good quality."

Absent-minded, bespeckled, tousled, Ludovico dominated my adult life even though our intimacy lasted only a few years. He gave me the most hedonistic love, that of sharing all the good things in life. (For what is hedonism if not a love of life and an ability to share it with others?) He made love to me among the ruins of Hadrian's villa near Rome, while goats romped nearby; with him I felt my way in the dark down the stone stairway at Giorgio's tower for a midnight swim. Years later, he held my first child at the wheel of his Lancia - and perhaps somehow transmitted to the second his love of architecture.

On the rare mornings when we woke up together, Ludovico would whisper in my ear, in order, he would say, not to wake me … Years later, Ram Dass's "What can't be said, can't be said, and it can't be whispered either", would open the door to the irrefutable glimpsed during those years with the man of my life.

[Ludovico]

Chapter V - Last Tethers

Rome, November, 1957

Today in Piazza del Popolo I realized that when it rains constantly, Rome is no longer itself. There are moments which, though fleeting, even light, are almost of despair. You never feel this in Paris, probably because Paris in the rain is so typically Paris. Rome in the rain is no longer Rome, but neither is it something else, so it's like being nowhere.

Ludovico had printed my small collection of poems, confronting me with the proof that I was made for a different life. Knowing that I could not survive on secretarial work, any more than bathtubs and cars could be my criteria for happiness, he wrote that he loved me 'active and intelligent'. But at a time of life when most people who could were preparing for work that would be fulfilling, I had put my emotional needs first. At twenty-four it was too late to think of going back to school. I had to jump on the train, somehow.

I was convinced that men were indispensable to my happiness, but had depleted my energy fighting for love. I had married Jean at seventeen, then invested myself totally in trying to help Leo. It was clear that I could never hope to live with Ludovico, yet I could not cut off my relationship with him by sheer will to seek happiness elsewhere.

The situation I mulled over during the long solitary evenings and weekends that Ludovico spent with his family resolved itself when an acquaintance of his invited me to a dinner party. Very quickly, I felt a connection with another guest, a young diplomat whom I'll call Giovanni. He offered to drive me home. A few weeks later, Ludovico accepted the inevitable without withdrawing his affection. His love was definitely of good quality.

Modeling, however, was not appropriate for a woman being seen about town with a promising young diplomat, so I enrolled in secretarial school, vaguely aware of the irony. Before the course ended, I saw an ad for secretary to the director of the French News Agency, and promptly got the job.

My boss was a rare person in the world of journalism, with a style that only an Anglofied French Protestant could have: upright to the point of being sometimes harmful. In June of 1940, he had been one of four French government officials in London (one of the others being the poet St. Jean Perse), who had refused to swear loyalty to the person of Colonel De Gaulle. They had correctly guessed that he was gathering a personal following with a view to a political future. Now, as a principled anti-Gaullist, M. was cordially despised by the top brass of the government news agency that employed him.

On my first day at work, sitting opposite him as our two desks were face to face, I witnessed a sudden distress as he opened a letter. He informed me that it announced the death of his great love, an American woman he'd met before the war and lost contact with. The incident created an immediate bond between us, and a few days later he asked me to reorganize the manuscript he'd been working on for several years, which told the story. Since he'd been spitefully refused a private secretary, he paid me a small salary out of pocket, supplemented by room and board in the family apartment that communicated with the office ihis wife and children being scattered around the world. The social advantage of a prestigious address a stone's throw from the Victor Emmanuel monument never occurred to me, but I loved having breakfast on the terrace that joined my room to the kitchen, the sun filtering through a pergola. Our colleagues' wild speculations of intimacy were a source of amusement, since M. and I were both enmeshed in other affairs of the heart.

Until that time, because Ludovico spoke good French, I had not learned much Italian. As part of Giovanni's circle, which met often to attend or discuss cultural events, my Italian soon became fluent. I found reading more difficult than in French because what

you hear is not always what you see, but Italian became my favorite language.

M. soon realized that I would never be a good secretary, but since my months-long reorganization of his manuscript enabled him to find a publisher, he decided I would divide my time between the cable desk and features on the movie industry, which was then in its golden age. I was happy in my work, but emotionally, I had gone from the frying pan to the fire: not only was Giovanni, like Leo and Ludovico, not really 'available'; unlike either of them, he was cruel. Although we had a lot to talk about and much pleasure in being together, after being in love with an older, married woman, Giovanni was less inclined than I to welcome a new happiness.

The news desk brought politics back to my attention. As in France, a third of the electorate were Communists, but since they were not on speaking terms with the Socialists, who also had a large following, it was the Christian Democrats and their allies who governed, under Washington's watchful eye. In a way, my situation too was similar to the one I had experienced in France, when I went from a resistance family to a royalist one, only the other way around: Although the Christian Democratic government was the source of much important work, Ludovico was essentially a humanist; but conversations with Giovanni were more often about local power plays than about Italy's relationship to the wider world. It was when I began to cover the cinema that I discovered the large, multifarious left that counted almost everyone who was anyone on the cultural scene: writers, film directors, academics. Eurocommunism had not yet received a label, but Italian moviemakers were typical of its mentality.

A popular gathering place was the restaurant aptly named *Alla Concordia* but known to its patrons simply as Otello's. A carriage door on a narrow street in the center of Rome opened onto a large courtyard with pergolas, and the dining rooms were decorated with paintings local artists had exchanged for sustenance. Otello had sparkling black eyes, a big nose, a red face and a mane of white hair. Near the cash register (and under the watchful eye of wife and daughters), he presided over a table d'hôte where directors, actors

and others involved in movie making pooled their solitude. A good twenty people gathered there, mainly in the evening, the waiters knew our quirks, and during hard times, served us pasta and cooked greens, upon which the olive oil flowed as usual.

[Interviewing Rene Clement, photo by Pier Luigi]

In 1958, during a short trip to visit Giovanni, who had been posted to Athens, I learned that like their French and Italian counterparts, the Greek Communists had spearheaded the resistance against the Germans, emerging from the war with widespread support. But the cleavage between popular revolutionary aspirations and a feudal ruling class had led to a civil war that lasted until 1949. Although the Greeks revered a culture in which ordinary people could be heroes, the country had not yet adopted 20th century democracy. Notwithstanding the marvelous light, the cypresses, and the Parthenon, I suspected that the ancient Greek sculptor Praxiteles lacked a modern successor. From the nondescript aspect of the capital - where any resemblance to a cosmopolitan city was limited to a radius of about 500 square yards - Greece appeared to be just another little Balkan country whose silent crowds whiled away centuries of unemployment. To understand, I would have had to be

aware of the five hundred year Turkish domination - the same which, I later discovered, had made Eastern Europe a back-water.

During that trip I realized I was not the ideal wife for a promising young diplomat in Christian-Democratic Europe. Being American was a plus, but being divorced with no money was not. During my stay, a young noblewoman was introduced into my lover's Athenian circle. She would eventually, though not happily, become his wife.

Back in Rome, under Ludovico's now strictly fatherly influence, I briefly considered returning to the United States, but knew that material comforts would never be able to compete with my need for aesthetic surroundings. Gray sky and rain on my terrace etched the neighboring buildings as if they were drawn in charcoal rather than whitewashed. *The Four Seasons*, which often did not leave my record player for an entire day, seemed to translate rain better than any other sensation, and remains for me the perfect love music.

October, 1958

For the third or fourth time in the past weeks, I've re-experienced the odor of my first months in Rome, a sensation I associate with a city I am just discovering, and which usually disappears forever. Perhaps it returned because the autumn, which I am only now experiencing, although it has been almost two years since my first visit to Rome, resembles that end of winter when I first arrived. It is as voluptuous as spring, often similar to the brisk, cool autumns of my childhood, the countryside turning to red and yellow. It's as warm as Paris in May or September, and on sunlit mornings the sky is a summer blue, the air well-washed and gentle. In late afternoons or evenings the air

is so soft that it catches in the throat, a
caress that reminds me of my honeymoon trip
to Nice, a gentleness just brushing the skin
and that you breathe, as you walk in a light,
open coat...

One evening, with time on my hands between a gallery opening and a dinner date, I crossed the wide deserted Piazza di Spagna. I would have liked to sit on the marble bench that surrounds the fountain, or simply stand on a street corner admiring the Spanish Steps. But Fellini's *Vitelloni*, aimless young men seeking distractions, were always there, on foot or in cars, skeptical of any interest in architecture that a lone woman might have.

Superimposed upon these delicate sensations was the impression of being inside a kaleidoscope, in which relationships between truth, honesty, appearance and their interpretations, in my own life and the lives of others, were constantly challenged. Although the situations were different, I saw in them the leitmotifs of truth and falsehood, and wanted to understand their place in the scheme of things, having until that time seen only the outer manifestations of problems. My reflexes were geared to helping anyone who suffered, and moral support was as obvious as assisting a sick or wounded person in the street. But sooner or later I suffered for the feelings of others as if they were my own.

Although I had always had one or two close friends, my problems with the women in my mother's family did not dispose me toward indiscriminate closeness with my sisters. In groups, women usually hated me, sensing that I disapproved of their catty behavior. My friends were exceptions. They knew we were astride two regimes, that we suffered for wanting to be feminine at a time when men were forcing us to be stronger than they, even as they used feminine mannerisms to avoid the responsibilities implied by the authority we continued to grant them. We lamented the fact that the sexual inequality of women was being replaced by the psychological inequality of men.

I was beginning to find Roman society boring, but was not yet ready to give up the Mediterranean. I knew that some day I would have to cease improvising, but was unable to regret that I would never be a good secretary. I resolved to become fluent in Italian and to visit the rest of the country, Then I might allow myself to live in Spain for a year or two before making a compromise with life: a serious job in a cold place like London or Paris.

In December, after another disastrous trip to Greece, hoping Giovanni would ultimately prefer a wife with mind to one with money, I considered suicide for the only time in my life. Luckily, though not fully in charge, my left brain told me that it would never be too late to die. I could afford to wait and see what happened next.

Accordingly, from Athens, instead of going back to Rome and the recent past, I went to New York, a neutral if largely unfamiliar place. Howard was living in a townhouse on the upper East Side with his third wife and a new baby daughter whom he'd "named Geena as in Deena". Whether in New York or Philadelphia, nothing had changed. I knew my place was still elsewhere, but I also knew that I could not return to my previous incarnation. Lamenting the time when I had looked no further than eating, sleeping and making love, I sensed that I had to find an agreement with myself on a new level.

When I returned to Italy, in early 1960, Rome was still abuzz over *La Dolce Vita*. Since everything had been written about the film during my absence, I decided that my paper for the AFP would focus on director Fellini and his collaborators. Fellini liked the fact that I neither fawned over him as most journalists did, nor treated him aggressively, as did a few. Having invented full disclosure before it replaced the pretense of objectivity, I considered it common courtesy toward someone who had granted me an interview to show them what I'd written before publication, rightly confident that nothing had been distorted. I said what I thought, which wasn't always flattering, but I was never gratuitous or insulting. Fellini appreciated my insights, and offered me a job on his next film.

Given such an opportunity, most people would have gone out to learn scripting or something. Candidly, I told Fellini I didn't know

how to do any of the things involved in making a film; then, after thinking about it for a few days I suggested I could write a day by day account of his creative process, and he accepted.

Fellini's offer seemed to come just in time, since due to budget cuts, M. could no longer pay my salary. In the end, I waited more than a year for Fellini to gather the psychological and material means to launch himself into another full-length film, making do with freelance work. A few days before the start of the Olympic Games, the police restricted parking in the center of Rome, but forgot to post the new rules near the Pantheon, where I lived. On the first morning, finding a huge fine on my windshield, I phoned *Paese Sera*, the evening paper. (Everyone in Rome read it although it was published by the Communist party. In Parliament, the left could only put spokes in the political wheels, but its papers could play up minor stories.) *Paese Sera* invited to me write about the parking situation, then asked me to do a series on Americans in Rome.

Though busy with work and meeting people, again I realized how alone one can feel while surrounded by others. I felt acutely the need to live with someone - but not just anybody, since personal space is necessary for a couple to thrive. You know the other person is there, even if he doesn't make himself heard, or felt, whereas unless it's very short, the solitude one wishes for after two or three days of socializing is neither restful nor invigorating because it is total.

The leitmotif of those years was: "Because I'm intelligent, men deny me the right to be weak." But I continued to believe there was only one real prostitution: that of the mind. As life continued with no other priority than to be available when Fellini shot his next film, I wanted no boring lover and no mindless work. One day when I was visiting Ludovico, the young architect who worked with him looked at me with such eyes that I was shaken. Roberto was handsome and talented, and although he tended to be a loner, both professionally and socially, he was charming and unpretentious. We started to see each other, uneasily at first, under Ludovico's benevolent gaze when I came to the studio to meet Roberto.

[With Jerome Robbins at the Spoleto Festival, photo by Pic]

Alas, I was unable to match Roberto's deep feelings. During our two year relationship, he suffered, and I suffered to be the cause of his pain. Though not a masochist, I preferred being tortured to being the torturer. I remained deeply attached to Roberto, and was pained when, many years later he told me that even our intermittent correspondence had to cease because of his wife's jealousy. (I have never understood why women who came after a relationship or a marriage had ended, were invariably jealous of me.)

One special moment of that period endures: sitting on the Gianiculum Wall overlooking the city with Roberto, waiting for dawn to break after a party, the unbearable slowness of a process that you know will happen but that seems determined to take its time. Since then, it has been difficult for me to resist following dawn's trajectory if I happen to be awake.

The habit of writing to Ludovico established during our liaison continued, first in the sturdily bound black notebook whose ugliness contrasted with my colorful, casual penthouse decor, then in a succession of nondescript others. One day, Jean-Paul Sartre came to speak against the Algerian War. Although I shunned crowds, I knew I had to be there. Mesmerized, I realized that not only things

could be beautiful, but ideas also. Sartre's ugliness underlined the beauty of his mind, which was as clear and sharp as a diamond. That encounter with raw intelligence was a decisive moment in the transition from right brain to left. I can see from old notes how even then, right brain sensitivity was served by a left brain capacity for detailed analysis - whether concerning the nature of my relations with Ludovico, or the quality of the air in Rome. The tendency to isolate myself that flowed from the contours of my life had allowed me to follow each idea wherever it might lead. Now it began to develop into a systematic form of inquiry that would lead me to places geographical, intellectual and emotional far beyond anything I could have imagined.

Chapter VI - New Druthers

[Entrance to Fellini's office, Rome]

By October Fellini had set up production offices near *La Concordia*, and Piero Gherardi had decorated them with orange curtains, green lamp shades and the oversized couches he had designed for *La Dolce Vita*. The assistants, lost in a vast, more casually furnished outer room, endlessly sorted photographs scattered on a long antique table. Fellini would open the padded

double doors that separated him from his staff, greet me with typical Italian verve, and show me into what he called 'the poet's retreat', assuring me that work on the picture was about to begin.

As the wait dragged on, I accepted an invitation to meet Howard in London, stopping for a few days in Paris. It seemed incredible that I once had known this city intimately. At each return, Paris struck me in a different way. At first, I was still at home, but in a home I had abandoned, like meeting an old friend and having the feeling that you're seeing his ghost, the anxiety was almost insurmountable. Gradually I became more detached: my home was building itself elsewhere. Now, the anxiety caused by no longer being in a familiar setting was replaced by a different perception, difficult to pinpoint at first: Paris was going modern! I was able to ask for a document from the civil registry over the phone and have it handed to me while I waited. Unheard of only a few years ago, it was probably part of De Gaulle's plan for recapturing la grandeur.

In London, I discovered why the English tap on the glass that separates them from the driver with the pommel of their cane: knuckles can't be heard, and as everywhere else, chauffeurs were ready to take you by way of China. (At least, the soundproof separation ensures that chauffeurs do not eavesdrop on passengers' conversations…)

I first heard God Save the Queen in a fashionable restaurant where Howard had taken me dining and dancing. Suddenly, the orchestra struck up the national anthem. Instantly, the waiters froze, talk and laughter stopped, people put down their glass and stood in rapt attention. The second time was at the end of a film in a neighborhood theater. The moviegoers were already moving toward the exit when the music came on. Immediately, everyone turned toward the screen, whence the music was coming, and froze. Howard had told me how the English had thumbed their noses at the blitz; now I realized that it was precisely because they are capable of being totally serious about a national anthem that they survived.

During my first visit to London, with Ludovico, I had almost strangled in the Heathrow ladies' room, trying not to laugh out loud at the sight of the notice printed across the corner of each piece of

toilet paper: 'Property of Her Majesty the Queen'. When Ludovico had asked for ice tea, the waiter had looked at us incredulously, and finally, after a long wait, slammed down a big pitcher of tea in which floated a gigantic block of ice hacked from who knows where. Now, I discovered that the English feared nothing so much as being too warm: the windows in the halls of our old hotel were open day and night, in contrast to its homey style. No public place seemed to remain at a comfortable temperature for more than five minutes: quickly, someone would come and open the windows.

By the time I went to London with Howard, I had been speaking French and Italian for so long that I had a tendency to mix metaphors (a problem that worsened when I acquired a few more languages). One day in the hotel elevator I said to him: "I hope you're not going to take me on a wild duck hunt." But this was also a Freudian lapse: in my wistful version, my father took me on a duck hunt, when in reality, he had sent me on a wild goose chase.

How little I've said about Howard, given that until middle age I considered him to be the cause of my problems! His gigantic figure had towered over my life like General de Gaulle towered over France. Was my father not handsome, charming, intelligent, gentle, authoritative and talented? Now I realize that it was not so much his several wives, but his way of treating all women as though they were his lovers that determined my later relationships with men. Devoting little time to female relatives, with whom sex was merely a fantasy, he denied me a true father-daughter relationship. During one rare and hence all the more unsettling burst of anger, he revealed that his behavior toward me was largely dictated by his hatred for my mother. I realized that unexpected reactions had been triggered by a look, a tone, or something else in me that reminded him of her.

In early 1961, as I continued to improvise a living, Fellini told me he would not be able to concentrate on his new film until he'd finished dubbing *La Dolce Vita* in English. Then came spring, and he decided to get *Boccaccio 70*, which was scheduled for release in December, out of the way so he would be able to take all the time he needed for *his* film. (Little did I suspect that the film would be about how much he needed that time.) I continued treading water,

with sporadic free-lance work and no boy friend. Finally, around the end of 1961, the production office for Fellini's still untitled film moved to quarters near the Villa Borghese where he had prepared *La Dolce Vita*. Anyone wanting to see him would be told to come to the office after six. I would usually find the chairs in the waiting room filled with aspiring actors, and when I sat in on interviews, Fellini would tell the younger ones that alas, there were no parts for them. "This picture is full of old people", he would sigh, as if there was nothing he could do about it.

The preliminaries continued to drag on. In March, 1962, we began to discuss what job would allow me to write a book about what he was doing. I resisted his suggestion that I be his script-girl, since I'm not good at details, and finally he decided I should be the press officer. At that point, Fellini really needed a few good people to help him get through those final weeks before shooting started, and I made myself useful wherever someone with no film experience could.

My contract designated me as press officer on the set, but a few days after shooting started, Fellini decided the set would be closed to journalists. Most of his entourage thought the rule would be short-lived, but I suspected it would endure, and in fact, he made very few exceptions during the eight months of shooting, during which I had nothing to do but observe him at work.

My relations with Fellini had been set once and for all during our first encounters. He very soon knew who I was, while I was never to really know who he was, although I often guessed what his decisions or reactions would be better than people who had worked with him before. Our relations were of mutual respect, perhaps because he sensed that I was different from most hangers-on in the film world, square, not as a woman, but in being literal-minded, unpretentious and unflappable. He also appreciated the fact that I totally lacked the killer instinct of the successful journalist: if he didn't want to answer a question, I didn't press him. If he wanted to give an ambiguous answer, I went away with that. I used my own mind to try to get answers, rather than pick at his. He never made the slightest pass at me, but could poke a finger between two buttons of

a blouse to see if what was underneath was real, simply out of playful curiosity.

Unused to getting up at dawn and not wanting to miss anything, I went looking for a magic potion. Perhaps it was a placebo effect, but high potency vitamins did the trick. For good measure, I went to bed right after dinner, a small sacrifice after waiting so long for this opportunity.

The shooting took place in an old studio known as La Scalera, which consisted of several two-story office buildings and workshops, and one or two sets. My favorite spot was the small garden where all the important decisions were made. Seated on wooden benches surrounding the fountain, cameraman Gianni di Venanzo, set designer Piero Gherardi, Clemente Fracassi, the executive producer known as Whirlwind (or rather 'Tourbillon' since the Italians had adopted this French word to describe his ability to be everywhere at once), Fellini and the various assistants, hashed things out without protocol, groups forming and transforming in a constant flow of questions and solutions. The fountain area was surrounded by oleanders, and it was here that we spent most of our evenings, that spring, summer and early fall, as the pink Roman sun gradually abandoned the party.

I soon developed a close relationship with Whirlwind, who had been among the long-time collaborators I had interviewed for my AFP article. Alas, he was devoted to an aging mother, and refused to believe love could be part of his life, but I was content to know he was there during those twelve to fourteen hour long working days. On early nights we sometimes had dinner together, and Fellini's good-nights on those occasions were tinged with affection for Whirlwind rather than his usual teasing. Tourbillon was one of the few people in my life whose friendship survived geographic separation.

Filmmaking is a tiresome business, which is probably why every occasion to celebrate was seized upon with childlike enthusiasm. Whether it be the official launching, the first day of shooting, or someone's birthday, a few hours were taken off in the middle of the day as stars and staff headed for the nearest trattoria.

Fellini would appear to have put out of his mind the challenge that haunted him; but in the midst of the merry making, a ghost would flicker across his face, a brief absence whence he returned with an almost guilty smile, as if to apologize for betraying the company.

[Fellini Team in garden, photo by Gideon Bachmann]

On a movie set, patience is the primary virtue, from the lowliest carpenter to the stars. Patience and tolerance, for rarely are shooting conditions comfortable. You have to weather the heat, the dust, the sun, the rain, the lights, the dark (when you can't even read), and for the actors, makeshift dressing rooms. There is a special quality to the human relations that develop between actors and technicians who are thrown together for several months, and must get along if they are to do their job. At least it was that way for the shooting of *8 1/2*: people made an effort to be cheerful and accommodating, and if someone did fly off the handle, it was short-lived.

Fellini himself was a paragon of good humor and diplomacy. He rarely used anything but sweet or joking persuasion on his actors, yet had a remarkable ability to get what he wanted from them. As I

watched him point a finger at a figure sitting in the shadows, or moving a piece of furniture, and put him under the lights for a walk-on role, I often thought he could get a chair to act. He knew instinctively who could do what, who would look right as what. The cardinal is played by a man he found in an old folks home, and Guido Alberti, who plays the producer, was a mature business man who had never acted in his life, but went on to a lengthy movie and television career. Fellini knew what kind of face he wanted for each role, what kind of clumsiness or grace, and he took it wherever it could be found. A housewife could play a major role, and a star could find herself so transformed she was hardly recognizable. We couldn't guess what it was about Sandra Milo that made Fellini want her for the female lead, but soon she looked completely different from her usual self. (Fellini asked her to gain a lot of weight. She ended up getting pregnant, which was fine for a while, but threatened to complicate things toward the end.)

What surprised me most was the way things that appeared so problematical managed to come together, through the input of dozens of people, each doing the right thing at the right moment in the right way. It was like living an ongoing miracle. The most interesting thing about watching Fellini work was trying to guess what he was going to do next, or how a decision would affect what followed. To do that, one had to take the pulse of his anxiety, which paralleled that of his hero, who was also trying to make a film without knowing where he was headed. 'Il Maestro', whom everyone called 'Federico' and addressed in the familiar form, as he did them, could penetrate a person's psyche like a nail being driven into a precise point. This is particularly evident in his early films, *The White Sheik*, for example, where he ridicules his main characters in a way that stops just short of cruel. By the time the shooting of *8 1/2* was over, I had developed a sixth sense about the Maestro's intentions.

[Whirlwind and Fellini]

While I pulled the book into shape, my linguistic abilities allowed me to remain on the payroll through the dubbing process, translating the English and French dialogue tapes into Italian. I was subletting an apartment from a cameraman who was off shooting in Africa. One day, he showed up on my doorstep. His film had been interrupted by a revolution, and he had nowhere to stay. The apartment had two large rooms, each with a bed. I knew this man only casually from Otello's, but sensed we could get along. Our table mates teased us when they learned of our arrangement, but only once did it break down, on a rainy Sunday afternoon. Though merely a ripple on the surface of our companionable cohabitation, for me it was a civilized interlude in a lengthening period of sterile encounters, a tiny oasis in the vast desert of promiscuity.

When I saw *8 1/2* again thirteen years after it had been made, it seemed remarkably unified and compact. I realized that although it was complex, it was not loose, but rigorous in a classical sense. The dialogue that came back to my ears was familiar, not because I had heard it hundreds of times, but because of its tone, which is that of classical theater. Fellini had superimposed upon his multileveled

exploration a dimension unrelated to the images or the action, but which as an attribute of the dialogue pervades the entire work. By elevating the dialogue to a theatrical tone, which normally has no place in the cinema, and is in fact what separates film from the theater, Fellini manages to unify the present, past and imaginary scenes. But that edge in the actors' tone has another implication: it makes the action appear to take place in a compact time frame, another characteristic of the classical theater that conveys a sense of inevitability. The succession of events taking place in different time frames gives the impression not so much of time fleeting, as of time compressed. What seemed like a rambling, unstructured work from close-up, now showed a classical conciseness perfectly suited to the challenge the director was facing.

Our suspense during the planning and shooting, in particular during the days when final decisions about the ending were being made, was trifling compared to Fellini's uncertainties, which came disturbingly close to those of Guido. Fellini didn't know where his eighth and a half film was taking him, but from the first day of shooting, he had found a way of turning his dilemma to advantage, making the confession of his professional crisis into a classic of that very art of film-making that the crisis was about.

None of Fellini's subsequent films seem to belong to the same family as those that led up to *8 1/2*. If was as if, in that work, he'd been breaking with the past, moving into a new world, whose disarray would be translated by grotesque masks and make-up, or oversized ships going nowhere, and whose characters, hitherto very down to earth even in their most lyrical dimension, seek guidance from spirits.

Fellini ate, slept and breathed film-making twenty-four hours a day. From time to time other interests penetrated his consciousness, but his passion overrode everything else. Hence the depth of his crisis. And yet, Fellini had used that eerie ability of being able to pierce people's facades and defenses, on himself. For the creator who has reached a turning point of this magnitude, it must have felt very much like stepping into another life. That's probably why Fellini hesitated so long over the ending of *8 1/2*: for all his desire to believe

that life goes on as before, and that he would continue to be the same Fellini as always, he knew that was a fairy tale - or a circus. What other meaning could the press conference have, with its nightmare of suicide, followed by the rebirth of Guido as a little boy?

The courage it must take for a man to put such a crisis on film is what allows us to go on loving and admiring him, even if we do not share his interpretation of the world. For most artists, courage consists in presenting solutions to social problems: Fellini never wavered from the conviction that this was not his role. (Perhaps coincidentally, artists who choose that path rarely seem to reveal anything personal.) For Fellini, courage consisted in baring a major turning point of his life, in which he could no longer represent the world as the humane place he loved, but had to show us in his own way what a terrible place it had become.

During the nine months I worked with Fellini, I thought little about what was happening in the world. But by the time I had finished my book, *The Two Hundred Days of '81/2'* a new curiosity had taken hold of my mind. The terrible things I had been reading in the papers about Cuba conflicted with what people who had been there were saying. While still at the *AFP*, I had worked on a story for *l'Express* with a well-known news photographer who had done several features on Castro's Cuba, and during a visit to Paris he had introduced me to the correspondent for the newspaper *Revolucion*. Their accounts had a ring of truth that I did not perceive in press reports. After spending anguished years wondering what to do with my life, finally breaking into journalism through a fairly large back door, and writing a book, my early, traumatic brush with dissimulation required that I now verify the credibility of the corporation I had joined.

However much the Mediterranean meant to me, Italy was really no place for a divorced foreigner going on thirty who hoped some day to have children. With no idea where I might end up, I was ready to leave the cocoon of Rome for whatever the future might bring. The Fellini book had been sold to an American and a German publisher. While excerpting it with an editor at *Paris Match*, I mentioned that I was thinking of investigating the Cuban revolution.

It turned out that the magazine wanted to do a series on political personalities, and would welcome an interview with Castro to start it off. There should be no politics, just 'the man'. I accepted the *Paris Match* offer, on condition they alter not a comma of what I might write.

[Tower for 8 ½ under construction]

A brief stay in New York reinforced my allergic reaction to America. I was reminded of an admonition read somewhere as an adolescent that pregnancy is like a roller coaster: you can't get off until the ride is over. Being in the United States was like being on a technological roller-coaster. Charting my way through elevator banks going to different floors, confronted at the last minute with ambiguous exit signs on turnpikes, and navigating the undefined spaces of the Pennsylvania Railroad Station, I experienced a feeling of helplessness I had never known in a foreign land. Ironically, I noticed that Americans liked everything foreign, on condition it had been Americanized. Chinese take-out looked like a dentist's waiting room. Children of two or three ran out of stores alone, eating ice

creams, singing and dancing, and you could paint shoes. I wondered whether the goal was for every Hindu and Zulu to have the privilege of joining our rat race, buying a television on credit that would exhort him to acquire an endless succession of Things in the same way.

Howard was convinced I would not return from Cuba alive, but he was too obsessed with my wildly sexy five-year-old sister Geena to talk me out of going. I obtained a Cuban visa on my French passport, and after the requisite visit to family in Philadelphia, I flew to Mexico City on my American passport. The following morning when I returned to the airport for the flight to Havana, and saw the elaborate screening system the Mexicans had set up in deference to the American government, I began to fear that at some point, someone might wonder why the French passport with the Cuban visa that I was presenting to leave the country, showed no evidence of my having entered it.

The checking, rechecking, photographing, and waiting, in a huge sealed off area, took about four hours. Finally, I was told to proceed to the ticket counter. Did I already have a ticket? Was I worrying that the ticket agent would check my passport? I have no idea, because the moment I came up to the counter, all my circuits froze: I was standing next to a tall, suntanned blond with a way of smiling with his blue eyes that almost made me blurt out: "This is not possible."

There was no dearth of things to talk about after what we'd just been through, and it turned out that my follow traveler - a Norwegian cameraman who had emigrated to Australia, acquiring an inimitable accent - was an old Cuba hand. His teammate was a journalist, but in a reversal of the usual professional relationship, Claus was the leader. Responding to my reasons for going to Cuba with the typical cynicism of hardened journalists, they were determined to set me straight. On the Viscount turboprop, Claus hustled us into front row seats facing two soldiers with submachine guns standing before a colorful map of the alligator-shaped island that I would call home for most of the next two years.

Chapter VII- Fact and Fantasy

[With Fidel and Vallejo, photo by Korda]

Less than a year after the Missile Crisis, the United States was still trying to corral the renegade island back into its southern yard. The *Revolucion* correspondent in Paris had cabled my arrival to the Foreign Ministry press office, but there was no one to meet me, so I was all the more grateful to be expertly escorted. At the Havana airport, the desks were strewn about randomly, and a mini-version of the Mexico City ritual was conducted by cigar smoking, bearded men in olive fatigues. When we emerged into the suffocating sub tropical heat I realized that they all looked like the huge portrait of Fidel Castro that adorned the airport façade. We piled into a taxi, one of those dilapidated American cars that would come to symbolize the Cuban-American standoff. The sun was tingeing the sky a robust pink, as Claus threw a knowledgeable *Habana Libre* to the driver.

The next few days were spent making requests at the Press Office and waiting for them to be granted. Claus and I carried our political disagreements together with our attraction to bed. Years

later, reading over the carbon copy of a twelve page letter I wrote to Howard during that first trip to Cuba, I discovered that we had been close enough to move to a little hotel in the old city that was cheaper than the *Habana Libre*. (After a day or two the Foreign Ministry offered us a discount to return to where they could keep an eye on us.) When Claus left after a week, I was still convinced that few things were more boring than promiscuity, and wasn't even sure of his last name.

I continued to badger the Press Office about my request for an interview with Fidel, and now that I was strictly on my own, I began to meet some Cubans. I became friendly with two upper class divorced sisters about my age who shared several children between them. One of them worked at the Czech House of Culture, and invited me to be there when Fidel was scheduled to meet the visiting Assistant Minister of Culture. Fidel didn't show up, but I took to Milan Tabor the minute I saw him cut the dark bread he'd brought for his hosts as if he were at home. He too was staying at the *Habana Libre*, and a few days later we went the beach. This was my first contact with someone from behind the Iron Curtain, and although the young minister seemed painfully on his guard, he gave me his number, in case I ever happened to be in Prague – a remote possibility in those days.

As I explored Havana, Fidel made unannounced appearances everywhere I was not, including my hotel at three in the morning while I slept. With my funds running out, I began to lose patience with the Press Officer. I booked a flight to Madrid, then, with nothing to lose, vented my anger on him, whereupon he called the Vice-Minister and told him there was a Western journalist who was probably going to write yet another negative story about Cuba. That very afternoon Pelegrin Toras called and asked me to come by. I realized as soon as I walked into his office that he was an experienced diplomat. We chatted for about an hour, and he promised to set up an appointment with someone who was in a better position to forward my request to interview Fidel: Cesar Escalante, head of the propaganda department of the Cuban Communist Party. The appointment came through for the next morning, almost

conflicting with the time for my departure. Bags packed, I went to the meeting, more out of a habit of leaving no stones unturned than anything else.

[Cesare Escalante]

I had a 'what-am-I-doing-here' feeling as I entered party headquarters, but immediately liked Escalante, even if he did brain wash people into believing communism was good for them. A wiry man with horn rimmed glasses and a shock of gray hair, he looked like a schoolteacher - or a Eurocommunist. Our conversation was more of a sparring match than the one with Toras, but it was also more spontaneous. After a while, I told Escalante I had to catch a plane at twelve.

"Listen," he said, "I can't promise anything on behalf of Fidel. But if you want to stay on for a few days, you can be sure he'll get your request."

"I appreciate your offer, but unfortunately, my money has just about run out."

"Be our guest. It's no problem. On the other hand, if you want to leave, I'll phone the airport to hold the plane."

I explained that journalists were not supposed to accept anything from people they were reporting on. Escalante raised his arm in a 'too bad' gesture and said he was sorry I hadn't pulled out the stops sooner.

Time was short. I thought back to when I had modeled for artists in Paris, knowing it wasn't what you did but who you were that counted. After about thirty seconds, I chose the story over journalistic correctness. When I returned to the hotel, I found a telephone message under the door. Fidel's aide de camp would call back later. At eight I was paged to the phone in the bar.

"This is Vallejo. I'll be by shortly."

When I got off the elevator, there was a tall, salt and pepper bearded man with twinkling dark eyes lounging on the bench. Making an instant transition, he strode down the long corridor after me, then, with an easy American accent: "May I sit down?".

Our talk was to the point. I explained my project, and my difficulty in getting through. After a few questions he got up and said: "We have a dinner for Boumedienne (chairman of newly independent Algeria's Revolutionary Council). We'll be by later." Before I knew it, he was out the door and down the hall. Similar exits would punctuate the next two weeks of my life, and be repeated often during the next two years.

I had dinner brought up to the room, but with no television, I could only sit and wait, numb from the early morning meeting and the day's nervous fatigue. At about midnight I heard the sound of boots in the hall, then a knock on the door. I opened it to find myself facing a huge chest that started at eye level. Vallejo, with his friendly smile was just behind Fidel. We shook hands, and the two olive clad men strode into the room, which fortunately, was furnished like a bed sitter.

We sat in a triangle, with Fidel at one end of a sofa bed, leaning on the end table. He picked up a newspaper, glanced at it and commented on a front page story. Then, with Vallejo acting as interpreter, he wanted to know who I was, what I'd done, how I

lived, what I read, and whether I owned anything. This was his way of gauging my probable reaction to the Revolution. Although I hadn't come to any conclusions, I tended to feel that the people who described Cuba in positive terms were closer to the truth than press reports. Still, I spared no criticism, in particular of the Stalinist running the Press Office (I would later learn that he had been moved to another job). After ten or fifteen minutes of questioning, Fidel agreed to let me do my story - though not exactly as I had outlined it:

"You can't follow me around all day - nor all night", with a mischievous wink. "But I promise to give you whatever time you need to do your paper over the next two weeks." I hadn't expected to owe that much to the Cuban government, but I wasn't about to pull out of this adventure now. I accepted the offer, and Vallejo promptly got up and left.

Was this some sort of signal? Actually, I was less worried about my father's dire predictions than about the loss of my interpreter. My intuition told me that tI was safe, and in fact, what ensued was a three hour talk fest. The Spanish I remembered from my ten year old crash course in Paris, plus what I had picked up during the last three weeks, was still mainly Italian. Undeterred, Fidel rephrased his statements until I understood. I briefly considered breaking with my custom of not taking notes, but decided that tried and true techniques were preferable to experiments that could fail. So I concentrated on understanding, wondering how my verbatim memory would work in Spanish.

We covered a multitude of subjects that night, ending with a breath of fresh air on the balcony at 3 a.m. When Fidel suggested I accompany him later in the morning for a swim, I was delighted. As soon as he was out the door, I fell into bed, assuming he meant late morning. Alas, it was only eight o'clock when the phone rang.

"This is Vallejo. I'm downstairs. Hurry up, Fidel's gone on ahead. And don't forget your bathing suit."

I pulled myself out of bed, wondering how I was going to keep my eyes open. Vallejo was waiting in the lobby when I came out of the elevator, and by the time I'd said hello we were in a limo parked in front of the door. Vallejo drove, I sat in the back seat next

to a guard negligently holding a sub machine gun on his knees. Realizing my feet were resting on several other weapons, I moved them gingerly about, as if that could make a difference.

Fidel's house was on a public beach. One of the things the Revolution (always capitalized) was very proud of was that beaches, which had been reserved for whites only, were now open to all. As we walked through a grove of ocean pines where a few people were picnicking, we came across a couple in a tight clinch. The woman stood up as we approached, the man did not:

"Get up, it's Fidel," the woman urged.

"It's also Sunday", remarked Fidel as he walked by.

On the beach people came running from all directions. Carrying on an uninterrupted conversation with one person then another, Fidel moved toward the water and waded in, with Vallejo, me, and several guards in tow.

We spent about two hours in chest-high water as the waves rose up and down, and Fidel answered questions. At one point a particularly big wave crashed upon us. I came up gasping, and everyone laughed. By the time we headed for the beach cafeteria, I was starving. But Fidel had to hear all the questions and complaints, and pay a lengthy visit to the kitchen before we got anything to eat. Back at the house, he showed me to the bathroom and demurely took out clean towels for my shower. As we were getting ready to leave, someone mentioned baseball, which I now discovered was Fidel's passion. Few people are as bored by baseball as I am, but tired, sunburned, hot and thirsty, I sat dutifully in the neighborhood grandstand and watched him play, endlessly dissecting each gambit.

Our next meeting took place ten days later. Fidel had spent the afternoon reassuring small farmers that they would not have to collectivize, enthusiastically describing the miracle of chemical fertilizers. I had waited patiently on a wooden chair in the wings of an assembly room in the presidential Palace, and suddenly, Vallejo appeared and we were sitting in a black limousine, exiting into the darkened street, with Fidel declaring he wanted dinner at the beach house in Santa Maria. Over tall glasses of grapefruit juice freshly squeezed by two of the escorts, Fidel told me his father, a landowner,

had disapproved of his student politicking. Seeing an opening, I posed the key question: "So you were already a Marxist?"

"I didn't realize it, but I was a utopian socialist. My economic studies had made me realize that a lot of talent was going to waste in our country, both in terms of work and money, and we had to organize, make long-term plans.

Suddenly, we were on the road again. Clenching a spent cigar in his mouth, the chauffeur held the car at robot-like speed as Fidel turned toward me from the passenger seat. I asked him jokingly whether he burned up as much energy studying. "I used up as much energy, but I studied mainly toward the end of the semester", he answered with an impish smile.

"When it's for something worthwhile, you can do without sleep. The Americans haven't realized it yet, but imperialism is over, and for us, nothing is more important. We'd be perfectly happy to sit down and talk to them, we've been ready since the beginning, but all they want is to attack us. They need to understand, once and for all, that we won't give an inch. Imperialism has to be liquidated. After that" - eyes shining - "I'll write my memoirs."

Our last meeting took place in Varadero. We were speeding down the highway when Fidel suddenly yelled at the chauffeur to stop. As he got out in front of a new apartment building, people came running. But Fidel didn't want to be adored, he was furious because the tenants had filled in the spaces between the stilts, ignoring the elegant design. Fidel scolded them and told them to take the walls down before he returned. Getting back in the car he grumbled: "That's poor administration! Why does capitalism work? Because they know how to choose people, that's the secret. There's no reason why socialism shouldn't work as well. It's a question of getting the right people."

At a secluded beach house, we had a late afternoon swim and ate grilled lamb chops, one of the escorts being an accomplished cook. When around ten o-clock Fidel put me in a car with a driver, I had an invitation to return. The radio played Tchaikovsky's violin concerto all the way to Havana, and I had the feeling that I was finally doing something worthwhile. Not because Fidel was a

celebrity, but because what was happening in Cuba was, in the scale of things, more important than what happened in Cinecitta.

[On the road with Fidel, photo by Rene Vallejo]

Back in Paris I spent the night before my story came out making sure the editors at *Paris-Match* made no last-minute changes. Just when I thought it was all wrapped up, I caught the second page title insinuating I'd slept with the *lider massimo*.

In Rome, I translated my article for an Italian weekly. Talk of the Venice Festival seemed trivial after seeing people passionately trying to find solutions to real life problems. I didn't know whether the Cubans were going about it in the best possible way, but I was convinced they were in good faith.

Notwithstanding my headline veto, *Match* offered me an internship, and after the article appeared, the Cubans formally invited me back. I planned to finish my stint at the magazine before returning to Cuba to research a book for an Italian publisher. The idea was to find out whether Fidel and his followers had been communists before the revolution, or whether events had gradually led them that way, a burning question at the time.

I had only been on the job in Paris for a few weeks when John F. Kennedy was assassinated. It happened on the night we were putting the magazine to bed. A few of us were having a drink in Pershing Hall, opposite the office, when the news broke. We rushed

back and rewrote half the magazine. Jean Daniel, a well-known French journalist, had just carried a message to Fidel from Kennedy, and there had been hope of winding down the confrontation. Now anything could happen. As I edited material from Dallas and Washington, I suspected that Johnson was part of the plot. When Oswald's Cuban connections were revealed, I activated my invitation. I wanted to be on the spot if anything should happen.

From Paris one had to travel either to Prague or Madrid to take a Cuban plane. With a mental nod to my grandmother Regina, I opted for Prague, boarding a Caravelle at eight o'clock in the morning, cursing the hour and the absurdity of the detour. As the plane climbed above the dirty clouds of the Paris Basin, as it is called, I remembered my youthful train journeys to Germany and wondered when we would be flying over Vitry-le-Francois, where I had been hauled off the train in the middle of the night. We were served breakfast, then, almost before I knew it, the plane started its descent. I was astonished to see that Prague was no further from Paris than Rome, and could be reached in the same amount of time it took to cross the city by bus, or wait one's turn at the dentist's. Remembering how my father had sent me back to the States in 1950 fearing the Russians would roll across Central Europe, I began to suspect the accuracy of the phrase 'Iron Curtain'.

Who could have guessed that Czechoslovakia, a small country walled into the center of Europe, would some day develop close ties with an island on the other side of the Atlantic? As the daily flight from Havana touched down on that gray autumn morning, Cubans and Czechs embraced. In the baggage room, blond girls with red cheeks and blue eyes wearing brightly colored parkas and ski pants loaded bags onto a carrier. A Valkyrie-like hostess helped carry mine to a bus whose door seemed resolutely closed. She called out to the driver, they exchanged a few cheerful words and the doors opened. That would never happen in Paris!

The *International Hotel* on the outskirts of the city was a Stalinist era concrete eyesore. The Czech passenger next to me made the remark in the same disparaging tone the Romans used to point out similar Mussolini era buildings. In a telephone booth in the lobby

someone had scratched 'Cuba si, Yankee no' and, more eloquently, in Cyrillic characters 'Kyba'. At the bar, in front of an expresso machine, extraordinary canapés were piled on starched linen-covered plates. Czech and East German newspapers were spread on low tables. In the restroom a long paper ribbon barred the toilet bowl with the word "disinfected" in Czech, French, English and Russian. I was reminded of the royal owner of the toilet paper in Heathrow airport.

I exchanged three thousand francs at the desk, and upon hearing the taxi rate to town, decided to take the number seven trolley that revolved in a lazy circle in front of the door. There were two cars, with boxes for the fare. The conductor made change. The dark wood paneled interior was fitted with matching benches; on the windows, small blue advertisements for soap and socialism.

The street was gray, almost deserted. At each stop a housewife clambered on. The trolley wound through a wooded hill and into a busier neighborhood, old buildings huddled together. Two high school girls got on, one wearing a skirt, stockings and heels, the other in pants, socks and white sandals, both with short, teased hair. They leaned over a book together. Facing them, an elegant young woman also read a book. Leaving behind the deserted neighborhoods of the outskirts where life seemed suspended, the trolley took on factory workers. In the center of town store clerks and office workers got on. There was little difference in the way the various groups dressed: everything was average but nothing was poor. Two young girls and a boy sat near me; typists maybe, with the brother of one. From the way they laughed, they were probably gossiping about sex.

Downtown there are few automobiles, and people throng the wide sidewalks. Gradually the trolley's peaceful rhythm overrides the shop lights, the windows filled with toys, books, clothes and pastries, the women in the tram with long leg hairs poking through stockings, like Italian women a few years ago. The trolley with its peaceful rhythm insinuates itself into my subconscious, makes its way through corridors of forgetfulness, seeking obstinately but surely its way to memory, where it finds the hundreds of wooden trolleys of my childhood, as the United States entered the war that

would eliminate the human dimension of things such as trolleys, filling the streets with automobiles and the skies with rockets.

I had arranged to meet Milan, the Czech vice minister of culture who had given me his number in Havana. Notwithstanding his reserve in Cuba, he had lost his job in a Stalinist reshuffle, and had plenty of time to show me his city. Our first stop was a retrospective of the work of a diplomat, writer, painter, cartoonist and illustrator, who had been a friend of Picasso, Cocteau and Malraux. The Adolph Hoffmeister show was the event of the day in Prague. People filed by slowly, stopping before each window, each picture frame. War cartoons published in England, caricatures of his Paris friends, subtle and audacious collages, paintings, mathematics books for children, an extraordinary energy, an authoritative stroke.

We stop briefly in a 'second category' restaurant, founded in the 13th century in the old town: vaulted rooms, frescoes, tables and benches of dark wood. In a 'fourth category' cafe restaurant filled with students and workers, the wine barrel fastened close to the ceiling shows 12°. We order beer, pork chops smothered in onions, and rich chocolate cake. The woman in charge is Hungarian, and will not allow Milan to pay. The clients call her boss, although the place is owned by the state. All the tables are taken, it's warm, people talk animatedly, eat and drank at ease. Near the door, four men: "The thin one with dark eyes founded the Czech Communist party. Now he's retired."

Coming from Cuba, where Communism carried a permanent aura of conflict, I realized with some astonishment that real people were living ordinary lives, laughing and disagreeing about the details of a structure that we thought was monolithic.

The neighborhood is full of wine cellars. In one, an orchestra plays in a large vaulted room. In the smaller room, three proper looking young women drink beer while the waiter, in black morning coat, tells them about his visit to America. Another waiter goes by nodding to my friend: "After the 1919 uprisings in Eastern Europe and Germany, he led the student revolt against the Communists.... "

At night in the old city lovers lean against bare trees along the broad Moldau, near the Charles Bridge lined with ancient statues.

The fog from the river fills the deserted 15th century streets: "Dvorak lived there, Apollinaire over there; there, Mozart.... in that house with the rose colored curtains lives Jiri Trinka, the greatest clown of the century; unfortunately he can only be understood by thirteen million people. Look! Trinka's turned out in the living room, he's in the kitchen with his wife and children. His last film is about a little girl who wanted a perfect grandmother, so they gave her a cybernetic one. She did everything perfectly, but had no heart. Over there is Beethoven's house."

"Beethoven? Mozart? But they were German!"

"Right, but Germany included Bohemia. Now we don't say Bohemia, we say Czechoslovakia."

And the rest of us think it's another planet....

From Prague the trip to Havana took two days, with an unscheduled night in Shannon to wait for a defective plane part. I was met at the Havana airport by Vallejo, who dropped me at the hotel saying: "We'll be by later for the cheese."

Fidel was particularly fond of French cheese, and I had brought a whole wheel of it. Exhausted, I decided to get what sleep I could before he showed up. At one o'clock in the morning there was a call from downstairs. By the time I'd put on my bathrobe, there were four men in olive drab and cigars at the door. The third was Commandante Dermidio Escalona, the fourth a guard, who hesitated in the doorway. Fidel turned to him and said:

"Aren't you coming in?"

They each took an armchair or a seat on the other sofa and there was no place for me to sit but on the rumpled bed. Seeing me bleary-eyed, Fidel smiled in mock commiseration:

"Poor thing! Look what we've done to her!" He was in high spirits, having just come from a showing of *Divorce Italian Style* with Mastroianni. "Every time he has to make a decision, he goes like this" - and he imitated the impotent man's facial tic.

I brought out the cheese, but knew that would not be the end of the visit.

"Kennedy was an enemy we knew. Johnson has to keep the elections in mind."

I agreed, and said I thought this might incite him to do something spectacular that would make him look as tough as the Republicans. Fidel thought he would be more interested in getting the liberals on his side, and would not invade Cuba. He was glad the Cuban Embassy in Mexico hadn't given Oswald a visa to travel to the Soviet Union via Havana. It would have made the Castro-Communist connection more credible. Vallejo interjected with a UPI story that Oswald had first been sent to the Soviet Union as a spy.

Fidel promised they would cooperate with my book project, but for the moment, Kennedy's assassination had been overshadowed by a major cyclone, and that was what he really wanted to talk about. He waxed lyrical over people's solidarity, and suggested I go to the western part of the island to see the damage first hand. I reminded him that on my previous trip, I'd scarcely been out of Havana. With a wink he assured me that since then, rules about western journalists had been relaxed, and they would let me know as soon as they could arrange for someone to accompany me. Fearing it would be a bureaucrat, I suggested Fidel's personal photographer Alberto Korda, who would be more fun.

Fidel shrugged: "Find out if he wants to go."

By three o'clock I was back in bed. The next day I got a call from the Cuban National Institute of Cinematography, known as ICAIC, enquiring when I would like to view the cyclone footage. I asked to see the film on the literacy campaign as well. Although the cyclone was a dramatic event, and all the top brass were out there helping to rescue people, it was the literacy campaign that interested me most. The way the Cubans went about teaching seventy percent of the population to read in one year truly embodied the spirit of this place. The first hurdle had been to get the teachers to the students, since many of those who didn't know how to read lived in remote areas with no public transportation. To the Cubans, this was a detail: the box cars used for hauling sugar cane were fitted out with wooden benches, and traveling in them, the teachers got a taste of the conditions under which they would work.

Housing in those remote places consisted of huts with roofs of pine leaves, called *bohios*, candlelight and no running water. The

young teachers were put up with each family in turn, usually teaching a child or two, who then taught the parents, freeing the teachers to move on to the next family. Some of the adolescents joined the teachers, or continued their education in the schools set up on the coattails of the campaign.

Time and again during my stay on the island I would recognize the Cuban hallmark. It was something you might call 'pragmatic creativity', adopting whatever works in a given situation, oblivious to whether it has been done before, or what it will look like. In a way it was like saying "damn the torpedoes..."

[Sierra Maestra foot path]

That same impression continued on the trip that I took with Alberto Korda to Santiago and thence up the Sierra in a jeep. One day I decided I'd been bumped around long enough and thought I would prefer walking down the mountain. Korda's 'the-customer-is-always-right' attitude allowed the customer find out she was wrong. The path was narrow and winding, and suddenly, with no warning, cattle or donkeys laden with coffee would appear, forcing us into the prickly side brush as they went by. I'm very fond of the picture Korda took of me dunking my feet in a stream at the bottom of the mountain, and when I look at it, I remember exactly how exhausted

and hot I was that early evening, as tiny lights went on in the village of *bohios*.

To find the answer to the question that every journalist and political analyst was asking, I planned to interview all the people who had been with Fidel since the beginning. One of the most picturesque was Commander Manuel Fajardo, who didn't know how to read or write when he joined the rebels in the mountains. Now he headed a gigantic cattle raising operation, complaining in colorful language about bureaucratic directives from Havana, which he ignored with panache. As Korda and I traveled, we witnessed the rebuilding of roads by night under giant projectors, and admired row upon row of cane reapers from the Soviet Union. They probably weren't the last word in cane reapers, but they were impressive looking beasts, with gigantic arms reaching toward the sky.

[At the bottom, photo by Korda]

Later in my series of interviews, there was a Commander who insistently repeated "caterpillar, caterpillar", waiting in vain for a complicit laugh. In the face of my incommensurable ignorance of things agricultural, he finally explained that for him, getting around

the American embargo meant purchasing Caterpillar tractors from "a sympathetic country to the north", meaning Canada.

[Cyclone Flora road repairs]

Korda and I met some wonderful people during our ten-day trip, but gradually something I had sensed without quite being able to formulate it, came into focus like a picture in a camera lens. I realized that 'The Party' was seen as a God by those who believed in it, and especially by those who worked for it. But unlike a personality cult for a human being, this was a cult to an abstract entity. 'The Party' was a faceless, soulless God who neither spoke nor heard, and whose edicts had no accountable author. Since party officials embodied the authority of this divine entity, each one felt himself cloaked in a shred of its mantle. But because, nonetheless, supreme authority resided in 'The Party', they did not take responsibility for their actions. The mantle gave them the right to judge others, yet they passed the buck to whoever was above them. And while they were not necessarily superior, everything they did, good or bad, was sanctified by 'The Party'. (Superior people are

never part of the herd: they organize it, for a divinity can only rule if there is a herd to carry out its word.)

Also, however well-intentioned most Communists are - and this fact is something Americans still haven't understood - they fail to realize that you can't force happiness down people's throats, as would later be vividly illustrated for me in Eastern Europe, where there was no revolution to be passionate about.

Another example of the Cuban spirit was a school for pregnant teenagers. Some of the country girls who had been chosen to go to school in the capital arrived pregnant. Fidel suggested they be gathered in a place where they could continue their studies while being with their children. An abandoned mansion was turned into a school with dormitories and nurseries. A staff of older women took care of the babies while the mothers went to class. After school, the girls took over, learning how to care for their children.

When I visited housing developments, farms and schools, I couldn't help noticing how well balanced the children seemed. It was ironic that while Cuba supported the Palestinians, in many ways its attitude toward children was similar to the Israeli's. One of the bogeymen stories Cubans were told was that their children would be taken away from them, and the government made a concerted effort to persuade people that this was not true. Many opportunities were created for educating children that involved them leaving home, but not until they were ten or twelve; they came home for vacations, and Cuban families remained as close as ever.

In those early years the revolution accomplished really spectacular things, like building convivial, functional teachers' training schools in remote areas. Or the beautiful and daring art school on the Havana golf course designed by Ricardo Porro - who later worked in France. Or turning the mansion of the former president of Cuba into a boarding school for kids from the country, leaving a lot of the furnishings and fittings intact as a political lesson.

From November 1963 to August, 1964 I interviewed all the surviving Commanders who had been part of the group known as the original 'twelve', plus several who had joined them in the early days

in the Sierra. These conversations are recorded in my book *Cuba 1964: When the Revolution Was Young.*

[Castro brothers' country school]

This was still the 'pachanga' period of the Cuban revolution, where high spirits were set to the rhythms of salsa music. It was only after Che's secret departure for Bolivia in 1965, that the more rigid period which some ascribed to his influence began. I'd heard stories about Che and glimpsed him from afar. While Fidel had appeared at the 1964 New Year's reception wearing a gala uniform made by Khrushev's tailor during a trip to Moscow, hair carefully combed like an adolescent at a first communion (but with a half smile at the idea of dressing up for a reception), Che arrived a bit late, in olive green drab open at the collar, the usual beret smashed over messy hair, and made straight for the Chinese ambassador - perhaps the only guest who might approve of his appearance.

A few weeks later, when Che left for an international economic conference in Geneva, where military uniforms could not be worn in public, the U.N. had to step in and tell the Swiss government that Che wouldn't be 'in Switzerland' but in United Nations territory.

[Raul Castro's photo]

On another occasion, Raul Castro was driving me to his house for an interview. As we passed a low, rose-colored tract house with a garden across from an empty lot, Raul pointed excitedly: "Look, that's Che's house!" Later, explaining the summary trials and executions of Batista's thugs carried out in the provinces on the heels of the revolution, he said: "Of course people said a lot of bad things about me, but that was because they couldn't criticize Fidel. They took their anger out on me, who was closest to him, and on Che."

During my interview, seated across a small desk from Raul, I took pictures as we talked. After a while, the head of the armed forces reached into a drawer, pulled out a camera and started to take pictures of me, remarking that it was only fair. He then proceeded to illustrate the main differences between himself and Fidel: he was an organizer who delegated, Fidel liked to follow everything through himself.

One evening I saw Che stride resolutely across the lobby of the Habana Libre, followed by two guards whose step was significantly more relaxed. With a curt nod to the writer he had steadfastly refused to see, he marched up the big stairway to the mezzanine. I found out later that he'd been on his way to give a speech to the congress of his ministry's Young Communists. He admonished them not to take on the sinister party heaviness, losing their spontaneity and freshness. "And don't spend your time

debating what the attitude of young people should be with respect to this or that problem. Revolutionaries should instinctively know what's right." When someone asked why the party had been slow to organize the youth, he said it was because it was full of people with a bourgeois mentality, which there would be no point in propagating.

[Raul Castro at home]

During all this time, there was an on-going discussion in Cuba over the question of material incentives to production. Under Che's system, factories put their earnings into one account and took their operating expenses from another. That meant they couldn't give bonuses to outstanding workers. Under the system espoused by the economist Carlos Raphael Rodriguez, each factory was a separate legal entity that could sign contracts, keep its own books, and reward productivity. Che maintained that a society trying to build socialism should emphasize the idea of work as a duty of each toward all. Carlos Raphael agreed with the principle, but believed people

couldn't be changed all at once. When I asked him about that disagreement during an interview in his book and painting lined study, Carlos Raphael mused:

"Che, Che, He's an intelligent man, very well read, the only thing is that, how shall I say, he's very demanding. He demands a great deal of himself and others, not because he's harsh, but because he sincerely believes that if he can do something, others can too. That's why he persists with his system. He believes that since with him, it yields excellent results, it should be the same for others. He can't conceive that other people are not as conscientious as he is. Did you know that Che goes to cut sugar cane under suicidal conditions?"

"How is that?"

"Because of has asthma, he suffocates from breathing in all that dust. It's crazy, but Che says: 'If I can cut cane, everyone should be able to do it, and no one should be excused from cutting cane.'

It was obvious that Carlos Raphael had thought a lot about this: "Fidel is also unconscious of other people's weaknesses, but the outcome is different, for example, our yearly climb up the Turquino mountain is no big deal for him; but when he realizes you can't do it, he doesn't try to make you keep up with him, he leaves you with someone to take care of you, give you an injection, everything you need, and he picks you up on the way back. Like Che, Fidel doesn't realize that everyone doesn't have his physical capabilities, but he doesn't say: "If I can do it, other people should too." In a theoretical case like material incentives, he has a lot of confidence in the people, but at the same time he's more realistic than Che when it comes to evaluating their capabilities. He knows how people are."

Pause: "But Che is as good as bread, really. He's an extraordinary person. I remember one time in the Sierra, before he went down for the invasion, there was a doctor who was a bit old, a bit fat, and Che didn't think he would survive a campaign. He hadn't said anything, but the man realized he wasn't going, and was devastated. Finally one day he said to me: 'Please take me with you the next time you go to see Che.' So I took him with me, and do you

know that just looking at him, Che understood his pain, and said: 'Okay, you're coming with me.' That's all, just that one sentence."

"You should read his writing, for example, the story called *Death of a Dog*, or *Lydia Twelve* about two messengers who were sent to Havana from the Sierra, and stupidly, they hid in the same house where some other boys were hiding after stealing a Madonna to prevent a religious procession from taking place. Batista's police traced them, and none of the bodies were ever found. You have to read those stories to understand Che."

My interview with Che Guevara, then Minister of Planning, took place on February 11, 1964 and was the most difficult of my career. As I had been warned, he was not only extremely intelligent, he had a devastating sense of humor. I was no match either for Che's erudition or his wit, which could be expressed as just sitting there waiting for a meaningful question. Since he was reluctant to see me, I could have saved myself the ordeal; but that would have left a hole in my revolutionary rosary....

After waiting for several months, I had finally messaged Fidel, and the next day Vallejo called to say that Che was resigned to meeting with me, on Saturday, at eleven. When I told my Cuban friends, they inquired as one: "a.m. or p.m.?" Because of his drug resistant asthma, he feels better at night.

The interview took place in Che's office, in the morning. I arrived ten minutes late, and was shown into a huge irregularly shaped room, with wood paneled walls painted dark gray, the whole thing in a state of disorder, books everywhere, on shelves, on tables, on the sofa. We sat in armchairs, a foot apart.

"Thank you for seeing me. You show great constancy in refusing to meet with journalists.

"You can waste a lot of time that way, and in the end they misquote you." He gestured as if to say this was inevitable.

"Well, since you mention it, I'd like to know whether you really said, in a recent meeting with some Italians" (perhaps the Italian publisher Feltrinelli), "that you wanted to kill off all the imperialists from age fifteen up."

[Che in his office]

Slight smile. "Yes, I said that, but it was in answer to the specific question: 'What can other countries due to help Cuba in the event of an attack?' I don't like to kill people, or to encourage others to do so."

"Well that answer makes you look like a monster."

Now he really smiles: "If that were the case, they'd have to kill the newborns too."

"Would you please explain what you really meant?"

"I meant there's no point in people demonstrating in front of an embassy, or writing letters to their representatives saying: 'We energetically condemn the attack on Cuba.' There's only one thing you can do in case of an attack on Cuba if you want to help: kill, in every country, the greatest possible number of imperialists in age to inflict damage. It's the only language they understand, the only thing that could make them think twice.

"I understand you fire on sight at counter-revolutionaries."

"Who told you that?"

"A friend who works on a collective farm in Escambray. Also, when I was in Bayamo with Korda, they arrested him because he was wearing olive green pants with a red sweater, and one of the policemen told us that the week before, they'd killed a counterrevolutionary who'd come down from the mountains dressed like that. They pretend to be barbudos, so real barbudos have to dress correctly."

Che laughed, slouched in his chair, head back on his shoulders, fingering the shirt hanging over his belly: "That's true, and it's also true that you shouldn't wear your shirt outside, but it's more comfortable... No, those people aren't shot unless they resist. They're arrested and tried by a popular tribunal on the spot."

"Which automatically means shot."

"Not necessarily. It depends on what they've done. If they give themselves up, and it appears they can be re-educated, they're sent to school or to a collective farm."

"But you used to shoot the barbudos in the Sierra for rape."

"If the women denounced them."

"Are you saying that knowing they would be shot, the women denounced them? In the Sierra, where couples lived together all their lives without being married? Where girls are mothers at fourteen?"

"Well, but it's different if she didn't want to! And sometimes it was the parents who denounced them. We had no choice. We had to be scrupulously correct in our dealings with the peasants so they would realize that the rebel army had nothing in common with Batista's."

"What do you think of the Russian sugar cane harvester? It looks like it will need a lot of improvements."

"I don't think so. Machines can always be improved, but this isn't the first one of its kind, so it's relatively well developed. There are two types, one that does everything, and the other that pulls a flatbed while the tractor part cuts the cane."

[Che's photo]

Che rummaged among the books and papers on the low table, where his secretary, Manresa, had put the coffee cups and glasses of ice water. He turned over a piece of paper rapidly to see if there was anything on the other side, and began to draw: "I'm not good at drawing, but I think you can see it."

The drawing was highly simplified, four little circles: the wheels; four lines: the body of the machine. Next to it, looking like tall commas, the cane. As understated as his way of talking and writing.

"How many new factories are there?"

"Sixty-two."

"I read about a factory that made spare parts for capitalist machines. You can't really eliminate the effect of the embargo, can you?"

He smiles, gestures: "It's good for something, otherwise we wouldn't have built it."

"The other day a friend who goes to the party school said it was thanks to the Communist Party that the Cuban revolution took

place. The school teaches that without the party, the revolution wouldn't have happened. But those who fought in the Sierra tell a different story. What's the official position?"

"The official position is not that of your friend. The party played a part in the revolution, which can be defined quite precisely. At first it was against guerrilla warfare."

"You mean the difference of attitudes between those in the cities and those in the Sierra, between the bourgeois and -"

"We're all bourgeois. This revolution was carried out by people who were all bourgeois, starting with Fidel."

"Right, but how does the party reconcile its past attitude with the needs of today?"

"There's no problem."

"But in the schoolbooks -"

"What about the books? Manresa! Bring me the party book that has Fidel's speeches, the pink one."

Slouched in his chair, head down, Che flipped the pages. It was the only chance I had to take a few pictures in the room shaded against the sun. Afterward, I sent him the one I liked best, a close-up that shows his uncompromising, mocking intelligence. When we met on the reviewing stand during one of Fidel's speeches, he said it was horrible, and when I dared him to do better, he took a picture of me that made me look like a kindly grand-mother.

"Do you know the speech about the origins of the party?"

"Yes, the three speeches."

"Well?"

"There's nothing specific about that."

"Did you read them?"

"Yes I did. They talk about everything but that."

He continues to turn the pages: "Here."

I look at the passage. "I don't see anything here. I read it. I remember it well."

"Read it again."

"Okay, but meanwhile tell me about the role of the party."

"If you can stop interrupting me, I'll tell you everything in five minutes."

"Promise."

"The party's attitude can be divided into three phases. The first, from before the departure for Mexico until we left Mexico. The party agreed on the need to fight, but they thought it would take more time to prepare an armed guerrilla. Fidel had said that in 1956 we would either be free or dead, so one way or the other he wanted to land that year. (The landing took place in December.) The party thought we should wait for the general strike planned for the spring of 1957, when the sugar harvest would be over and many people would be out of work. Fidel refused to wait."

"And who was right? Fidel or the party?"

"How long does a women's promise last? Fidel was right, as the facts demonstrated. The second phase of the party attitude corresponded to the first year of guerrilla warfare. The party was convinced that you couldn't have a revolution from a base in the Sierra, therefore it limited its activity to underground work in the cities. In 1958, there was a general strike, but the heads of the 26th of July movement didn't want to organize it together with the party, so they didn't participate, and the strike failed.

"Afterward, Fidel called a big meeting of the heads of the 26th of July Movement in the Sierra. The movement was reorganized to coordinate our activity with that of the party. That was the beginning of the third phase of the party's attitude, its full participation. Of course the revolution continued to be led by the 26th of July; they had started it and they remained in charge, since the party, in a way, arrived late.

"After we won, the enemy was no longer Batista. The first goal of those who backed the revolution had been to get rid of Batista. Once that happened, the number one enemy became imperialism, which moved from the background to the foreground. All those who'd wanted to get rid of Batista weren't enemies of imperialism, but the 26th of July movement and the communist party were. From that moment on, they were together in a struggle against the same enemy, and therefore everything that happened from then on is perfectly logical."

Suddenly, the colors were brighter on this core issue. The movement wanted a revolution, and was potentially anti-imperialist. The communist party was anti-imperialist, but didn't believe in the possibility of a revolution until the 'historical conditions' were met. Fidel doesn't give a hoot about conditions; damn the torpedoes, he forges ahead. Around him other parties take advantage of the machine he sets in motion because they too want to get rid of Batista. When Fidel realizes the party is ready to cooperate, he imposes that cooperation on his friends."

"Would it be more or less right to say that before the revolution had won, you believed vaguely that communism would eventually come to Cuba, and that once in power you realized that 1) there was no other way to do what you wanted to do, and 2) contrary to expectations, after a few years, the people were ready to accept that choice?"

A drawn out "right". I don't know whether Che has reservations about my analysis or whether he's surprised that a woman (especially one who interrupts!) could come up with anything so complex. Some of Fidel's speeches from 1959 might help, but they're out of print. I turn next to a report in *Revolucion* on Guanacabibe, the prison on the Isle of Pines.

"Why did you send that soldier who shot in the air to Guanacabibe?"

"It's forbidden to shoot in the air."

"But he said he didn't know how the rifle worked."

"Right, but what were the circumstances? Was it during a maneuver, when he could have killed someone? How many times had he done it before? If you don't give people a sense of responsibility -"

"How long do they spend in Guanacabibe?"

"From a month to a year."

"Why do you say it's voluntary?"

"Because it is. A factory head can either go to Guanacabibe or lose his job."

"A factory head who made mistakes because he doesn't know better?"

"We don't send people to Guanacabibe for inability, but for bad faith."

"For example?"

"For example if someone sleeps with his secretary. The secretary can do what she wants with her body, but suppose he gives her a raise? We can't tolerate that."

"But how can people come back to their workers after being in Guanacabibe?"

"They're sent somewhere else. It's better than not having a job."

"Guanacabibe is your idea. Why?"

"I wrote something that explains it, but it's an article about economics, and I don't think you'd understand it, and in any case you prefer to hear things rather than read them."

"Only when the written thing is vague. You can get a person to explain until it's clear." I use his anti-feminism to pose a different type of question:

"Cubans who have been to China say the Chinese attitude toward relations between men and women is very puritanical, that a man can't even look at a woman in the street, and that if you ask the interpreter how you can meet a woman, she blushes and changes the subject. What do you think about that?"

"I was in China with a delegation and I didn't notice anything special."

There was no way I could get him to say anything that wasn't diplomatic about China. Not even about something that had nothing to do with politics.

"But I do believe that flitting about is bad for the revolution."

Apparently sex does have something to do with politics: "Why is that?"

"To have first one woman then another and so on, you'd waste a lot of time, you'd have to court her, bring her flowers, and all that takes time away from the revolution."

Now I was wondering if he was really serious: "That's okay for the leaders, who sacrifice themselves, but you can't ask it of the man in the street."

"I don't say you can ask it of everyone, but before, women had little choice but to sell themselves if they didn't want to go hungry. Was that better?"

"Let's not exaggerate. People are dying of hunger all over the world, but they still make love. I don't think people will ever agree to give up sex for food."

"When everything is all right, of course, but let's not forget that we're in a time of danger."

"Its true there could be an invasion, but the revolution has already been here for five years. You can't ask people to live as though they were forever on the brink."

His last words brooked no response: "What about the bomb?"

Several months after this conversation, Celia Sanchez confirmed the insights I had arrived at while talking to Che. During an informal five hour conversation, I asked Fidel's right hand woman whether during the war she had been sustained by the conviction that one day they would reach this point, or whether the way things turned out was like an unexpected gift, something that had seemed unlikely as they fought for what they expected to be a much more modest result. She replied impetuously: "We didn't think it would happen so fast."

Waiting for interviews required a great deal of patience, and the more important the subjects were, the longer one had to wait. Foreign visitors - mainly, but not only, journalists - were put up at the Habana Libre, and all were guests of the Cuban government, for the simple reason that otherwise they would never have agreed to spare the time. We called ourselves the 'Waiting for Fidel Club', and inevitably, the members of this cozy band became involved in various affairs. For me, promiscuity had been going on for too long, but this was part of the far-out adventure we were all living. It was fun to evade the ladies posted in the emergency stairwells of each floor to enforce the rule against promiscuity inspired by Che's puritanical attitude. (Desk personnel, on the other hand were generally discrete accomplices.) At that time, the revolution pretty much refrained from interfering with the natural inclinations of the

population, but this began to change at around the time I left, which also coincided with Che's departure for Africa, then Bolivia, where he would be killed.

From July 1963 to July 1965, I witnessed the trial of a young man who had betrayed a group of rebels during the war; several intellectual battles; the sequestering of Cuban fisherman by the U.S. Coast Guard, and the threat of an invasion, or at the very least of an air attack, during which I discovered how much of a coward I was. Abysmally ignorant of the laws of physics as well as of warfare, I was convinced that because I lived near the top of one of the tallest buildings in Havana, I would perish under the first bombs. The crisis had started when American U2s were seen flying over Cuba. Then there were provocations by the Marines at the base in Guantanamo. Celia Sanchez, whom I had come to know and admire, said Fidel wouldn't hesitate to shoot down a U2. As I reflected on events, I tried to see past the surface. Here are some of my notes dated May, 1964:

In this gentle land, harshness is not a contradiction, but a counterpoint.

Only middle class leaders can be generous enough to make a revolution. The working class basically wants to trade places.

Leaders can bring people to any extreme. Fidel's merit is to have provided his people with a high ideal.

Countries need inspired leadership during exceptional times, such as a war of liberation. But leadership ceases to be inspired if it remains in power beyond the critical period without opening the way to democratic government.

Fascism is the extreme of capitalism, communism is the extreme of socialism. Clearly, some form of socialism is of benefit

to the majority, although it may not suit the minority who put freedom to travel above freedom to eat.

Typical of the difference between American and European attitudes toward Cuba is that De Gaulle doesn't waste time fighting Communism in the name of moral principles. He knows ideas cannot be vanquished. Working with the existing situation, he recognized China and maintains good relations with Ben Bella's Algeria. to ensure that France benefits. Aside from that, nothing is more important than the glory - and influence - of France.

Because the U.S. is a melting pot, Americans tend to ignore differences between groups of people, assuming that the world can become a melting pot under our direction.

American attitudes toward Communism are like those of a person in need of psychotherapy. They think knowledge about Communism is fatal; a book about it is like a hot coal. The American press gloats that: "Castro's people hate him because as a result of the blockade, he can't even give them houses with elevators." The travel interdiction that goes with the blockade prevents Americans from witnessing a government that is trying to improve living conditions for the majority of its people.

Attitudes toward socialism and capitalism turn on the definition of rights. Capitalists say that "all men are equal" , meaning that each has the inalienable right to arrive at the

maximum of his abilities, which implies free enterprise. Socialists say that if all men are equal, the state must make sure they receive the basics. Both fail to define responsibility.

Some people are more clever than others, but that should not give them more rights. In an ideal world, the relationship to work would be direct. No one should have to work for others.

Democrats can think like Republicans because they are not fully attached to the principles which, when taken all the way, could turn them into socialists. Both parties banish ideology, not realizing that this too is an ideological position. They believe that somehow the world can be better off while some remain entitled to deprive others. Intellectually, Europeans know socialism is more just; pragmatically, the wealthy are opposed to it because they would stand to lose.

That last paragraph could have been written today!

Part II: Raulito, Regina and Me

Chapter VIII - Fantasy and Reality

During the Waiting for Fidel period at the *Habana Libre*, I was seriously involved with two men, one of whom was free and wanted to marry me, the other married but wanting to have his cake and eat it. Then, in the spring of 1964, I met a Polish economist on loan to the Cuban government, who changed the course of my life. Notwithstanding the various husbands and lovers I've had, I am incapable of chasing a man; but I did notice a handsome, blond, green-eyed, seemingly single man in the hotel restaurant full of mainly Mediterranean types. After several days of glancing at each other from our respective tables for one, we found ourselves in the same elevator, exchanged a few words and discovered we were on the same floor.

Andrei was everything I had been missing: unpretentious, bright and tender. He had been married for five years to a woman whose heart condition prevented her from having children. At twenty-two, he already had a graduate degree, and was a consultant at the sugar ministry. Though his Spanish was rudimentary, our bodies needed no interpreter. Within a week we were living together in perfect bliss.

[Andrei]

Should I have foreseen that Andrei would cause the same suffering to our child as my father had caused me? Unlike my parents' relationship, ours was one of complete harmony. The only time I saw Andrei looking slightly annoyed was when we attended the 26th of July anniversary celebration in Santiago, and he was left out of my long arguments with the American journalists covering it. English was not one of the languages he understood, but I translated while trying to keep up my end of the conversation. Even the mildest man is bound to feel diminished in this type of situation. During the entire duration of those festivities, I was hemorrhaging, but never imagined that I could be pregnant, although seen with hindsight, a picture Korda took shortly before I was due to leave for Italy with my finished manuscript hinted at my condition. Celia had asked me to act as interpreter at a dinner for the head of cabinet of the King of Morocco. There were a dozen of us seated around a huge table, as Korda hovered discretely in the shadows taking pictures. Aside from the fact that this was a formal dinner, my décolleté was almost always in view in Cuba, due to the mild weather. One picture shows me looking across a gentleman in bournous as I interpret to Fidel, while the gentleman glances sideways away from Fidel down my unusually generous décolleté.

Pictures are funny. After shooting hundreds during those years in Cuba, I realized they reflect the brain of the photographer more than the actual subject. As with painting, photography is mainly a question of *seeing*. The picture of Fidel and me in front of the houses with the filled-in walls, which was taken by Vallejo from the other side of the car, shows me in much sharper focus than Fidel, even though we are at the same distance from the camera. I had already guessed that Vallejo had more than a professional interest in me, but I could no more marry into a revolution than I could marry into money. He remained a true friend until I left Cuba with Andrei's child, at which time, sadly, he was dying of cancer. As for the Moroccan on the other side of Korda's lens, he was young and quite handsome, but when he invited me to visit his country, I demurred, not only because of Andrei, but because I suspected I would not be treated with the same respect as in Cuba.

[Interpreting for Moroccan official, photo by Korda]

I left Cuba in August 1964 to deliver my book to my Italian publisher. In Rome I saw a gynecologist and discovered that I was three months pregnant, too far gone for anyone to perform an abortion in a country where it was illegal. After waiting all those years to have a child that would grow up loved and happy, I found myself in what the French call a Cornelian dilemma (a seventeenth century version of damned if you do and damned if you don't). I had to choose between aborting the child of a man I loved and whom I knew would make a good father, and allowing the pregnancy to continue amidst major uncertainties. The greatest emotional challenge of my life occurred as I was discovering and analyzing new ideas, completing a switch from right brain to left. But the Cuban ethos had revived the gusto of the belly-flopped girl on the sled: I would not give up this child. Nothing in my life has ever generated the same upbeat determination.

Andrei assured me by phone that he would get a divorce and all would be well. He had invited his wife, Casimira, to enjoy an exotic vacation, during which they would deal with the matter like civilized people. Meanwhile I tried to speed up my plan to visit Latin America for a book the Cuban government wanted me to write. I believed the southern American hemisphere would eventually follow

Cuba's example, yet for most Americans it hardly existed. I would call it *The Phantom Continent*.

Leaving my manuscript with the Italian publisher to edit, I returned to Cuba in early December. I should have foreseen that Cuban 'mañanismo' would eventually make it too late for me to engage in more plane travel. And perhaps also that Casimira would busy herself getting pregnant, declaring she would only get an abortion in her own country. I had grave misgivings, but too much respect for Andrei to have it out with her.

Casimira went back to Poland, and Andrei and I were assigned an apartment near the Habana Libre, high up overlooking the city and the harbor. We went to the warehouse where furniture abandoned by Cubans going into exile was stored, and picked out a few simple things. Friends in Mexico sent bottles and a sterilizer through the diplomatic pouch, as well as basic tropical baby clothes. A huge Donald Duck from Celia was put to bed in the basket that awaited our child, whom we wanted to be everything the duck was not, that is, beautiful and intelligent. To encourage his pre-natal development, we wrote out comic strip dialogues and placed them near the duck's face, and when we went out at night, we put sunglasses on his nose and a book on his chest. Although Andrei was a quiet person, he confessed he expected his child to come into the world knowing integral calculus.

Raul was born twelve minutes after midnight on my grandfather Jake's birthday. He was overdue, so they had to induce the delivery, and at one point they wondered if it would turn out all right, only managing to avoid the forceps by calling in a big hulk of a guy to bear down on my belly. At last Raul lay on my chest, and we looked at each other. All I could say was 'chico', gripped by an uncustomary apprehension.

Andrei told me that a few minutes before hearing that Raul was born he had shed his illusions: He would be just like any other kid, he wouldn't talk or know logarithms. "A nurse came out of the delivery room with a baby and said it was mine. I looked at it and, somehow I knew that baby wasn't mine. Then she brought out Raul,

he looked so much like me, but he was so ugly! I felt guilty, but after they dressed him in a white robe, he looked a little less ugly."

In the afternoon we went down to the nursery to see him. Predictably he was the one with slightly fairer skin. I liked him better than the others, but worried at not experiencing a surge of maternal feelings.

I had the baby settled in my room, as recommended by *Dr. Spock*; but when the obstetrician came, he told me there were some contagious cases on the VIP floor we were on, so once out, the baby could not be put back in the nursery. We had to go home. I was feeling so well that it didn't occur to me that women who have just given birth are supposed to spend most of their time lying down. As a result, my episiotomy became infected and for days I couldn't sit. I turned to Raul for help with my diary:

My name is Vladimir Raul. Only time will tell whether I was born in the right place at the wrong time, or in the wrong place at the right time, or whether I was indeed born in the right place at the right time, only to be brought, at the wrong time, to an interminable series of wrong places.

[With Raulito overlooking Havana, 1965]

Perhaps you're wondering how I come to be familiar with these events. Well, I often receive firsthand accounts from my mother, and before my birth she was the only person who believed I paid any

attention. Like the Chinese, she considered that I was really born at the moment of conception, since I existed in her mind long before that, and that transcendence enables me to pass with ease from one life to the other. Things come to me from many sources, in a continuous flow, not, perhaps because I'm especially perceptive, but because I've been willing to play the game, listen to what is said, and to what comes to me intuitively, instead of letting myself be confined to a world of milk and more milk, where children rarely see or hear.

Actually my Donald Duck was called Fidelito. Although my father had said in the beginning that he wanted a son named Raul, by the time the duck appeared on the scene, certain complications had led him to discard his favorite name. He and my mother more or less settled on Fidelito, since if it hadn't been for Fidel, I wouldn't have been there in the first place.

But why did everything change again and make me turn out to be Vladimir Raul? As you can see, Raul came back into favor, but with some reserves, since it was degraded to second place. Officially that is, for in practice I've always been called Raulito, Raulinko, and even Raulka, no sexual innuendo intended.

What happened was that my father thought he would be able to handle the complications, so he decided he wanted me to be Raul after all. At the same time, he had become aware of the fact that Raul Castro, whom the name inevitably evoked, was supposed to be a tough character, whereas he fancied me as the gentle image of himself. My mother suggested they put Raul in second place as a sort of secret name; that left the problem of what to put in front of it. Obviously, one couldn't put Fidel and Raul together (although we learned later from a neighbor that the Minister of Sugar, who lived in our building, had a son name Raulfi) and besides, my father was afraid that so much live fame would inhibit my development and prevent me from becoming famous too. That was how they came to consider Vladimir. My mother liked Russian names, and my father, who was born and bred a communist, of course found it appropriate. Upon further investigation, it didn't remind either of them of someone they had disliked intensely or loved unhappily, so it seemed

a perfect choice. So perfect that it has never been used, except by my mother in the first few days of my life, in its Polish form Vodek, perhaps prompted by a desire to have everything in its place that could possibly be there, since those things were so frighteningly few.

The first week of Raul's life was one of disorder, discomfort, little sleep, constant vigilance and stunned introspection. The first few times I showed him off I would point to his big feet, but soon forgot about them because his hands were so long and beautiful, and his eyes looked at everything so intently. His skin was pink and his slender body was rounding out. I realized that was how maternal feelings developed, happily monitoring them as they settled in.

At this point my parents began to misunderstand each other's psychology. My father was convinced that, having always been a virtuous person, he had fallen into evil ways, and that he was too weak to impose his will on the person who had led him into disgrace. She had refrained from rebuking him for the moral connotations of his infidelity, having always been convinced that chastity is neither a man's highest virtue nor his most common one, and more than willing to grant attenuating circumstances in this particular case. With her perhaps overly simple logic, she was incapable of imagining that anyone would allow himself to be blackmailed into staying in a marriage, and she feared for the child who had been created only to make trouble.

As our personal drama was unfolding, the revolution forged ahead, Fidel surprised everyone, including my father, who evidently lacked as much faith in the productive powers of the Cuban economy as in his own, by producing an astonishing number of eggs, as he'd told my mother he would. Everyone went around cutting sugar cane, and during the week I was born, the Council of Ministers took itself to the cane fields, leaving Raul Castro in Havana to answer the telephone.

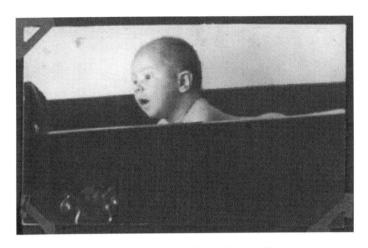

[Raulito's bed-in-a-drawer]

But wait! There's still something missing with regard to my name. You see, my whole name is Vladimir Raul Karvina y Boyer, Karvina being my father's name, and Boyer having been the name on my mother's passport at the time of my birth. In Cuba people take both parent's names, and this made the declaration of my birth a problem, since the name on my mother's passport had only been left to her by courtesy of her ex-husband. Finally, there was no way to prevent it being entered on my birth certificate, but since I wasn't going to live in Cuba, it was not worth making an issue over.

Although my divorce from Leo had not given me the legal right to use his name, years later, one of those bureaucratic absurdities of which only the infinitely nationalistic French are capable would give me the right to pass the French citizenship he gave me on to my children. But I'm getting ahead of myself. For the moment, things were getting ugly with Poland.

When my parents went to declare me as a Polish citizen, they were met with icy indifference. My father was still married to his Polish wife, and my mother, besides not being his wife, wasn't even Polish. Legally I was entitled to Polish citizenship, but we were met with icy indifference just the same. That left me with Cuban

nationality, which no one could refuse me, since I was born on Cuban soil. To the Cubans, the fact that someone who didn't have to be, should have been born on Cuban soil, was a tribute to the Revolution.

I've omitted a final detail. My mother's original nationality is American, but she felt more at home in the old world. I should have been forewarned of things to come by the fact that having considered first France, then Italy her home, she had failed to settle in either. Finally, for whatever it's worth, I look distinctly Slavish - or Anglo-Saxon to those who haven't traveled broadly enough to differentiate at a glance.

Andrei was in a state of shock. He told me his arms shook when he carried the baby, and one night when I asked him to fetch him and he didn't come back, I found him sitting on the floor, cradling him. "What are you doing?", I asked him. "I want to stay with him", he answered, and he sat there for a long while. "Sometimes I'm afraid I'm going to drop him, kill him, I don't know. I never thought he would affect me so much." In my state of blissful fatigue, I failed to notice his ominous tone.

Although I was with Raul all day, taking care of him, looking at him, I was not really conscious of having made him, that he was my child, probably because he didn't look like me. One day, clumsily changing the navel bandage, I poked him with the scissors. It was as if I'd almost killed him; I became catatonic. My mind told me the slight bleeding was normal, yet I feared that it would never stop. That if I put a bandage on the tiny wound and left him for a moment, I would come back to find him dead. Finally I applied a folded piece of gauze, watching it for several minutes to see if the blood soaked through, still unable to believe it wouldn't if I turned my back. Never had I experienced such a feeling of guilt.

April 30

Dear Mexican Friends,

Yesterday the sterilizer came and Mommy said it looks like a spaceship. She's very pleased with everything, including the little

panties. I'm not big enough to wear them, but mama says they're just what she wanted, and she knew I was going to be a giant. I have enormous feet, arms, and legs like Charles de Gaulle, but mama always shows off my hands with their long pinkies. She says I have daddy's hands, even though his aren't beautiful. I don't understand this but Mommy and Daddy say I shouldn't worry, life is full of contradictions.

They've accepted the fact that I didn't come out talking and doing logarithms and they're thrilled when I look around with a knowing air or an expression of curiosity; or when instead of sleeping, I lie in my basket with eyes wide open, deep in thought. I can't tell you how impressed they are with that little trick, especially my father. Mama is more blasé because she reads books about babies, but deep down she's the same. (Every time she doesn't understand something, she looks it up. When she find out that I'm "in the normal range", she closes the book with a satisfied look and and tells daddy. They want me to be "different" and at the same time exactly like all the other millions of kids. What a job!)

Mama has asked me to tell you a propos the Mennen Oil that she hasn't used it yet because it has a synthetic smell like recently disinfected airport restrooms. She knows she's prejudiced, but she still hasn't dared to use it on me. Besides, she knows I don't like to feel wet. Every time someone touches me with a wet cotton I cry until I feel the towel drying me. So please send talcum powder, which is very hard to get. She thinks you forgot a few things on the bill, but since I never let her sleep more than three hours in a row, she can't think straight. She's going to send you $50 and ask you for a few more things.

Well friends, I'm going to stop now. I enjoyed writing to you, and hope we'll meet soon. Daddy says to say lots of hellos because he always tells mama and she forgets. Daddy is a bit shy, and doesn't like to bother people. There was no problem with the package sent by the pouch, but what do you mean that "Mama is the betrothed of the Minrex"? (I could hardly have been expected to know that Minrex stood for the Ministry of Foreign Affairs!)

I'll sign off now, if these two let me - they're always asking me to add something. Why don't they write their own letters? With lots of love to aunt Elena, and bravo to Max who's going to Cannes!
Your U.N. nephew Vladimir, alias Raulito.

When Raul had his first attack of colic, for which nothing could be done, his suffering was unbearable. And if I simply found him one day with hands a bit cooler than usual, I imagined all sorts of terrible things, turning to the paperback edition of Dr. Spock I had picked up before returning to Cuba fo reassurance. I followed Dr. Spock no matter what Cuban mothers did. They dressed their infants in starched, ironed clothes (even ironing the diapers!), Raul usually wore nothing but a diaper and a loose camisole tied at the top. They fed their babies bottles straight out of the refrigerator, I heated mine. The cleaning woman predicted I would spend forty nights listening to my baby cry, Raul never cried until he had colic. Cuban babies were taken out in carriages. I carried Raul over my shoulder.

Three weeks after Raul was born, Andrei was given a tour of some of the cane fields and sugar mills whose production he'd analyzed. As he settled the baby in a portable bed in the back seat of a government Cadillac, he answered proudly to the chauffeur: "What do you mean 'is he coming too?' He's the most important member of the family!"

We ate in the cane fields at noon and in the mess hall at night, sleeping in rudimentary quarters, none of this bothering our baby. It seemed to prove that my childhood determination not be tied down by children could become a reality.

A few days after our trip to the cane fields, I was walking out of the apartment building with Raul in his usual position on my shoulder when Riccardo, an Italian friend stopped me in the revolving door:

"Come up to my place. I have something to tell you."

Riccardo sat me down and took the baby: "I was at the airport this morning getting a package from Italy and I saw Andrei being escorted to the plane for Prague." I was dumbstruck, but knew he couldn't be lying. It may seem as though I have a heart of stone

because I didn't sob or faint, but what was the use of crying when one could not rewind the film?

Though I couldn't bring Andrei back, I was determined that our child not grow up without his father. I scarcely ate for the next few weeks, as I tried to piece together what had happened. Instead of getting an abortion, Casimira had fomented a major scandal at Andrei's ministry in Warsaw. Andrei had confided in a Cuban psychologist he was seeing, but not in me, that he was being sent home. Though the Cubans could not change what had happened, they were fully supportive of my desire to repair the damage to Raul.

Shortly before Raul was born I had received from my Italian publisher the edited version of my book on Cuba. So much had been cut that it read like a series of newspaper articles, and I felt it did not do justice to the extraordinary access I had been granted to the revolution's actors. The publisher agreed that I could reinsert the equivalent of about fifty pages in bits and pieces, but for several weeks, under the shock of Andrei's departure, I was unable to focus on that task.

It is certain that had I remained in Italy through my pregnancy, I would have been able to work closely with the publisher to bring out a work that would have satisfied us both. But that would have meant renouncing a father for my child, and because of my own past, this had not been an option. For weeks, I could do no more than take care of Raul and plan our departure for Poland. Adding in the time it took for mail to reach Italy from Cuba, I failed to meet the publishing deadline, and the contract was rescinded. As a result, that book remained in a drawer instead of moving my career forward, and ultimately, Raul ended up without his father anyway.

A few weeks before Raul's birth, I had expressed my joy at having a child by drawing a ceiba tree with its big red flowers. The story I wrote about it was premonitory:

The Red Tree

One day, on a faraway planet, a child was born who didn't look like any of the others. After thinking about it for a long time, the elders decided he must be a descendent of an Earth man who a year before had fallen to the planet from a space ship. Unable to adapt to the atmosphere, after some months the Earthman had died.

The mother too had died when the child was born, and the elders, faced with this fragile little creature, became very concerned. Should this descendent of an Earthling who had been unable to survive on their planet, remain there? The elders knew that on Earth human life did not have the value it should, but felt they had to give him a chance in his own world.

He could not be accompanied by one of their own because Earthlings did not believe that other planets were inhabited, and every previous mission had been met with hostility. Accordingly, they prepared a special space ship that would disintegrate before anyone saw it. The only problem was deciding which country to send the child to.....

Only the presence of the child I had always known I would have could overcome the despair of Andre's departure. Like my father's disappearance, it had been stealthy, cloaked in dishonesty. And as with Howard, it did not prevent me from loving him even if, for a short while, his disappearance clouded my love for Raul. Although I was determined that he should be near his father, this was no simple matter. The Polish embassy had not only refused Raul's right to Polish citizenship, they had insinuated that it would be an

extremely lengthy business for us to be granted a visa. Wondering whether the embassy in Havana had communicated our undesirability to other Polish embassies, the Cubans, who were taking care of the arrangements, first considered sending us to Warsaw via Moscow, but finally opted for Prague.

Gradually, despair gave way to reorganization. Spock said one didn't have to live on a six-ten-two schedule, so with no one to relieve me at night, I decided it would be four-eight-twelve for us. When it came time to skip the four a.m. bottle, Raul tried to sleep through the midnight one. I dunked him in tepid water to wake him up. When Dr. Spock said to start oranges, there were none, so I gave him lemon juice - without sugar, so he wouldn't get a sweet tooth. He drank it as if it was water. He was a long baby, and when carrying him, I often bumped his head on door frames. Dr. Spock said that if mother didn't panic, baby wouldn't either, and he was right. (At seven months Raul would still be unperturbed by a shot in the arm.)

While I was engrossed in these mundane matters, Che left the country in secret. Riccardo and his wife Graziella, who'd been in Cuba for seven years, began to be very worried about the way things were going, and foreigners gathered at their place like anxious parents over the crib of an ailing child. I've never been able to determine the duration of the Stalinist period that began around that time, but many foreigners left soon afterward, Riccardo and Graziella eventually taking over my apartment in Rome. The poet Padilla, whom we all knew, was sentenced to a prison term, and eventually exiled. In the years that followed, when any of us who had lived through those years in Cuba met in other parts of the world, we were aware of having been involved in something extraordinary that had affected all of our lives.

Chapter IX - Fatherland

As you know, my mother was obsessed by the idea that I not grow up without a father. The material obstacles that stood in her way were formidable, but she had not needed coffee klatches to become liberated.

Everything having finally been arranged by the Cuban government, we left Havana for Prague around mid-July, passing through the formalities at the Jose Marti Airport in Havana, with a minimum of delay. Then, as a woman with babe in arms we were boarded before everyone else, occupying the front seat with plenty of leg room. At Gander my mother gave me canned pear juice in a teaspoon, then bought paper diapers. Back on board, learning that a Czech woman had a supply from home, she didn't know whether to be sorry for the money spent, or glad that paper diapers had breached the Iron Curtain before us.

In Prague we were escorted to the Cuban consul's apartment, and the officer working on our visas reported they would take about two weeks. Double checking at the Polish airline, my mother was told this might be because she was a journalist. She thought that might be a cover for what was really being held against us. A call was put through to Warsaw where my father promised to see what he could do to speed things up. Meanwhile, why on earth didn't we go to his brother's, to flesh and kin, instead of some stranger's?

After dinner, my mother took a taxi to a neighborhood on the outskirts of Prague appropriately called Solidarity, where her 'brother-in-law' lived. By the time the taxi found the street it was half past nine. An elderly woman in a night-gown opened the door cautiously, and at that moment my mother realized she had not a single word at her disposal. Hopefully she uttered my uncle's name. The woman smiled and went to fetch a younger woman, also wearing a nightgown. The sound of a flushing toilet was heard and a white-haired man appeared, obviously not the brother-in-law. A whispered consultation gave the impression he would never return, however my mother was ushered into the parlor where a sleeping two-year old

flaunted a familiar profile. Soon a key turned in the latch and my uncle appeared, bringing with him a few words of English.

They called Warsaw. My uncle and father agreed to try on both ends to hasten our visas, and if we really did have to wait two weeks, we would come to stay at Solidarity. My mother felt it wasn't worth moving for a few days, and besides, she wondered where they would put us, since there were only two rooms. Grandpa slept on an old sofa in the hall, next to a big closet with suitcases piled on top. Grandma slept on a sofa bed in the parlor, and the young couple occupied twin beds in the bedroom. Little Stashu slept either in a crib beside his parents, or with grandma.

While these negotiations were taking place, my mother was served plum cakes and tea at a large round mahogany table. She studied the room, equating it with other mahogany sideboards and grandfather's clocks, lace doilies, the slow gestures of an elderly man who must once have been strong and handsome, the maniacal tidiness of the consort, and so many other things that made her feel as though she had been here before and didn't want to come again.

Prague was an altogether different matter; with its baroque architecture and relatively tranquil streets she felt it would be a pleasant place to live, away from the relentlessness of Rome, Paris or New York. The beer cellars with their vaulted roofs and frescoed walls were warm and cozy, the food was, if not exquisite, almost as familiar as grandfather clocks and lace doilies; the people were neither servile nor arrogant, and the language had a humorous sound which she liked. The fact that it was a communist country didn't enter into her assessment.

Aside from a brief stopover when I had been only a suspicion, and my mother had walked across the Charles Bridge under a bright September sky, almost missing the plane to Rome, she was seeing the city in the sun for the first time. Teenagers in the colors of the Spartakiads, the East's version of the Olympics, swarmed over Vaclav Namesti as white-haired ladies in straw hats, crocheted gloves and parasols from the spa scene in "8 ½", crossed the Museum Platz adventurously between two oncoming trams. Toward evening, as my mother and I walked down Vaclav

Namesti under the shade trees (I in my usual position over her shoulder, seeing everything backwards), Baden Baden gave way to the Beatniks: long-haired, unkempt adolescents aware of their incongruity.

Sometimes, leaving me in the care of the consul's cleaning woman, my mother would go out for lunch to the nearest Potraviny, where Baden Baden, Beatnikery and the wholesome Spartakiads receded in the face of so much salami, mayonnaise and Russian salad combined in fantastic layers that made my mother wonder if the Czechs had invented the sandwich. (That theory was later contested by a Dane in Warsaw.) In these canopy temples, white clad maidens served hot sausages of all lengths and widths with beer and colored drinks, but one had enjoy them standing at high tables.

One of her favorite destinations was the children's department store, where she could dive headlong into the adventure of trying to buy 'long white woolen socks for a three month old', or 'pajamas to sleep in, not for daytime', or a sweater and trousers 'of soft wool' from clerks whose German did not include the same words as hers.

Or she would climb up Stepanska street in search of soup greens, tomatoes and peaches, discovering a vegetable that looked similar to the fennel she knew from Italy, but which no one here would dream of eating raw. (It was kohlrabi, which, with fennel, would eventually make its way to America.) In the Czech equivalent of a supermarket she would buy paper diapers, plastic panties and shampoo in a plastic tube. Outside, oranges and flower stalls alternated with carts selling hot greasy sausages to eat a l'allemand with your two fingers, or a la Czech between pieces of bread. The oranges were expensive, yet there was always a line, and soon they would disappear 'til the next day.

When it became clear that the visa, if we got it, would take its own mysterious course, we moved to Solidarity. Although we had been warmly invited, when grandma saw us arrive with all our luggage and not knowing my mother, she probably feared we would settle on her for good.

At eight a.m. the older folk were in bed, grandma reading religious literature sent by an American church organization; at nine-thirty the younger couple retired, then all was silent except for the ticking of the grandfather clock in the parlor where we slept, Grandma having doubled up with her daughter-in-law.

At five o'clock grandfather's alarm went off, and a few minutes later we heard him moving around in the kitchen, striking a match to light the gas water heater, and another to light the gas stove. (This was strictly forbidden by grandma. Once the water heater was lit you didn't strike any more matches, but coaxed the fire out on a long, wound-up piece of newspaper, just as the French used to do.) Soon after, Aunt Vera would join him, Uncle Stasek would spill water down his neck in the bathroom and the three of them would be off to work.

Grandma and little Stashu led an easier life. They got up at about eight. As for us, we would have sleep on, had grandma not sent Stasu stomping through on his way to the balcony. When that failed to rouse us, she would stand at the foot of our bed and announce loudly:

"Acht und halb."

Once grandma was sure we were up, she would go food shopping, leaving Stashu in the care of these strangers with whom he could not communicate, except to cry. Then it was my mother's turn to shop, and finally, the necessities of life ensured, the two of us would climb onto the number eleven tram and ride into town. There we would meet Milan and his friend Susan. After Milan had lost his job, his wife had left him. For a while he'd been almost destitute, an ancient Skoda and books his sole possessions. Then he met Susan, become happy again, grown a beard and begun writing screenplays. Susan was the most beautiful woman we had ever seen, with her strawberry blond hair, green eyes and pale, porcelain-like skin. And she was as kind and fun loving as she was beautiful.

The afternoon was usually spent washing my things - including diapers when we ran out of paper ones. I would be put out on the balcony to sleep, and mother would fill a big aluminum tub with water from the shower, then heave it onto a wooden stool and

plunge in the washboard. She filled the tub again and again to rinse, until she realized that worsening relations with grandma were, among other things, due to her spendthrift use of water.

The bathroom evoked early fifties France. Dirty clothes were piled on the floor, doubtful towels hung from wooden pegs next to bathrobes and house dresses in various states of wear and tear. The combs and brushes on the shelf above the sink were dirty, and the toothbrushes were old and soft. As in France, the toilet was in a separate, unheated cubicle, and large squares of newsprint hung from a nail on the wall.

Also reminiscent of Paris in the early fifties were the look of the girls whose faces had discovered makeup and home perms but whose bodies were still plump with unshaved legs. There was the wide-eyed admiration for the foreigner; the yen to buy the refrigerators and televisions that had splashed into the shop windows; the desire to make money and catch up with the richest. Western Europe had emulated the United States. Eastern Europe emulated Western Europe.

One thing that wasn't reminiscent of Western Europe was family life. There, meals were rituals, even in the poorest homes. Here, although the members of the family usually arrived within fifteen minutes of each other, no one waited for anyone else; each wolfed the food prepared by grandma on a corner of the kitchen table. Even on Sundays there was no common meal. My mother realized why she had been the only one served tea and cakes on that first night.

Paradoxically, the working day, over at two or three in the afternoon, would have left plenty of time for family life. But at Solidarity, the big passion was gardening - a solitary passion. We would sit on the balcony and watch the neighbors coming home from work along the cement path through large garden plots. The grass grew thick and green, and the ground floor tenants each had their own garden, where petunias, marigold, phlox and roses grew pell-mell. The odor that floated up to us was another of those things that caused my mother to fall into a trance. (I was used to her sudden absences, as she sat in front of a small green box, punching little

black pegs hour after hour, making a monotone, rhythmic noise.) The odor and look of Regina's garden had never really left her senses, mixed in with grandfather's clocks punctuating peaceful boredom, lace doilies and plum cakes.

I had asked May whether my letter announcing Raul's birth, twelve minutes after mid-night on Jake's birthday, had arrived before his death. She answered that it had, adding: "When I read it to him at the hospital he said: 'Mrs. K. will be happy to know that Deena has a son.' It was obvious from this remark that his brain, in the grip of atherosclerosis, was well advanced in its fatal march toward death." My mother's use of medical terms showed how important her father's death was; that of Rose had been announced without flourishes. True to herself, flying over a beautiful plain to land head first in a bog, May saw Jake's reference to Regina rather than his own wife as evidence of a failing mind!

Jake's mind may have been wandering, but he knew he was dying - a thought May refused to entertain for herself – and his hallucination fluttered in my head like a butterfly in a Renoir field. 'Mrs. K. will be happy to know Deena has a son.' May had put those words in the trash with her father's hardened arteries and wrinkled skin, his eyes veiled with death, as part of the indecency that surrounds dying in our world.

"How can you be so dumb!" I wanted to shout to her across the ocean that separated us. A ray of sunlight lit up that death chamber, my beloved grandfather died smelling Regina's acacias on the Danube plain, and you didn't see it!" I was not there, I was the grandchild whose affection for him must have been the least obvious, since, when still a girl, I had fled his world, then, at intervals granted it a few days' visit, fondness delivered as playfulness. Yet I was probably the only one who perceived the light that brushed Jake's forehead on his deathbed. The light called Regina, who was as tolerant as he. Whenever their children's mismatch permitted them to spend a few fleeting moments together, as I was solemnly handed from one set of mismatched grandparents to the other, she would sigh wistfully: "He is a good man!". Jacob

Oxman, husband of hysterical Rose, was at last going to rejoin Regina Kadzan, wife of grouchy Morris, and he would tell her that I had a son!

Although I was setting out for Warsaw rather than Regina's Budapest, any place in Eastern Europe would conjure up the precious times spent in her home. She had made me aware that I came from a particular place, and instilled in me a desire to know it, as she had. Within the prism created between the ages of seven, when Jake announced there would be war, and eleven, when I suggested to Queen Elizabeth that countries learn from one another, her quiet demeanor made observation of the different ways in which live together second nature.

We spent the afternoon before our departure for Warsaw (suddenly, the visa had arrived, and at the Polish consulate everyone was all smiles), in town with Milan and Susan, arranging our flight, buying things in Dom Dietzka and ending up in a tavern in the old town. The plane to Warsaw was almost completely chartered by a group of American tourists being led through the socialist countries by a Catholic priest. I couldn't resist telling them all about Cuba. They listened, nodding their heads politely, and one of them said, in a genteel voice: "You know, we were surprised there were no beggars on the streets in Prague." Beggars indeed! I snorted inwardly, as I managed a polite smile. Czechoslovakia was not affluent, but its people were properly clothed and fed. I'll never forget the brief visit to a pharmacy in search of an aspirin on my first trip to Prague. When I saw the person in front of me receive medication with no quid pro quo, tears welled up in my eyes.

We had a touching family reunion at the airport. My father held up a nylon net bag and announced proudly: "Paper diapers."

It was about ten o'clock at night when the airport bus left us at the Hotel Bristol. Our room had only one narrow bed, so my mother decided I should sleep in the bottom of the closet. (It was more comfortable than the drawer I'd slept in in Cuba, since it could be padded with the seat cushion from the armchair, which was then placed in front of the open door to make sure I didn't fall out.) My

father thought I should sleep with my mother, as he had done with his, but my mother was adamant. For all her anti-Americanism, when it came to child care she was ready to defend Dr Spock against all the grandmothers of the continent.

The euphoria of motherhood that I described with such complacency in Cuba having suddenly come to an end, I began to lead a double life, noting every smile and look of Raul's, meanwhile trying to bring the man I had chosen to be his father back to reason, and failing that, prepare for what I hoped would be a permanent home.

While Casimira was in the hospital having her baby, it was decided that we would stay at the grandparents (what was one more absurdity?). We had been received by my putative mother-in-law on two occasions with coffee and cake, and she had wept discretely when we left, making sure however that we did so before her husband came home. Now, a few hours after we were installed in his old room, Andrei, returning from his daily visit to the hospital, took us ceremoniously into the living room saying: "You mean you haven't greeted my father yet," as the older man and I sized each other up.

Later, as I relaxed in a tub of hot water, Andrei knocked on the door, put his head in and admonished, with a gaiety I hadn't seen since we arrived: "Hurry up girl, or you'll miss the telly!" Disappointed that in a socialist country, where people should be less eager for tinseled entertainment, television wasn't partaken of in a more detached way, I refused to rush.

The living room was actually a dining room with a large couch, where my mother-in-law and her youngest child, twelve year old Sophia, slept. There was a big round table like the one in Prague, a TV, a buffet laden with various examples of folk art brought back from grandpa's official travels to fraternal countries, and which, in one's right mind, one would call kitsch.

Andrei and I were left the love seat - a folding extra bed, staple in every Polish household - while grandma and grandpa lounged on their tummies on the big bed and Sophia lounged beside

them in her nightgown. Andrei's five brothers occupied straight chairs or the floor. Every once in a while one of them would disappear into the kitchen, returning with a cup of tea and a plate of sausage. They sat by the table rather than at it, eating and watching TV in such a desultory way as to make American eating habits look formal.

The Poles got up very early and had tea and sausage. When they came home from work, about four in the afternoon, they had vegetable soup, tea and various kinds of cold cuts - mainly sausage. Later they had more of the same as they watched TV. As at Solidarity, each one had his main meal in the afternoon, grandma serving on a little red tray and doing the dishes, too. To be fair, Polish mothers bought blenders and made drinks for their children with milk and fruit. And carrot juice, made by grating carrots finely, then squeezing them out in a thin handkerchief reserved for this purpose, was a staple of the infant diet.

During that summer, grandma got up at six to fix breakfast for the working members of the family, then went back to bed, where she and Sophia slept until about ten. When the television came on, they would sit up and watch the morning film, then grandma would send Sophia out shopping. (A broken foot had never healed properly and she took only an afternoon constitutional with grandpa.) Then the heavy woman would make her way to the kitchen where, seated on a stool near the stove, she phlegmatically peeled potatoes and other vegetables, letting the peelings fall into the garbage can at her feet. She accomplished a few other gestures with pots and pans in an offhand way, and left the meal to cook itself. The menu varied from day to day, but always the gestures seemed to be the same.

Although I enjoyed my mother-in-law's vegetable soup, especially when she added pickles, I have to say that Poland and Yugoslavia vied for first prize as the worst places to eat, the first because every restaurant reeked of cabbage, the second because everything floated in oil. One day in a supermarket I noticed packages of meat being poured into the cold display. Everyone in the store rushed toward the counter, then drew back in unison. I inched

forward to see what horrible thing had put them off. It was steak; nice, lean, tender steak: the Poles craved only pork.

In Czechoslovakia I had loved the big round dumplings served with fresh summer fruits cooked in their sauce. (As for the Hungarians, they eat cold soups in summer made by boiling cherries or peaches, adding sugar, lemon, cinnamon and sour cream and refrigerating - but I didn't know that yet.)

Although there appeared to be a sufficiency of life's necessities and a reasonable amount of frills in both communist countries I had known so far, sleeping was a different matter. Cramped quarters resulting from the housing shortage dictated that there be at least one sofa bed in every room. These contraptions could take various forms, but they were uniformly uncomfortable. In Poland, they were made of three sections, one separation hitting you under the shoulders, the other under the thighs, any resemblance to a bed being purely coincidental. (And yet, oh, the eiderdowns of Eastern Europe, an invention the French thought good enough to emulate!)

Alas, life was not the warm, soft haven it could have been for us. I became cranky for the first time in my life. Grandma and Sophia held me on their lap for hours on end, and Sophia was reluctant to put me down even for a nap. My mother refrained from fighting this battle since it would be only a matter of days before we would have to cede the place.

Any attempt to enlist grandma's active help in resolving our situation was hopeless because of the absolute language barrier. Father became grimmer by the day and although my parents spoke a lot, no decision was reached. One afternoon my father was sitting at the dining table reading the paper; Sophia sat next to him, idly lighting matches and letting them burn down. My father noticed the game out of the corner of his eye and when the next match was struck, he moved the paper so that it caught fire. After a moment of paralysis, he ran with the flaming pages into the kitchen, then bolted out the front door, returning only after several hours.

We left a week later. With the help of my father's youngest brother Vodek, our suitcases were once again loaded into a taxi, and I was wheeled to new quarters. A friend of my father's was going on a two-week vacation and had agreed to let us stay in her apartment. My father commented in a vaguely disapproving tone: "She got married three months ago, got rid of the husband and kept the studio."

Casimira discovered our presence in Poland when she came across an ad Andrei had run seeking a furnished apartment for 'a foreigner with child'. One day when he failed to return home on time while helping us move yet again, she packed a bag and went to her mother's. My father received the news over the phone and swept me into his arms. Holding me high in the air, he laughed and chanted: "My son, you are my son!" When he called home later, he was crestfallen. His father had fetched Casimira back.

My mother-in-law, who continued to provide us with a steady supply of carrot juice after we left, was probably on our side, but with this incident, Casimira had ensured that nationalism prevailed.

We were not surprised to learn that Casimira now demanded our immediate removal from the country. My father communicated the news without taking sides. An estrangement between my parents ensued, which was to deepen over time. A few days later, Casimira made Andrei accompany her to the Militia, as the Foreign Registration Bureau of the Ministry of the Interior was known, to find out whether they were going to allow us to remain in Poland. The official declined to answer, and Casimira declared that if we didn't leave, she would return alone to plead her case.

We were then staying with a woman doctor who had just put her unfaithful husband out. My encounter with her thirteen-year old daughter was an important moment in my life. As I lay on a couch, she bent over me with her long golden pony tail and her long golden lashes and blue eyes. She smiled at me and I smiled back. It was then that I discovered that one doesn't smile in the same way to a beautiful woman as one does to other, perhaps kinder people.

I planned to see if I could get a job, and if I did, we would immediately go to Rome to fetch my old car and the things I had left in the apartment taken over by Riccardo and Graziella. After a week of suspense, I obtained an interview with the Polish Radio, and was told I could be given a job if the Ministry of the Interior allowed us to stay. The Ministry told us we would probably be allowed to stay if I got a job. When I told them that we wanted to go to Rome for two weeks, they said that unless we first obtained a reentry visa, we would have to wait for a new one in Rome longer than we had money for. It would take them about a month to decide whether we would be allowed to stay in Poland, and therefore, whether to give us a reentry visa. It was only by dint of perseverance that I finally managed to align the two edges of this Catch-22 like a skittish dress seam.

I had assured Andrei that I would never keep him from being a father to his daughter if he decided to leave Casimira, however he still couldn't face the idea of a showdown. He hoped she might leave him, as she had threatened, and if not, that she would at least accept our presence in Poland. To foil her attempts to interfere with our negotiations with the Militia, Raul and I set out each day after breakfast with a bottle of pear juice and a toy. We spent many hours in a long corridor with bright yellow linoleum, red and black modern chairs, magazines and Poland's ubiquitous potted plants - nothing like registration offices in other countries in which I had been an alien.

Nicole, a French-speaking woman my age, was our immediate contact, and she confirmed that Andrei and Casimira had been there and that Andrei had asked her in an aside to tell his wife that we would not get the visa, even if it wasn't true. Nicole informed him that the Militia couldn't get involved in his private affairs, and obtained an interview for me with the head of the foreigners' department. Several days later when I phoned him, he told me that Casimira had made a follow-up visit alone. When we met, he relayed everything Casimira had said, allowing me to rebut her story. The day before our temporary visa was to expire, we were

still waiting in Nicole's office for the decision at lunchtime. When Raul began to show signs of hunger, she opened a drawer and pulled out a ripe tomato. He was sucking it contentedly when a smartly dressed young man came in, tickled him under the chin and said everything was going to be all right.

I probably would not have made such strenuous efforts to settle in Warsaw were it not for the fact that we would have more financial security than in a Western capital. My languages meant I would always have a job, and also, things were organized so that mothers could work, with priority to single mothers. I hoped Casimira would gradually be neutralized, at least insofar as Raul was concerned.

With my reentry visa in hand, I booked a plane to Rome. Our landlady, fearful we might miss our flight, her regular boarder due back that day from vacation, bundled us into a taxi at six o'clock in the morning. Raul was almost five months old, and in the two months we'd spent in Warsaw, had had eight homes and four beds. Andrei had come to say goodbye the night before, sitting glumly on a chair complaining of leg pains which a doctor had said were psychosomatic. He asked me what my plans were, and upon departing, kissed my hand up to the elbow.

At the airport there was some haggling about the overweight. I hefted Raul into the arms of a hostess and toughed it out. When I realized they had carried my baby off, I at first refused to get on board until they brought him back, but the stunned look on everyone's face convinced me he was not being detained. I found him cooing happily in a basket suspended from the cabin wall, and once the plane got off the ground, his cooing turned into a lusty chant that lasted all the way to Rome. I reveled in his enthusiasm for life, in the midst of its now obvious uncertainty.

Chapter X - Italian Interlude

Rome invaded my senses the minute we stepped off the plane at Fiumicino Airport: the warm, dry breeze, the feverish activity on the landing strip, the sparkling glass corridor flanked by espresso machines, the conversation level, and the crackly loudspeakers.

We stood in the security line, Raul flung over my shoulder as usual. He had grown heavier since our flight from Havana, but the immigration officer wouldn't let us in because he didn't have a visa. As we stood in the visa line, I realized I had never been a woman with babe in arms in a Western country. In a socialist country, even the worst cheaters allowed a woman with baby to the head of a line. I snickered inwardly at the Western barbarians as I heaved my load pointedly from one shoulder to the other, to the utter indifference of those around me.

My friend Mimi was not there to meet us. After making a few calls, I realized it was probably the last good Sunday for the beach. M., my former boss at the French News Agency couldn't leave the office, but offered to put us up until we found a place to stay. We took the airport bus, and soon M. and I were feeding Raul bottled pear juice and farina, cooked in a tiny aluminum coffee pitcher over a huge fire in the deserted restaurant downstairs from the French News Agency in Palazzo Colonna.

By evening, I had made contact with Mimi. True to form she had hoped we would have a change of plans, since there was no running water in her apartment, and suggested we bathe at the agency. When we arrived, there were several people drinking whiskey, including a few frustrated mothers who enthused over Raul.

When I woke the next morning my mother was leaning out the window with a Chianti bottle in each hand. Suddenly, she cried "Stop" (with a short Italian o), and I saw water dripping from a green garden hose hanging above her head. Aunt Mimi was on the

other end, and they were filling bottles of water from the hose on the terrace while the plumbing in the apartment was being fixed.

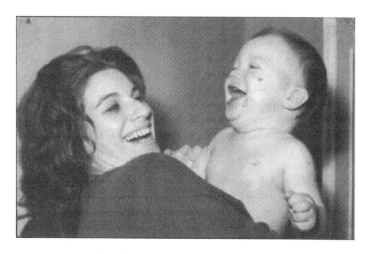

[Raul, five months, in Rome]

My mother's first objective was to be reunited with her automobile. On route to the garage she stopped in a children's shop and bought me a baby relax chair. I immediately made clear I didn't like it, but with cars swirling around us she could only offer me a reassuring pat and a promise.

Traffic in Rome was different from Havana, Prague or even Warsaw. In Havana mechanical limitations forced drivers to be indolent, in Prague they had a way of rushing at pedestrians, but there weren't enough of them to be really dangerous. In Warsaw traffic was staid, just like the couples marching their prams. In Rome nothing was staid. Even St. Paul's was somehow part of the general chaos, with its absurd colonnade and the Lancias, Fiats and Maseratti's swerving unerringly around the fountain in the middle. Every time my mother saw that place she remembered the closing shot of The White Sheik, her favorite Fellini film. It shows the provincial couple that has narrowly escaped scandal marching proudly to an audience with the Pope. Now, after several years' absence, you couldn't tell whether Fellini had portrayed Rome, or taught the Romans their lines. After a few days in this environment,

my mother had lost the ability to differentiate between a Fellini and an Antonioni soundtrack, and realized it was not the first time that habit trumped perspicacity.

My favorite places in Rome where those where I was given food. In case the reader doubts the quality of my care, let me state here that no matter what my mother was doing, one part of her mind was always focused on feeding me somehow, somewhere, something healthy. And it's much more fun to eat Buitoni's pasteurized meat if you can gaze at a plate of spaghetti, or a luscious watermelon. Every day we were taken to lunch by one of my mother's Roman Guardian Angels, as she had dubbed her male friends, regardless of the type of relations she'd had with them in the past. As people turned to stare at the fair-skinned baby in the wicker basket that had replaced the relaxing chair, it crossed her mind that they probably thought that even so, HE was the father and that HE was probably feeling uncomfortable and at the same time rather flattered.

My mother would order mashed potatoes to go with my jar of meat, and when I was full I looked up at the pergolas, or listened to a passing guitar player, or to the carefully calculated soliloquy of a street vendor or beggar. For my mother, the biggest problem was whether to have spaghetti, agnelotti, fettucine, cannelloni or rigatoni, and sometimes, how to resist having them all. In the end, nothing else mattered. I suspect it was the pasta that made Italy sacred in her eyes.

At my old haunt, *La Concordia*, rampant joviality was still rare, but only in Italy could a table d'hote bear up under the symbol of concord, antipathies humming beneath the surface. My arrival with baby in tow caused no small sensation, since the last time I had had been there he had gone undetected. When I learned that Otello had made a trip to Moscow, I assumed that with John XXIII as Pope, the Eurocommunists had vowed not to nationalize the restaurants.

Even so, given Italian machismo, I didn't want to spend the rest of my life in Italy, and it still didn't seem like a good place to bring up a child. As I decided which things from my old apartment on Via Garibaldi would be indispensable in the next·stage of my life,

I imagined Raul playing on the hillside street like a regular Trastevere urchin, aware that the Gianicolo park above would be a better place, but also, that the two bathroom flat with terrace and maid's room, afternoon tea at Piazza del Popolo, courtesy of some elderly gentleman represented a way of life that I rejected.

Most importantly, my own history dictated that my child be within visiting distance of his father: We would travel first to Prague to pick up the record player and two suitcases left during our lengthy transit from Havana to Warsaw. Then it would be on to Poland, our future home.

Two hundred and fifty books had been made to fit on the turned-down back seat of the Fiat 600. Framed prints and oil paintings had been stacked on top, blocking the rear view. (My mother was not so much concerned at not being able to see, as at the possibility she might be fined because of it.) Six suitcases were securely fastened to the roof of the car and covered with a heavy sheet of plastic. A pile of woolen blankets encased in a plastic bag occupied the passenger seat; several small lamps stood daringly on the back floor, an antique Venetian mirror wedged in between. A huge Mexican raffia bag with odds and ends, including a sewing basket that didn't close and an iron, was stored in the trunk next to the gas tank, a week's supply of paper diapers was on the floor in front of the driver's seat just behind the driver's legs, the plastic flight bag with my bottles filled with boiled water and a can of powdered milk was found to fit up against the driver's door without hindering the clutch, while the record player and typewriter fit in front of the passenger seat. Last of all, the wicker basket, with me in it, was placed on top of the blankets (it fit perfectly between the back seat and the dashboard), and a silver bell was tied to the handle. This last item was a gift from one of our guardian angles, a music box which played "Il était un petit navire". It would save me from many boring moments during the trip, and from total disorientation in the months ahead. By the time this arrangement had been completed, the only unoccupied surfaces in the car were the driver's

seat and the pedals. My mother placed the relevant parts of her anatomy on these, and we drove off.

We headed uptown, if one may use such an expression to describe a city like Rome, which is not up and down, but round, to the mind's eye at least, depending for its ups and downs on half a dozen hills, seven, to be exact. We crossed the Olympic Bridge onto the Via Flaminia, and soon reached that paragon of superhighways, the Autostrada del Sole, which runs the length of the boot. There, on the familiar road to Milan and Paris that the little Fiat had often traveled, thoughts and feelings were allowed to break through our mundane concerns, a kilometer at a time. They were bound by two parallel compulsions, the small signs ticking off each thousand meters, and the larger ones showing the number of kilometers that still separated us from our destination (or destiny). And so we drove on towards Florence, past the innumerable hilltop villages of Lazio and Umbria that looked down upon sentinels called Agip, Pavese, Essoservice.

Towards the middle of the afternoon, while we were refueling at one of them, a violent storm broke out. The rain came down with such force that it was impossible to see ahead. My mother sat there, as precious minute-kilometers ticked by. I was sleeping with my head toward the windshield, and when the clapping thunder and the rain beating on the plastic monument above finally woke me, I lifted my head and got my first view of raindrops on a windowpane. For a long moment my mother allowed herself the luxury of not thinking about the schedule: she leaned her elbow on the steering wheel and watched me watch the rain: I looked at the dynamic pane of glass, then at her, with delight.

We got only as far as Bologna, a mockery of the plan, according to which we should have spent our first night somewhere near the frontier, or at least close to Venice. The ever-so-polite officials in charge of foreigners' comings and goings in Poland, had allowed my mother to set the date by which she would return, for the round trip visa. We had six days left in which to reach the Polish border, hence the importance of the plan.

After spending the night in a Jolly Hotel, we had lunch at a little trattoria on a winding road to Venice, under a parasol in the gentle September sun. Near Venice, we stopped at a tourist information booth where, in a totally un-Italian manner, we were refused information as to best place to cross the frontier, probably because of the dispute with Austria over the South Tyrol. My mother consulted her map of Europe for the nth time, and finally chose the road which led through Cortina d'Ampezzo, where she had got her first taste of Italy twelve years ago. It seemed fitting that we should leave Italy for good through this particular place.

Chapter XI - Eastern Detour

As we climbed the foothills of the Dolomites, night was falling, and once again I awoke at a time of scenic importance: dark purple mountains were silhouetted like a great wall against a blue-white sky. My mother wondered if I would cry, but the trouble came from beyond our cozy world: a carabinieri stopped us and enumerated all the things that were wrong with our lights. We were eligible for a heavy fine, but managed to avoid it by telling him that we had to get to Poland on fifty dollars. For this twentieth century man-of-arms, the idea of a woman with baby driving from Italy to Poland was as dangerous as was sailing to the horizon to Pre-Columbian navigators. Cautious for once in her life, my mother refrained from pointing out that Warsaw was closer than Oslo or Lisbon, in return for which, with pointed chivalry, the carabiniere escorted us to the nearest garage where our lights were fixed almost for nothing.

At about seven o'clock, as we started up the mountain towards the frontier, a tire began losing air. Women's lib notwithstanding, my mother had never changed a tire. Luckily, we were just passing a restaurant, and the two women who seemed eerily alone there got a neighbor to change it while we ate. Only then did my mother remember she had no more lira with which to pay for these services. The women offered to rent us a room for the night. In the morning the garage in Cortina, where she had once tried to ski, would have fixed the tire, she could change money and pay for everything. Glad to have gotten off so easily, my mother decided there was no use crying over lost frontiers. But when we piled into the car for an early morning start she was only pretending to be awake, and backed straight into a gas pump, jamming the trunk shut. It was noon by the time the mechanics in Cortina managed to pry it open.

The frontier turned out to be closer than we had expected; but it was a day of delays. During our week-long immersion in the Western world, my mother had forgotten that I was traveling on a

transit visa, and that it had expired. With the convenience of her French passport, she was used to traveling around Western Europe without any visa at all, much less a transit visa - which is what you get when authorities want to make sure you don't plan to stay permanently. Now she was discovering that as a Cuban I needed a visa every time I turned around. After a lengthy confab, the Italian border guards decided to consult distant authorities. My mother waited fatalistically while trying to wrench open a bottle of pear juice on the door lock. Finally, the guard playing good cop fetched a bottle opener and told us the alternatives that were being considered: make us drive 300 kilometers to the provincial capital of Bolzano - or maybe even all the way back to Rome - or let us out quietly. After about three quarters of an hour, they let us out quietly, and we purred along to the Austrian post, where my mother immediately confessed that I didn't have a visa. The Austrians took one look at me and waved us on without even stamping my passport.

All we had to do now was cross Austria and we would be at the curtain once again. In Austria there were no names calling out from the past to be revisited, no familiar landscapes, no places to bypass wistfully, no favorite dishes to eat in farewell. Austria was an entirely new experience. Separating the familiar from the half-known, this former seat of Empire, now a no-man's land between East and West, was schizophrenic to the point of exasperation. Prague and Warsaw belonged to Slav land, even to Russia, but you already know there is thicker blood mixed up in this. My mother's previous arrivals had occurred under the aegis of seemingly incongruous ties to a Caribbean island: now, the image of my great-grandmother Regina beckoned us toward central Europe's Asian enclave: Hungary, land of the Huns.

The Grossglockner, a first-gear mountain, got higher with each turn of the road. At the top we skidded frighteningly on patches of slush; on the way down, the few restaurants we passed were indifferent to the fact that motorists cannot keep regular hours. We stayed on our empty stomachs until about four o'clock, when in despair - yet marveling at my apparent equanimity - my mother stopped at a roadside cafe in the valley. From behind an expresso

machine, as we wolfed down sandwiches and baby food, the owner told us how to get to Linz. It was dark by the time we found our way around Salzburg to the autobahn. The signs pointed everywhere except to Linz, even to Budapest, but my mother resisted temptation.

Linz at ten o'clock at night was a garishly lit but deserted Main Street. We found a hotel room, but no garage. As soon as I was asleep in the middle of the double bed, my mother left the key with the night watchman, determined that the car, with its precious scaffolding, should not spend the night unattended. At the central police station, prominently indicated, an Austro-Hungarian type with a big white mustache made a few phone calls and directed her to an empty garage. It was after midnight when she returned to the hotel, where she dined on zwieback and lay down to a fitful sleep.

In the morning we discovered that our window overlooked the fabled Danube river. We drove over a bridge, and quickly realized that the Danube marked the frontier of that Central European plain where the stubbornness of the Alps, Europe's heart of stone, came to an end. According to the map, we were entering the Bohemian forest, but to my mother, who saw the picture through Regina's eyes, the rolling hills with intermittent groves were a variation on a plain, with undulating pastures and fields to give the land breadth, and trees to give it contour, in that quietly civilized manner of which Bohemia is synonymous. Although acacias did not bloom here, my mother accepted the Bohemian setting that had inspired the architects of Prague as an approximation of the land beyond, as if the acacias were immanent, just behind those distant hills, in the air. At once free of the Alps and as far from the sea as you could be anywhere in Europe, the air of the Central European plain was perfectly temperate, like the center of a good fruit before the seed. And it was the antechamber of my mother's expectations.

The sun shone obligingly on the fields of late grain and the sky was just the right shade of blue. Here on this road that symbolized the mellowness of Central Europe, she could not avoid a comparison with the landscapes of France, elevated by centuries of travelers' descriptions to the standard by which the beauty of all other landscapes was judged. This land would not usurp the status of

la douce France, but it breathed the dignified gentleness that Regina brought to everything around her. The Central European plain was comfortable to the eye, with just that fair amount of culture necessary for the creation of Prague's carved roofs, or the Medieval portraits in museums, where, in the forgotten heart of Europe, essential things existed.

As the kilometers rushed by, as we consumed more and more of the Central European plain, Regina circled us like hula hoops, moving away only fleetingly, back to her acacias, of which there were none on the road from Linz to Prague. Taking us northward rather than to the east, this was not Regina's road, but it was taking the physical part of us where we had to go.

Hunger was the only thing capable of breaking my mother's trance. We stopped in a dusty little village just short of the frontier to spend our last Austrian Schillings on lunch. There seemed to be no public eating place on the sun-baked, deserted plaza. We knocked at the door of a wine cellar and were shown into the host's kitchen, where it was agreed that for the money we had we could get a meal. Soup, meat, potatoes, vegetables and pie were served at the large kitchen table as the hostess and several villagers looked on. My mother conversed in pig German about life on either side of the iron curtain, while I was passed from shoulder to shoulder with undisguised admiration.

Down the road, literally in the middle of nowhere, was the frontier post, marked by a tiny wooden sentry box. A guard came out and took our passports. Under the effect of the voluptuous hot meal, my mother pointed out trustingly that I was traveling without a visa. But that was not the problem: my passport had no stamp to show I had entered the country. How could one let out what hadn't come in? If you think the guard was joking, it's obvious you've never been to Austria. He walked back to the sentry box to confer with his companion, and at length they both sauntered back to the car with an air of superiority. The second one, who seemed to have some rank, said:

"Do you ever plan to come back to Austria?"

"Well, I really don't know," murmured my mother, trying to see into the future as truthfully as possible.

"Well, if you do," snapped the solider, very pleased with himself, "don't forget your little Fidel Castro needs a visa!"

He thrust my passport through the window and waved us on with a gesture of contempt. We drove a few yards to the Czech post, where there was a refreshment stand, a bank window with pretty clerks, and several rosy-cheeked young officers who all grinned delightedly at the arrival of a Cuban baby with a Czech name accompanied by a French woman with an American name, six suitcases and two hundred and fifty books.

My mother confessed that both of us were without visas. The Czechs gave her some forms to fill out and asked for pictures, which my mother carried in good supply, and although it was very complicated and took forever, to our biased minds it didn't matter.

We drove in the late afternoon sun through a series of villages and towns with funny, unpronounceable names like Kaplice, Cesky Budojevice, Hluboka and Ohrada, arriving in Prague at dusk. We went straight to the Cuban attaché's house on Stepanska Street where our things were, and where we would be sure to find a bed. Jarringly, nobody was home. Our other resource in Prague, Milan and Susan, weren't likely to be home, but were. "Stay where you are", they said over the phone. "We'll come and get you."

Happy at the thought of seeing old friends, my mother lifted me from my basket and sat me on the steering wheel, where I laughed and laughed 'til Milan stuck his bearded face in the window and frightened me to tears. We followed his ancient Skoda to Susan's house, where Milan and Susan's brother dismantled the rooftop extravaganza that would have to be reconfigured to accommodate the new items. I was fed and put to sleep on crisp white sheets laid over the Cuban rubber pad we carried with us, under a huge eiderdown. Susan's mother watched over me while my mother, Milan and Susan went to dinner in a huge coffeehouse humming with conversation. My mother asked Milan if there was a counterrevolution afoot but it was too early for that. (When it did come, a few years later, Milan was part of it, but during the fatal

days of the Russian invasion, he and Susan were on a vacation in Italy that became a tragic exile.)

Next morning we woke up late to find Milan in the kitchen stirring a brew of mushrooms and herbs with which to make an omelet. It turned out that the Cuban attaché had gone home on leave for his wife to have an operation. Someone from the cultural center opened the apartment so we could pick up our things, then we fetched Susan at her office. By the time the roof was assembled it was mid-afternoon and our hosts insisted we have lunch. We drove in two cars to a restaurant in the center of town, then our friends put us safely on the road to Warsaw.

The frontier was almost 150 kilometers away, and as a precaution was to be crossed that night, since the deadline for our return to Poland was the next day. If the car were to break down in Czechoslovakia, my mother would be left crying on the wrong side of the frontier as our visa expired.

We made it, only to discover that our deadline was in fact the following day.

Except for that memorable storm on the first leg of our journey, in six days of travel, our road had been all sun, blue sky, and that balmy Indian summer air that always seems to be just the right temperature. As we sped through the sunlit Polish villages, my mother wondered yet again whether the wheat looked the same in that light as it did a bit further east, if the houses were similar, the air much warmer, or damper, in a word, whether Regina would have been at home here.

You may wonder how Regina could still be so important, after all these years. Please forgive me if I've been vague. It's difficult for someone who passes, as I do, from one life to another, to remember that some things require explanations. Although she died before I was in place, I could not be Regina's great grandson without knowing everything about her. For "she is the cats grandmother" as my great-aunt Shirley used to say, and I am more cat than anything else: cats have many lives, they leap, swerving sideways, moved by spirits on the other side of an opaque door whom others cannot see, although perhaps it is Regina, great grandmother to a cat, whose

father was born under Leo and died a coward, leaving me his lion's face and green eyes framed in grapefruit colored hair. (Had not my mother often said that my father looked as though he could have been a cousin?)

Often when Regina spoke to Morris, or to the brothers and sisters who had followed them across the ocean, she reverted to the syncopated tongue of those times. It had been the only thing that kept their faraway world from vanishing, for there had been no letters, no photographs, no visits. Everything had ended with that frightful rocking boat, forty, fifty years before. Almost sixty years before the grapefruit lion reached across the seas to Regina's granddaughter to put Regina's catlike eyes on my face.

Regina had gray eyes and black hair, a straight friendly nose (not a straight, arrogant nose), black eyebrows that were fine although they met in the middle, and a wide mouth such as women had before mouths were painted, or transformed by advertisements to mean sensuous instead of being sensuous. And once she walked off the ship on Morris's arm, she was never sick again. She became a grandmother who baked bread every Friday and wanted to be told that hers was better than any other.

It was in that kitchen that the acacias had taken root in my mother's heart, together with the emphatic first syllables that infiltrated the straight, square sounds of English, to lurk there until the day when, driving across the wheat fields of Southeastern Poland - that part of Poland which had belonged, in turn, to just about every central European nation, including Franz Joseph's Hungary - they would come rushing back, as though she had always been hearing them, even as she roamed other lands, hearing other tongues.

This land had been blocked off the maps of my mother's world just as she was venturing, little more than a child, into postwar Europe. Divided up among constantly changing combinations of peoples, for us it was Regina's world, to which she had never returned. Racing through the Polish fields in our tiny car, as we had raced through the Austrian and Czech fields, the wistful image of Regina dancing before us, we abolished past and present frontiers. The canon balls the Czechs put in their soups, and the

stuffed cabbage Warsaw restaurants managed to turn out better than most other dishes, were partly responsible for the way my mother eyed the unfolding scene with a proprietary air. I think she knew that one day we would get to the land of dill pickles and sour cream.

Chapter XII - Childfest

After successfully crossing half of Europe without losing our way, the innocuous looking little town of Lodz appeared to have no exits, delaying our arrival in Warsaw until midnight. When we finally arrived at the *Pensione Sgoda,* the room with kitchen I had reserved a before departing was unavailable. We woke a friend, who made a frantic series of phone calls and got us into the tourist hotel, a sort of upscale hostel, where we were told we would have to vacate eight hours later. Passers-by gawked at the scaffolding as I unloaded it, then did a double take seeing Raul contentedly asleep in his basket inside. When I had brought everything in, a supercilious clerk, standing at the far end of the lobby, announced for all to hear that Joan of Arc had been a little less crazy.

It took another ten days for us to get into the Pensione Sgoda, during which time we sofa surfed, but at least the job on the English desk at the Polish Radio had come through. Although the workday was relatively short, I had to leave Raul with a series of mostly young and inexperienced baby sitters, and when I was incommunicado in the broadcasting studio, I would be seized with panic.

October 1965

How many things have I forgotten already?
I've spent hundreds of hours observing you,
drinking you in, watching over your
happiness. My apparent brusqueness,
roughness even, counterbalances kisses,
caresses, songs. When something is really
wrong. I try to guess your desires.

Sometimes you tire of my patter, you arch
your back, you howl and get all red. When
you're right, I give in, and if I 'm not sure, I
give you the benefit of the doubt. But when
you're just having a caprice, I leave you

there with your antics, and it's amazing how quickly you realize their futility.

The rare times when you're really unhappy, and you cry with big tears, taking you in my arms calms you momentarily; but if the necessary remedy is delayed for too long, you start up again, unless your gaze falls on something you love (an electric switch for example, or a picture); then the pleasure of the senses or the mind overrides your more prosaic need.

You so delight in rediscovering the world each morning that you never cry for food. For an hour or two I hear you talking from the other room while I catnap, communing in your pleasures. When I finally make my way to the doorway and look at you, you're totally absorbed, trying to pull a chair into your crib, or lying on your back, your feet in the air, rocking lazily, a finger in your mouth, and cooing the song you love, da-i da-i on two rather high notes. When you're feeling phlegmatic or sensual you sing soft coos; other moods are expressed by sonorous basses like the one on the plane that drew such attention. I wonder if all babies have such a wide register.

I continued to hope that Andrei would be part of Raul's life. Alas, like the hero of my little story, my child's father seemed to have died to himself, a sad, heavy person who haggled over child support. Yet notwithstanding the tragedy that followed the arrival of a much-desired child, my left-brain, where rationality resides, continued to come into its own. It was difficult to follow events in

Cuba at the time, since I could not read the Polish papers, but years later, when Gorbachev consolidated his power, and Perestroika became a magic word, I was not surprised by Fidel's condemnation. However much I regretted it on an intellectual level, I understood his reaction. The socialist regimes in the Soviet Union and Eastern Europe were run by people who were several generations removed from those who had dreamed of, or initiated the change from feudalism to communist power, while Fidel had devoted forty years to the Revolution; it was his creation, how could he repudiate it? Yet I suspected that deep down, he knew the limits of what he had set in motion. Had he not confessed to Edouardo Frei that it was a shame to turn everything upside down?

Periodically, documentaries showed him forging ahead with ever the same enthusiasm, charisma and conviction, the same crowds turning out to welcome him and exchange with him. Given all the Cubans had been through, they must have felt the positive outweighed the negative. In Eastern Europe after about the same number of years, some of people were beginning to realize that exploitation tends to reproduce itself, no matter the means of ownership.

[Raul, nine months, Warsaw]

January, 1966

We've been in our own apartment since Christmas, but the young girl from Bialystock whom I hired as housekeeper carried away pieces of my Community chest silver.

When I paint my fingernails, you approve. You're happy to stay up until I go to bed, and thankfully, you sleep until ten. You recognize people you haven't seen in a month, and before drinking your bottle you caress it, singing a cantata to your sacred totem.

You discover the relationship between the light switch and the light, play 'Where is Raul' by pulling the sheet or the towel over your face. You love to pull other people's hair, and when we pull yours, you resist silently for several seconds before letting go.

March

When you awake your eyes full of sleep are larger than usual. You raise your head heavily and let it fall back again, you arch your back like a cat and rub the back of your head where the hair is almost kinky from sleeping on it, then you roll your head from side to side, as if to wake it up, caressing it in circles (I'm told infants do this, but is it always so charming?). You relax your back, tilt your head, eyes wide open, and pop goes the finger in the mouth, as if to say : "I could

*use some food, but I know you'll make me
wait 'til you've had yours! "*

*"My dear, I've been used to eating as soon
as I get up for thirty-two years, and since it
doesn't really seem to bother you....."*

The agent assigned to me as a foreigner by the Ministry of
the Interior took to visiting me at home, then to meeting me in a
hotel lounge, and finally in a hotel room. He had never had a
suggestive word or gesture so I wondered what this was about. One
day he commented: "You would do anything for your child,
wouldn't you?" I took this for sincere admiration, until, at the end of
the meeting, he mentioned that he wanted me to meet someone the
next time we got together. Alarm bells rang. I was frantic until I had
reached the Cuban ambassador's wife on the telephone. She agreed
to keep Raul at her house during my next meeting with the Militia
agent.

I was right to take this precaution. The two interior officials
wanted me to get a job at the French embassy and keep my eyes and
ears open. I told them demurely that I wouldn't make a good spy.
Toward the end of the meeting my keeper remarked that I hadn't
brought Raul. Just as nonchalantly I responded that I had left him
with the ambassador's wife so we wouldn't be disturbed. I'm sure it
was because Raul was in safekeeping that they didn't press the
matter.

April 11
*In a few days you'll be a year old. But today
I want to talk about you indirectly.*

*I've always felt that one has to situate one's
life in relation to the world. Of course, when
one has children, the logistics change, there
are imperatives of health, and later of*

school, etc. But what shouldn't change, yet almost always does, through inertia, is one's perspective.

Even in a non-traditional life, one should stay connected, participate, not limit one's life to raising a child (notwithstanding the fascination of every moment), because the child too should be linked to the world.

After a winter in which Raul seemed to catch every bug from the otherwise excellent nursery, it was decided that I would work mostly at home. I was glad, never having been much of an office person, with its intrigues and rituals.

May 30

It's as if each instant were dilated, each element measurable. I'm in my bath. I have nothing to do all day but make meals and shop. I have no work left over from yesterday, nothing to prepare for tomorrow, no unpleasant obligations, only positive things to do, things directly for us.

It's my favorite time of day for a bath, about six p.m. The door is open, your door faces it, and you watch me from your bed/playpen. I'm far enough away to be able to look at you without it being a real exchange, yet close enough to be able to see you clearly. You're seated facing me, legs hanging out of the crib, your face cut in half vertically by one of the bars. My face is probably also cut in half, so you lean forward slowly, your eyes still fixed on me to see what

happens. I play the game, subtle movements back and forth.

I continue to sit there contemplating you for half an hour, running more hot water in the tub from time to time. You know I'm there, but pay no attention as you practice pulling yourself up from more and more difficult positions.

I wet my hair, then soap it, wondering whether you'll cry like you did two weeks ago; but that fear has already passed. Head to one side, you look at me with a serious expression, perplexed, yet hopeful (it's not really a nightmare, is it?), then you smile just slightly.

When I get out of the tub and wrap a towel around my head, you burst out laughing. Now you probably remember the whole thing, and you know what's coming. I reach for the dryer, you greet it standing, very sure of yourself, and when I turn it toward you, you smile, another fear overcome.

That summer in Warsaw, perhaps due to my inelegant material and psychological situation, I became obsessed by questions of esthetics and wealth. Raul played contentedly on the balcony, while I watched the children in the playground below and wrote furiously in a notebook:

July 17

I can't seem to get my mind around the Platonic idea that the only true beauty is abstract, that it equals the just and the good. In Cuba there was no contradiction between beauty and life. In the West, one is painfully aware of beauty's link to

*wealth, one could almost say its 'alienation' in
wealth.*

*As an adolescent I once declared, without really
knowing why, that bourgeois life was a rut:
now I realize it's a state in which beauty is often
about status. The abstract beauty of the
philosopher may be embodied in the simple
objects that surround him, but he does not want
it compromised in the name of 'value'. Beauty
is not only in the eye of the beholder, it is 'in'
the eye of the beholder, as when we say 'in the
mind's eye'.*

After war and Stalinism, by the mid-sixties, most Poles, like
other Europeans, had a job, a family, a home and a garden, where,
communing with nature, they centered themselves. Ironically, it was
in Poland that I became aware of television for the first time, and I
saw that instead of linking people to the wider world, it was bringing
a senseless agitation. The benefits of communing with nature were
being lost, along with awareness of the just and the good.

From my admittedly limited experience, I sensed that
Poland's new middle class didn't care passionately about anything.
Families watched TV together to make up for the lack of shared
passion, and it de-linked them from the world almost as powerfully
as morphine or a sleeping pill. Work and love, probably the only two
things that arouse personal passions, had also become routines.
Parents 'loved' their children, but not passionately: and they worried
not so much about one-party rule, as about them 'getting ahead'.

July 18

*An eight page ad in l'Express touts the
advantages of an up market development in
Versailles, with color photos and detailed
descriptions. In this beautiful environment,*

created by intelligent people for people who are bored, one constantly adjusts one's appearance, changing one's clothes several times a day.

In Warsaw, during the occasionally hot summer, I put on a bathing suit and cook or wash clothes at night, when it's cooler. I do housework when I'm too tired to write. That would never go over in Paris Ouest!

The inhabitants of this 'integral luxury' go to Drug West (America in Paris...) where they can buy string beans, or a dress, with a credit card. It's really difficult to believe that this is the same France as 20, 15 or even 10 years ago. Or the same Express as five years ago, when it was opposing the Vietnam War. In my world beyond the Iron Curtain, as yet unmediated by electronic money, farmers call out their fresh-picked vegetables from horse-drawn tumbrels under my windows.

July 22
I may not know exactly what I want, but I know very well what I don't want. Then again, maybe I'm creating all these complications to avoid being bored. Never being bored is a quality, but not tolerating boredom may be a defect. Is there a link between the fact that wealthy people are usually boring and beauty's alienation in wealth?

Convinced that something is wrong if one can only have access to beauty with money, I have always kept possessions to a

minimum, but cared about their esthetic value. Now that I have realized that beauty is our consolation for the way things are, I feel much better about it than when I was struggling to analyze it in Poland.

> *July 31*
> *Riccardo's letter keeps coming back to me: "Only a few countries still have lovely smells." Here's a talented, successful, intelligent photographer, seven years in Venezuela, four years in Cuba, and now, back in Italy, he and Graziella are going to pack up again. They'll sell some of the furniture I sold them, go somewhere new, then perhaps somewhere else....As 'Herzog' says, good people no longer know where to go...*

It was in Poland that I realized I could probably never become middle class. (That's probably part of the reason why relationships that were important to me did not lead to marriage: the men involved wanted the real thing, but knew I couldn't adapt to its codes, whereas I thought I would be able to accept a diluted middle class life - with them.) But I did want a country, a language and a culture for Raul. I wanted a permanent home, yet was determined that life be flexible, adapting to what happens every day.

> *August 4*
> *M. wrote recently that I shouldn't spoil my child because when he grows up he'll hate me and he'll be right. I believe my way of bringing up Raul will save him from being spoiled. It's true that I show my love for him a great deal, but I also require that he leave me alone most of the time. Mothers who spoil their children are always worrying that*

something will happen to them. A child would be right to hate a mother like that.

August 23
One night in Cuba African priest Arcadio asked everyone what life is, and I was the only one to answer that it is movement.

Thinking now of the need to make order in my things: clothing, books, papers, I wonder if this is the beginning of a middle-class outlook, the inevitable temptation of the part of us that aspires to order in a disordered world. But too much order = peace is a prelude to immobility, and giving in to it leads slowly to death.

To be linked to the world is the opposite of dying. I'm reminded of a Roman friend, so passionate about the arts. When he dies, it will be suddenly, from high blood pressure. Until that moment, he will be as far from death as a child.

(Ten years later a letter from a friend informed me that that friend had died while soaking blissfully a hot tub....).

August 28
I'm still wondering whether thinking about the future for the first time in my life, making plans, something that until now had been inconceivable, means I'm becoming middle-class. Judging by the life we've led so far, we're far from it. But although one has to live somewhere, have a base, a child needs

the reassurance of familiar walls, a language, a culture, I don't believe one can become middle class all of a sudden, even with a child.

I wanted stable work, because the anxiety of not being able to provide for my child was unbearable. But I was also in love with 'the peninsula' and longed to see its two halves reunited, and Raul was forcing me to find the right place for all of that to happen.

While I was philosophizing, Andrei was deciding to stay with Casimira, on the pretext that I was a better mother and more able to shoulder the responsibility of bringing up a child alone. Though true, it was a bittersweet compliment. I went to court to obtain child support for Raul, Andrei challenged the amount, which was reduced, and I decided there was no point in remaining in Warsaw, where his visits, like the support, would be contingent upon Casimira's good graces.

As always, once convinced that a bad situation would not evolve into a better one, I lost no time deciding what to do: it would be preferable for my son not to know his father than to pine after him. Before he was a year and half, we had left Poland.

The decision to leave had been a simple one. Determining where to go had been another matter. The countries I knew in the West: the U.S., France, Italy, all seemed like impossible places for a woman to raise a child alone. I was not tempted to return to Cuba, which seemed to have lost the innocence of the Revolution's early years. Because of the social system - and the blond men - I was attracted to Sweden, but given my abhorrence of the cold and snow, I knew that would be a wrong decision.

After many months of reflection, Hungary seemed the best choice: I knew enough of the advantages and inconveniences of communist regimes - from the privileged position of a foreigner free to leave at any time - and in any case it seemed a pity to be so close, yet not complete the return Regina had longed for. I obtained several recommendations for people in Budapest from fellow journalists, and we took a trip in early summer by train. After about a week in

Budapest, I decided it would indeed be a better place for us than Poland, and I could probably get a job at the Hungarian Radio

We left Poland for good in September of 1966, in the little Fiat, through the back roads of Czechoslovakia (why go the long way on a good road when you can go the short way on a bad one?). The 500 mile trip took two days. We slept in a village on the Polish side of the Tatra mountains, on uncomfortable beds in what passed for a hotel, then made our way through unattractive little Slovakian towns with unpronounceable names peopled by abrupt, rosy-cheeked peasants. I was thrilled to discover that although very different in sound, Polish was almost the same as Slovak (and close to Serbian, Slovenian and Croatian, should there ever be a need).

I had hoped to arrive in Budapest in time for dinner, but by the time we reached a place called Banska Bistrica I knew that dinner would be a late one. We could only hope to make the Hungarian border by six, and optimistically, I calculated that the formalities and the road to Budapest would take another two hours.

The sky was clear on that September afternoon, as it had been during our romp through Eastern Europe a year earlier, and the sun was as tender and rosy as anyone could wish on a momentous day. The road from Zvolen to the frontier at Sahy was a good one, and it seemed we had almost reached home. (Home was not only where I hung my hat, but where Regina had hung hers...) I stepped on the accelerator with new determination, forgetting how old my car was and how tired I felt, scanning the horizon for the first sign of the land on the other side of the fence.

We arrived in Sahy, hardly more than a village, punctually at six. But there we drove round in circles following well-meaning directions, looking in vain for a frontier post. Finally, we came to a little hut in the middle of a wood. The barrier was pulled down, and on the other side was a truck, the driver showing his papers to the guard who seemed to be waving us off. I waited, my heart beating fast; at last the guard came over and said something that didn't sound like a welcome. I shoved our passports at him, wondering what could be wrong. He gesticulated furiously, handed back the passports and walked away. Unable to accept - or believe in - this rejection, I

called him back and spoke to him in Polish. To no avail. In desperation, I tried my limited German. At last he uttered a few words that I could comprehend: this frontier post was only for trucks, and local ones at that; we had to go to - and there followed a totally incomprehensible word, or series of words, with German you never know. That was all I could get out of him. Back in the village, with more German, I found out that the place where cars could cross the border - a mouthful to pronounce: Balassagyarmat - was half an hour's drive. At least I had discovered that decades of Soviet influence had not erased German as the lingua franca of Central Europe. I mentally shook a finger at Regina and turned the bruised and battered Fiat 600 into the forest path that had been indicated as the road to follow.

Half an hour later, we were still bumping over a dusty road along a wood that could have been a border. Finally, as the sun was setting and I was beginning to think this was all a dream, we came upon a beautiful old man sitting in front of a small house, leaning on a walking stick and smoking a pipe. With his generous white mustache, he looked so much as though he could be an uncle, that I would have invented a reason for stopping had I not had one. He came forward slowly, smiling as if he had been expecting us, the way Regina would greet people as they opened the screen door. He may have been Slovak, but borders were flimsy things when it came to blood, and this man obviously belonged on the Hungarian side. He smiled silently at first, acknowledging our communication problem: finally, he said slowly, in German, that we would soon arrive at Balassagyarmat.

Half an hour later, with night almost falling, we arrived in the strange sounding place and sneaked up to the barrier, hungry and tired. The lights were on in a low green house and it was warm inside. A Slovak and a Hungarian passport officer sat facing each other across two desks pushed up together in the middle of the room. I wondered how they communicated - in German perhaps, or else they had forged a special language of their own, having no common ancestor. One of them, pointing at Raul, said "baba", and I thought it was distorted English, not knowing it was Hungarian via Turkish.

As the Slovak officer flicked through our passports, I noticed that the Hungarian - probably a fresh recruit - had red hair and freckles. He smiled at us. I smiled back and tried my few words of German, only to discover it was not the lingua franca of the young generation. As my fellow redhead and I continued to smile at each other, I felt like settling back in the old, stuffed armchair the men had motioned me to and putting my legs up over the side, as I would do on Regina's porch to watch the rain, letting night fall without moving. Raul reached out to the little side table and picked up an alarm clock, then, hearing it tick, listened in ravishment. The Hungarian officer took our passports from his colleague, flicked through them and picked up his pen. For one searing moment, time stopped. From a point in eternity, a bridge was thrown to us from other, distant points in time; yet Regina would never know that we had come home.

Chapter XIII - Regina's Land

[Heroes Square, Budapest]

We arrived in Budapest around ten, and luckily the room friends had reserved in a central two-star hotel had not been given to someone else. By daylight, I saw that the Hungarian capital forms part of a quartet of cities, composed of Paris and Rome in Western Europe, and Prague and Budapest in Eastern Europe. These four gems are like two sets of non-identical twins, Paris and Prague being gray, Rome and Budapest red. What makes Budapest special is the contrast between its two halves, which for a time were separate cities: flat, commercial Pest, and green, hilly Buda, which hardly seems like part of a city. Linking the two are several bridges, but the one I always see in my mind's eye - the first one I came upon, and also the most beautiful - is the Elizabeth Bridge, rebuilt after the war with two graceful soaring white towers that seem to ease the transition from hills to flatland.

I soon realized that if the Uro-Altaic Magyars can be compared to any Europeans, it's to the Italians, at least on such a

superficial level as serving good coffee and making good wine, while their neighbors are mainly into beer. (The fabulous Hungarian pastry shops, on the other hand, come from neighboring Vienna...)

Other familiar things from Regina's house in Philadelphia included bicarbonate of soda as toothpaste, unstructured gardens, the smell and taste of paprika, and the music. Bartok and Kodaly, constantly heard on the radio as part of the Soviet-inspired emphasis on the national heritage of each satellite country, both based their music on the folk airs I had heard in 13th Street. The language too was familiar, but the challenge of learning even the limited amount required to move every day forward, was daunting. In one of the first rented rooms we occupied, Raul ran a high fever while the family was away for the day with the telephone locked in another room, and I felt incapable of communicating with the neighbors.

Regina's image lingered on the city's rust-colored facades. But it was the people, neither hurried, nor depressed who echoed my grandmother's world; and even as I struggled with it, the language, with its tonic accent on the first syllable, imparted a dignified musicality to my life as I did what was required to feed, house, and clothe a child whose metamorphoses never ceased to enchant me.

September, 1966

Your spirit illuminates the world like a diamond. In Hungarian they call you 'cilag', which means star, and your aura causes people to turn around in the street. When you're among other children, everyone looks at you, not with envy, because each parent thinks his child is the most beautiful, but with wonderment: your beauty and intelligence transcend other people's parental feelings, and they love you too. Strangers give you gifts, like that day at the Citadel with Milan and Susan, when a family gave you a big

balloon. You do make me angry sometimes, so I know this is not my imagination working overtime. If you weren't capable of being a capricious whiner, you would be a very suspicious little person.

As a French citizen who had spent two years in Cuba, I could hope to be allowed to establish residence and work in Hungary. While waiting for my situation to be sorted out, I was offered several interpreting jobs. One was for a UNESCO conference on art, which could best be described as 'international conference, national outlook'. Very few delegates were willing to take up someone else's ideas, much less learn from another country. The wet blankets of nationalism and chauvinism were thrown over the conference table, first from one corner, then the other. Each delegate was convinced that because his country was different, it was better, and worked hard to isolate it from the experiences of others. My teen-age advice to Queen Elizabeth seemed to have got no further than Buckingham Palace.

October, 1966

Instead of sponsoring all these organizations and conferences, Unesco should find a way to teach people to become internationalists. It's useless for citizens of different countries to confer if they can't hear each other. When someone suggested that artists living in Paris could help the French organize a workshop, I realized that the delegates should be like those artists, who had refashioned their original psyche into a cosmopolitan one. Until everyone goes through this transformation, people won't be able to be part of the world, listening to it,

cooperating with all its components. They will remain eternal purveyors of 'us-itis', each trying to sell his own world to the others, while defending it from them.

Paris is the foremost cosmopolitan city because each foreigner adds something of his own world to the original, like a sculptor smoothing little daubs of clay onto a statue. All international organizations should be located there, with international civil servants returning to their countries for short periods, instead of coming out for short periods to argue. There's already a breed called UN, UNESCO, or NATO man, yet Swiss, Swedes, English and Italians, who share a common heritage and live on the same tiny peninsula, are deaf to each other around a conference table.

Modern technology is giving each country a common denominator of outward appearances, gadgetry, and even practices. But these are shells which they insist on filling with their own idiosyncrasies, convinced that theirs is better, diversity is bad, and different is downright dangerous. The Italian painter drinks the same coca-cola as the English (the former at a cafe in the sun, the latter in a cold pub), but is convinced that since artists have always enjoyed a special prestige in his country, and the fractured left, while not in government, can unite long enough to push through laws protecting artists, Italy would have nothing to gain from a British idea to register all works of art in a computer.

The Swede, who abhors the conformity of his wealthy but cold country, almost physically pushes the British proposal away, fearing yet another blasphemous technological assault on art for art's sake. On the executive committee, he refuses the Secretary General's pleas for more money, fearing a growth of superfluous, ineffective bureaucrats, as opposed to the artist who creates. Never mind the people art is supposedly created for.

Happily, the Dutchman announces that The Hague City Council - in full Provo swing - has earmarked 100,000 gulden a year to buy works of art for children....

After months of uncertainty, the job at the Hungarian Radio came through, and we moved to an apartment in the building next to the Chinese Embassy where most foreign radio workers lived. My boss was a Scottish communist who had been in Budapest for about fifteen years and was married to a Hungarian woman. A no-nonsense type, Harold was a man of robust temperament who was always ready for a laugh and enjoyed an independent position among the heads of foreign departments. Because we both liked work well done, we got along famously.

April 26, 1967

It's time to take stock. Before you were two, you knew several letters of the alphabet, and guessed from the different lengths of the words whether piano music was by Bach or Beethoven.

You laced your shoes, crossing them correctly, and if I said one two, you'd say three four. You

like to look at yourself, comb your hair, suck on your toothbrush. A box and its cover, anything you can take apart and put back together, is very precious, you must have it. You even want to open tin cans.

You sing pipi, kaka but you do it all in your diaper. You dance like a bad boy, the way Itza, our gypsy cleaning woman taught you; you like to hear music, but even better to put the record in its envelope, again and again, or through the slit between the two parts of a folding door. You are delighted by children's voices on a recording of Hungarian songs.

When you come into a room, you make a beeline for keys beckoning on a cabinet door, or knobs on radio or tv. A year ago, you loved to make the volume go from loud to soft, now you defy the interdiction to play with electric switches and plugs.

You feed yourself, but you behave better at restaurants, where you visit other tables, especially ones with other children. You like beautiful clothes, but prefer to go naked. You like soft materials to bury your head in while sucking your thumb. You still love my hair, though it is very short now.

When you see scissors, you say 'nails'. It took me hours to cut your hair, which had grown quite long. Finally, we went to the kitchen, but when you saw me looking at the result of my handiwork with a critical eye, you ran into the other room.

You have an extraordinary ability to concentrate and are fascinated by books, photos

of children, and busses. You know that photos are made with a camera.

You seem almost superhuman, not only because you're so well built and handsome, but because of a light that emanates from you when you gaze at other people, a unique look of tenderness that touches everyone.

In the spring of 1967, while rubbing elbows with the nomenclature, Harold had met the director of the wood exporting conglomerate, who never missed an opportunity to get something from someone. His son had taken a crash course in English conversation and wanted to keep up his new skill. Knowing I could use the money, Harold asked if I would be interested, and that was how I met Matyas. Like Raul's father, Matyas was much younger than me, but he had black hair, blue-green eyes and an Egyptian style build. At first, his pushy ways annoyed me, but after several conversation lessons, I realized that he was also quite charming and intelligent, with a down to earth physicality that put an end to two years of celibacy.

Almost immediately, I became pregnant. Though Matyas and I got along very well, I felt that our relationship was too new to be confident of its future prospects. Matyas's father referred me to the hospital where party members were treated, and a Hungarian lady gynecologist performed a D&C without anesthesia. It was the only abortion that was legal and took place in a hospital, and the only one that developed complications. The other abortions I had had, two in Paris and one in Rome after I had tried to reconcile with Leo, had been performed by midwives or even amateurs, in their homes, by inserting rubber tubes. This time I bled for eight months, until I had another D. & C. (Though uneventful, these interventions were probably what had caused me to remain sterile for seven years. When nature reasserted itself, only the delivery system remained faulty.)

It was right after the Budapest abortion that May had been scheduled to visit, and she was very annoyed to find me in bed, unable to squire her around. Little did she realize that like their Polish counterparts, Hungarian beds were not conducive to feigning illness, being sofas that opened up for sleeping, with a gully down the middle where the seat and the back met. Matyas and I later replaced the one in our furnished apartment with the latest in creative bedding: a double bed-cum-storage box whose foam padded top felt more like a floor with two quilts on it than even a hard mattress. This box could be raised at an angle thanks to two enormous hinges on either side, and the bedclothes were stored inside - a blessing for someone who at an early age had rejected hospital corners. At any rate, indifferent to my bleeding, May hinted that I had purposely scheduled the intervention to coincide with her visit. Matyas was happy to act as her guide, and Raul was a beautiful and charming child who would have made any grandmother's heart melt; but not May's. Only later would she and her elder grandson get along famously.

Gradually, the wounds inflicted by Andrei healed and I became very attached to Matyas, who was also a good father. Looking back, my marriage to him was the most real. Starting with the housing shortage (which also existed in France and Italy), life in Budapest was not much different from that in Western European capitals. People went to work, more and more of them in cars, they gathered to argue in coffee houses over fabulous pastries, cheated on their spouses and grumbled about one thing or another. Matyas taught math at the university, Raul went to nursery school and I worked at the radio, where I had access to various foreign publications that enabled me to follow what was going on in Cuba and sometimes I wondered whether I had been right to leave that place where extraordinary things were happening. A major event of 1968 was the publication of French writer Robert Merle's book *Moncada*, in which Fidel justified the revolution's first attack on power and the eight-year struggle that followed:

"Nothing has changed in twenty years. It has probably been this way from the day the Republic was founded, and it will continue with no one doing anything about it. Over the years, more than theory, reality has convinced me of this. Everything we do in the area of education is useless if we don't rethink the economic situation. Let's say that with government help a young man arrives at a good technical level. He would drown under the narrowness of our present economic and social conditions. Karl Marx wrote about the same thing in The 18th Brumaire of Louis Bonaparte, a more romantic concept of history than the scientific, realistic concept of history in Das Kapital." And Fidel declared: "How I would love to revolutionize this country from top to bottom! I'm convinced I could bring happiness to all its inhabitants, even if it meant incurring the wrath of one or two thousand people, including all my relatives, half my friends, 2/3 of my colleagues, and 4/5 of my old school friends."

A speech on March 13th 1968 was, as often, a lesson in economics, full of ideas that would eventually become conventional wisdom:

"By the year 2,000 the population of Latin America will have increased 157%, from 265,000,000 to 690,000,000. In North America and the USSR, it would increase 42%, in Europe 25%. During the first 50 years of the English industrial revolution there was a population increase of 0.6%, in France, 0.4%,

Belgium, 0.7%, Germany, 0.8%, Italy 0.8% or a total of 4%.

In the first fifty years of industrial development, there was only a 1% per annum increase in the per capita gross product. To obtain this, 6% had been invested, and it was not until incomes were three or four times more per capita than those of today's underdeveloped countries, that they were able to invest 12%.

If a country had a 2.2% population increase a year, in 50 years the population would triple, and it would have to invest 12% just to keep up. In order to raise the gross product by 1%, 16% would have to be be invested. Yet in eighty years, a country would only double its income. In 1968, the income in Latin America was 10 times less per capita than in Europe and 20 times less than in the US.

To get a 2% increase in GDP, a country would have to invest 20%. But historically, developed countries have only been able to invest 20% when their income was five or six times higher than the 1968 income in underdeveloped countries.The population in Latin America is increasing by 3.2%. To obtain a 3% in-crease in the gross product it would have to invest 25%. No developed country is doing this."

The decision I had made to go from Poland to Hungary was the first one I had ever taken after thinking about it for a very long time, one that I had weighed, calculated, and planned, and although I had assumed future decisions would be made the same way, suddenly I was thinking about going back to Cuba. For even as Regis Debray's 'permanent revolution' was bringing France to a

standstill, Eastern Europe was moving decisively away from the direction Cuba had taken, which I believed was the more desirable.

Although communism did not make things difficult for me in Budapest, the priority Matyas granted to his relationship with his family did. I was glad that Raul had acquired grandparents, uncles and cousins, and enjoyed spending time with Matyas's mother, who taught me to cook Hungarian dishes, (his father had to be made to keep his roving hands in place), but I felt that barring emergencies, their need to be chauffeured around should not take precedence over our family routines. As with attachment to country, I was bucking a basic facet of Eastern European life. Luckily I got comic relief from the political jokes that were a typical aspect of Eastern European culture. During the Six Day War the 'in' joke in Budapest was: "What do Israeli mothers do when their children misbehave?" followed by the right hand being slapped over the right eye to evoke Moshe Dayan.

During the 1968 spring break, Matyas and I drove to the town near the Romanian border with the almost unpronounceable name of Nyreghasza to look unsuccessfully for a trace of Regina's family. I was disappointed by her acacias, but perhaps it was not entirely coincidental that I became pregnant with her second grandson there. Realizing that I had been contemplating a new uprooting the way men contemplate new wars, forgetting just how difficult the last one was, I happily gave up the idea of going back to Cuba to have Matyas' baby, one of the few times when thoughts of change were not followed by action.

It was almost easier for an American to travel to Cuba than it was for a French citizen to marry a Hungarian in Budapest. By August, the daunting paperwork was still inching along when Raul and I and my future in-laws accompanied Matyas to a mathematical conference at the southern tip of Yugoslavia. It so happened that on the day before our departure, the countries of the Warsaw Pact, including a reluctant Hungary, invaded Czechoslovakia, which had been practicing 'socialism with a human face' since the spring. In a vivid example of how much more powerful historical feelings about neighbors are than decrees of brotherhood, our superintendent broke

the news with ill-disguised contempt for the Czechs who, instead of following the Hungarians' discrete example under Kadar, had proclaimed their deviance from the rooftops.

Luckily, my Beetle didn't have an 'H' on it, and the license plates the Hungarians issued to foreigners looked the same as Belgian plates, for in Zagreb, where we stopped overnight, there were violent demonstrations against the invasion. Our car would surely have been burned had it been recognized as coming from Hungary so for added security, Matyas, his father and I made a point of speaking English, to the old man's halting delight. At a farmhouse where we found overnight accommodations, I saw olive trees, and got the farmer to sell us some of his oil. I had got used to Hungarian salads dressed with water, vinegar and sugar, but my longing for olive oil was incommensurable, like that for the Mediterranean. By the next day, under the southern sun, the corks had come lose, flooding the floor of my car, which forever after smelled of olive oil.

Back in Budapest, I confronted the West's determination to make life as difficult as possible for anyone living on the wrong side of the curtain – and the Hungarian tit for tat response, as part of the New Economic Mechanism, which had come into effect with the New Year. The goal of eventually make the forint convertible having put hard currencies at a premium, I had to get permission to send the equivalent of fifty cents to France to pay for the papers I needed.

The new system also gave managers more leeway to manage their profits, make investment decisions, pay for imports, etc. As I had intuited, the Hungarians had decided to move away from the Che economic model, toward that of Carlos Raphael. Theoretically, this would require greater protection for workers, but if democracy were allowed in the workplace to ensure that protection, it would lead to a demand for political democracy. Hence the necessity of what I called a lid. This arbitrary limitation on democracy was the primary intellectual focus in Budapest, but I was more frustrated by the tendency of our academic friends to uncritically imitate Western 'progress'. I simply could not get them to realize that life should not be about getting more 'stuff'. After months of trying to convince Hungarians that gadgets weren't everything, I attended a talk by the

movie director Andras Kovacs, who told me he used the cinema to air his political views. The talk was accompanied by excerpts from other directors' films which were also surprisingly political, and afterwards Kovacs discussed the directors' views with them in front of the large audience.

Thinking about how these intellectuals spoke out for what they believed a socialist society should be, it occurred to me that had they been Cubans, they would have been more strongly identified with third world struggles. I wondered whether this was because Eastern Europeans had such strong cultural roots – or were Cuban intellectuals simply lucky that the regime supports internationalist ideals?

Shortly after deciding not to return to Cuba, I was again hired as an interpreter, this time at a conference of the socialist leaning *World Trade Organization.* Although my Hungarian was still rudimentary, and I would never conquer the written, more sophisticated form, my four other languages were at a premium. (I still had only four, because although circumstances had forced me to learn rudimentary Polish, rudimentary Hungarian had swept every trace of it from my brain.)

As with the Unesco conference on art, in the plenary sessions each delegate spoke without taking into account what others had said. In the commissions, each saw only his own world from his own point of view. In a scene reminiscent of a futurist film, about fifty men were seated around winding tables - an extrapolation of the original round table - each with his own interpreter, some of which spoke into microphones, others in low tones into the ear of their 'client'. The sight of dozens of men enveloped in clouds of smoke droning on simultaneously, as great crystal chandeliers swung overhead epitomized their mutual incomprehension.

December, 1967

As you turn two and a half, I discover that children progress from being totally disconnected from the world, to being capable

of understanding any idea for which they know the words. This capability marks the end of infancy and the beginning of childhood, and it is a most beautiful and fascinating thing to watch. Last spring, when we went to a house at Lake Balaton, you understood that Matyas couldn't get the door open. The second time we went to Rome you learned the names of all our friends beforehand, and when we returned you knew what each one had given you. But you still didn't understand discipline. You ran wild in restaurants, wouldn't leave a toy in a store. Now you understand the concept of restraint. Before, when I said no, you obeyed because you knew you were vulnerable; now you can be persuaded to do things for a future reward. In the spring, you vaguely understood the difference between now and later, but you couldn't apply it.

You come home every day from the nursery with a new poem or song; you know more or less the same letters you learned in January, but now you can count almost perfectly to ten and you're practicing your colors.

You still have the last vestiges of your contrary period, which has lasted almost a year; you like to say, in fun: I need, I don't need.

You're not terribly interested in stories, but you have a passion for a huge book of photographs of life in Hungary, and you know which book has what in it.

When the puppet theater came to the nursery, you told me you had cried. The teacher told me

you had watched wide eyed, saying you didn't like it: I guess you felt like crying.

You've begun to ask for Matyas, but you don't miss him when he's not here. Your try at calling him daddy fizzled, but you called a friend's father daddy the other day.

You love your new pair of winter boots, and to rumple my hair. You enjoy using new potties and toilets, pulling the chain, wiping yourself, throwing everything away.

You love to eat, sleep, and run against the wind.

In the fall, Matyas and I got a lesson in capitalist economics when we traveled to a mathematics conference in Germany. Each week, in a magnificent complex in the Black Forest, Volkswagen held a gathering of mathematicians from all over the world, who could bring their wives and children for a small fee. Before meals - for which people were scientifically rotated to different tables - we would gather in the lounge, where there was a closet full of soft drinks, liquor and snacks. Guests were expected to write down what they took on a sheet of paper. If you made a long distance call, you asked the operator the price and put the money in a box. Also, there were no keys on any of the doors. The Germans seemed to have so much money they didn't know what to do with it, so they did silly things like piping muzak into carpeted village drug stores.

When it was time for us to leave the Volkswagen conference center, instead of having to pay for my and Raul's board, as we expected, Matyas was handed a wad of cash and an explanation: by driving we had used up only a small amount of his travel allowance, so the foundation owed him money. The story made the rounds of the Budapest mathematical community.

Raul was now in the 'fear' stage. Looking out the window he would announce gaily: "Mommy, I'm going to play in the garden." But after looking again: "I'm not going to play in the garden: there's

a wall." At times he claimed not to be afraid although he was. A neighbor had three kittens that he could stroke contentedly when they were in a basket. Then, suddenly they were much bigger and running around, and he kept pulling me toward the door, all the while insisting that he wasn't afraid.

He still preferred poems to stories. And he was anxious to become bigger and older so he could make my breakfast, an idea that definitely appealed to me.

The convictions expressed in the article I had sent to *Elle* were being confirmed daily, but now I saw women's lib in relation to the broader question of life-styles. I realized that women are sexually 'uncertain' in that they may or may not have an orgasm. Also, they may or may not make full use of their brains. At that time, because there was always a man in the background, many women failed to acquire a profession, content to work at a low-level job until they had children. They lived according to their biology, letting a husband support them while they 'just stayed home and raised the children'.

Many writers were convinced that only socialism could liberate women from the household grind, freeing them for productive work. Cynically perhaps, I figured that half of them would be caring for other people's children. In the end, I reasoned, it should boil down to each woman doing the job she's best suited for: i.e., caring for children, working in a factory, teaching, being a doctor, etc. I was skeptical of the idea that 'only socialism' could liberate women.

I mused that in the past, considering what was expected of children as they grew up, women were much more important in their lives than now. They were not only cooks, nurses, etc., but dancers, painters, weavers. Fathers, too, were more immediate models. I knew from observing Raul that children were highly sensitive to music at a very early age; yet most parents did nothing more to foster this than have the radio or a record on. A six month old noticed music and often stopped crying to follow the sound. One and two year olds had a marvelous sense of rhythm - all wasted because music and dancing were no longer part of family life, as they were part of tribal life.

In the sixties we heard music by appointment with a ticket to a concert. Now, perhaps because we have instant access no matter where we are, everyone is still not a musician and a dancer as in primitive societies. The need to express himself led primitive man to decorate his cave walls; each was his or her own artist. 'Great' works of art now reach more people, but artists who do not strike a critic's eye starve. Ordinary people have to stifle their creativity or join a club, expressing themselves at preordained times and places. In Hungary, I began to wonder how society could be organized so that a person could be an artist without having to be only an artist. How could we recapture the enjoyment felt by a baby, which should come partly from art, but can only happen if art is an integral part of living?

Living in a society where health services were free, I imagined them expanded to include sports and beauty facilities, and art. I dreamed of those living-resting-working-curing places decorated either by local people or artists from outside. Children would participate, and everyone could learn an instrument. I yearned for only necessary, esthetically pleasing things to be produced, and suspected that society would do just fine if people worked no more than four hours a day.

I felt that Dr. Spock's ideas about the isolation of women should be taken seriously by architects and urban planners. I wanted urbanization to be organized so that people lived in village-sized groups of semi-private-semi-communal one story houses, where children could play in common areas, with rotating parent supervision assisted by professionals, instead of being deposited like packages in nurseries. I thought that together with professionals, parents should also be teachers, with schools closely tied to the community.

I knew cities had been places where families were rooted, where people had personal and historical ties. But as they continued to grow, and mobility increased, I feared they would become 'only' monsters, even in socialist societies where crime was much lower than in the West. In a decentralized society based on anarchy, i.e., with an administration that served only to coordinate individual

responsibilities, there would no longer be capital cities, where the important decisions were made, where court was held, where the most influential and richest people lived and supported the arts. With the arts developing everywhere, gifted people wouldn't feel the need to gravitate to the big cities. In the absence of frontiers and capitals, they could wander from one town to the other. At that time, in Europe, many capital dwellers would have liked to live in small cities, whether Sopron in Hungary, Aix in France, or Sienna in Italy, all of which have a human dimension.

These last few years of familiarity with American suburbia have convinced me that the answer to sprawl might be precisely to accept that people like to live where it's green, and encourage the development of suburban communities interspersed with farmland, which would provide food locally. This is already being done in some places, and it will become more widespread when more people choose to live off the grid.

An idea that would probably be considered heretical by ecologists, is that strip malls are efficient ways of grouping places that people need easy access to. Big box stores, of which Walmart has now become the epitome, where you can get just about anything you need for daily living, have the advantage of making shopping a more matter-of-fact occupation, that of 'getting supplies', whether it be a skirt or food, because you need them, not because advertising tells you that you need them. But this should not imply that supplies are trucked in over long distances.

Matyas and I were married in November, with Michael due to be born in January or February. Although my anatomy was ideal for conceiving, as with Raul, doctors could not estimate the delivery date. This was a problem, because Matyas had been invited to do research in Holland for a year starting January, and in December, his passport still didn't have the requisite signature that would allow him to travel. If I gave birth before he departed, I risked being left behind, since my Hungarian child would not be able to leave the country. (As foreigners, Raul and I could come and go freely, but it was still unheard of for entire Hungarian families to be allowed to travel to the West together.) I was determined not to be left caring for

186

two small children alone for a year, but didn't know how to make it happen.

[Hungarian wedding 1968]

Though Howard and I rarely communicated, he came to my rescue by reminding me of our Dutch uncle, Pal, whom I had met when we arrived on the SS Rotterdam twenty-two years before. Slightly ashamed at having lived within a few hours' train ride in Paris for nine years without ever contacting him, I picked up the phone in Budapest and called him, doubling the surprise by speaking Hungarian. I announced that I was expecting a baby in the very near future and wanted it to be born in Amsterdam, which might require me to travel in advance of my husband. Uncle Pal told me not to worry about a thing. He would line up an obstetrician and help us find an apartment. Meanwhile, Raul and I could stay with him and his wife Ilse. I merely had to obtain permission from the Dutch government to have my baby there, since Holland zealously guarded the size of its population on land reclaimed from the sea.

My parents-in-law, uncles, aunts, and cousins, were nonplussed by my plan. How could I contemplate a twenty-five hour train ride with a small child in tow in my ninth month, to have my baby delivered by a strange doctor in strange place? Why did I not just let things happen?

Chapter XIV- Exoticism in Europe

Their gentle protests failed to move me. As for Matyas, he wasn't looking forward to spending a year in Amsterdam cooking for himself, so he went along with my plan. The only thing that really mattered to him was his work: as long as he could be curled up in a chair with paper and pencil, solving mathematical problems, he was not particular about the rest. (Early in our relationship he had stated as a matter of undisputed fact that mathematics was a kind of poetry, and I liked him for that assurance.)

All it took was a month or so of Hungarian paperwork for leaving the country, and by mid-January I was ready to depart. As I had foreseen, Matyas still didn't have his passport back with the necessary signature, but trusting that it would eventually arrive, I set off with Raul in tow. Changing trains in Vienna, we had dinner in the station restaurant surrounded by our five suitcases. Contrary to my earlier pregnancy, I was rather large, and everyone gawked. Actually, I felt fine, except that I couldn't eat salt. By then I was used to it, and my mother-in-law had baked a wonderful salt-free nut cake. We had a Wagon Lit, and though it was a long trip, I loved being on the train. My only fear was that I might suddenly go into labor, and my child would be born between stations. Luckily that didn't happen, and Pal was waiting for us in Amsterdam, whence he took me straight to the obstetrician. Though I saw no need for such precipitation, I followed him obediently: it wasn't often that someone looked after me.

The backwardness of Hungarian medicine was one of the reasons why I was just as glad to be giving birth to my second child in Holland. Hungarian notions of hygiene, even in the party hospital where Matyas and I were treated, were sometimes astonishing, as when a nurse stuffed a wad of cotton under her arm before swabbing me for a urinary catheter. I had come down with a simple vaginal infection which is cured in a few days with the right medicine in the States, but went on for months in Budapest while a burly Russian woman doctor prescribed gentian violet and a series of useless antibiotics.

The Amsterdam obstetrician was only as surprised by my venture as a phlegmatic Dutchman could be. However, he didn't seem any more clairvoyant than the Hungarian doctors as to my delivery date, and told me to come back in two weeks. Raul and I were warmly welcomed by Pal's wife Ilse at the top of a long flight of steep stairs in an old building in the center of Amsterdam. We were served oxtail soup on a long antique table which, like the rest of the furniture, enveloped us in a reassuring patina. The next few days were spent sight seeing and looking for an apartment, and when I realized it would probably take more than a few days to find one, Raul and I moved to the hotel next door, continuing to take our meals with Pal and Ilse, with the exception of breakfast, at which enchanting platters of thinly sliced assorted cheeses and cold cuts were served.

Strangely, it was not overly cold, nor was there any snow. We rode around on the trolleys, poked into museums, and even went to see *The Nutcracker* at the Konzertgebouw, an event that frightened Raul into wanting to leave before the end.

I found an apartment in a high-rise development just the other side of the Ei Tunnel, adequately furnished with simple modern furniture. I signed a year's lease, and a few days before my appointment with the obstetrics we moved in. The next morning I woke up to discover that my water had broke. Fortunately, Matyas had given me the address of a colleague who just happened to live in the building opposite. She came immediately, drove me to the hospital and took Raul to stay at Uncle Pal's.

The next few days were less stressful for me than for Raul, who found himself in the care of two people whom he scarcely knew, only one of whom spoke a language he understood. Michael was born the same way Raul had been, by intravenous medication, because after 24 hours, the birth process had petered out. But the atmosphere was different: the doctor was called by the midwife during his Sunday lunch, which he took time to finish. Then, wearing a white coat over his jacket and tie, he perched himself casually on the side of the wide delivery table.

When after a week's rest I asked to go home, the doctor was just as phlegmatic. Pulling down my eyelid he said: "You're a bit anemic, but you can go". Twenty-four hours later, alone with two children, I was flat on the couch. Pal's daughter came to the rescue and Matyas called to say that he was finally on his way by car. When he arrived the next day, I could hardly stand. Luckily, under the Dutch health system, a neighborhood doctor was on-call on Sundays. He took one look at me, gave me a shot of calcium and put me on iron pills.

A picture in my album shows Raul a few weeks after Michael's birth, holding his brother on his lap, his contrived smile seeming to say: "I'm not unhappy at all!" Obviously he was, because if I put Michael down on a blanket on the floor, he would lie on top of him when I left the room. Raul did try to be helpful, but Michael was constantly crying, and perhaps in those moments I forgot to have a word for the older brother who had been so little trouble, or perhaps he took his cue about the new baby from us. We called Michael 'fusspot cross-eyed Chinaman', but it was Raul who developed a lazy eye and had to wear a patch for months.

Of Holland I remember mainly the cold, which explained why the Dutch flocked to the Mediterranean in winter; the Indonesian Ristaffels, the only good food in the country, aside from thick pancakes served with molasses, and oxtail soup. I found Amsterdam to be incredibly 'exotic', different from any other European city I knew, and its inhabitants were uniquely open and cheerful. Raul was enrolled in the neighborhood kindergarden, and although I asked the teachers to speak English to him because I didn't want his head filled with another 'little' language, they ignored my request and he soon became fluent, insisting that Matyas and I speak Dutch too.

In the spring of 1969, my mother May and Maytas' parents all descended upon us at the same time. Things went remarkably well, our visitors being too taken with their grandchildren and sightseeing to make trouble, though May commented sourly that I had a knack for organizing others to do things.

[Raul and Michael]

During that visit, Raul switched from Spanish to English almost overnight. After we left Cuba, I had been unable to suddenly address my baby in a different language from the Spanish I shared with his father, but now he had been hearing English for two years, since that was the language Matyas and I spoke together, while communicating with Matyas and others around him in Hungarian. May of course could only communicate in English, and by the time she left, Raul was almost fluent. I continued using it with him, as I had done when May was there. A few days later he said to me, in English: "Mommy, why don't we speak Spanish anymore?" I answered him in Spanish, but he could respond only in English. For several days I tried to get him back to Spanish, but without much conviction, knowing English was more important. (Now it occurs to me that perhaps the reason why Raul found English more satisfying was because, without another adult to speak to, my Spanish had become somewhat rudimentary, and English gave him more room to grow.)

One day, Matyas and I were having a quiet afternoon when we heard something drop through the mail slot. Matyas went to see what it was. At the sight of a promotional bar of chocolate, he laughed and shouted "Communismus!" I believe this was the start of his realization that communism, like everything else, is relative. The

dispassionate attitude I had toward the subject, as reflected in my 1969 Amsterdam diary was to prove highly prescient:

> *What revolutions demand of 'the masses' is the unnatural maintenance, for a protracted period of time, of a natural high. The wonder of the Chinese, Vietnamese and Cuban revolutions is that, in different ways and under different circumstances and personalities, they've more or less succeeded in doing this. What will probably be the undoing of Soviet power is that for too long (since World War II), it has not. What impelled the other Eastern European countries to move relatively quickly toward middle class goals is that they never tried.*

> *The process by which each new generation of potential revolutionaries eventually falls back into middle class patterns must be the same as that which leads professional revolutionaries to become bureaucratic and counter-revolutionary. For both Fellini and Fidel, their actions constituted the very fabric of their life. But only a handful of individuals are revolutionaries or artists to their very core. It's disturbing to think that America may already have its future apparatchiks, who will have been following the party line since before the beginning, and who, in twenty years, will be telling the American people how to think.*

The fall was very cold and windy, and I didn't believe in walking around pushing a carriage to give my baby fresh air. We were on the 24th floor and had big balconies, so Michael spent long hours asleep in a warm snowsuit under layers of blankets, oblivious

to the world. One night he refused to sleep as Matyas and I were trying to work on a translation (we did mathematical texts from German or Russian into English, Matyas dictating, me correcting as I typed). We brought him into the living room and put him in the carriage, where he insisted on standing up, threatening to fall out. After a while, I put him in his snowsuit, covered him up and put the carriage out on the balcony where it was minus something. Within seconds he was out.

Matyas and I both enjoyed the year we spent in Holland, but by the time it was half over, we were thinking differently about the future. The only thing that would have made Matyas leave his country would have been anti-Semitism: though no more religious than I, he did identify with being Jewish. But this was the first time I had found myself in a place that seemed to combine the best of all worlds, and I was reluctant to leave Holland. We argued a lot, but Matyas wouldn't give in.

At the end of January 1970, we drove a two-car caravan over snow-covered roads to Budapest. Matyas had bought a Renault 16, more comfortable for driving his parents around than my Beetle, and the two vehicles were piled high with our bags and a dish washer. Matyas took the lead to Dortmund, where, thanks to his father's far-flung network, we were to sleep with Hungarian friends. Since he was a reckless driver, I had insisted on having both children in my car, but I had to keep shouting at Raul to stop torturing Michael in the back seat. At the German border, as Matyas held out his passport to the guard, I turned on my knees to give Raul a serious scolding. When I turned back, the Renault had vanished. "What a stinker", I thought, "taking off like a bat out of hell. He knows I don't have a map, or even the address we're going to."

Fuming, I showed my papers - which were in my maiden name, since I had not taken Matyas's when we married - and took off in hot pursuit. There was no sign of him up ahead as far as I could see. For several hours I doggedly followed the signs to Dortmund as the snow fell thicker, and strife reigned in the back seat. On the outskirts of town I stopped at a police station, barely remembering our hosts' names. Luckily, they were in the phone book, and I was

given directions. Pulling up in front of the apartment building, I banged on the horn, having worked myself into a frenzy after all those hours of driving on faith. Flanked by two old ladies, Matyas emerged from the building, gesticulating wildly and shouting before he was close enough to be heard from inside the car. I stepped out and we faced each other like two gladiators:

"Why didn't you wait for me?" we both shouted.

"Me? You're the one who took off like a bat out of hell!"

"You're out of your mind. They made me go and park in the back of the guardhouse, because Hungarians don't cross frontiers just like that, as you should know by now."

"I didn't see, I was turned around dealing with the children."

"I told you not to take them both."

"Why didn't you honk your horn to get my attention?"

We might never have stopped had the old ladies not signaled that this sort of thing wasn't done on German streets.

We made up and drove through snowstorms for several more days to Budapest, where we settled back into our apartment in the radio building. Luckily the two rooms we had were both very big, for with the thousand dollars Jake had left me, I had bought a hundred year old half grand Viennese piano and a washing machine, the latter now joined in the kitchen by the dishwasher from Holland.

One day there was a knock at the door. Two young strangers were standing outside. They were carrying a letter from Ludovico. I had been worried at not hearing from him, and it turned out he had been ill. He wrote candidly, without undue emphasis on suffering. Perhaps because his health problems had developed early, but more likely because he had the stoic's ability to face pain as part of life, he treated it lightly, asking me to drum up an invitation for him to give a talk in Budapest so he wouldn't have to make up an excuse to see me. I was unable to do this, and he died the following year. The letters of that time show with what tenderness he reconstructed the past we had shared, as I continued in my daily battles with the life I had chosen.

Part Three: My Left Brain

Chapter XV - Home Again with Goulash Communism

In 1956 the Russians had assassinated Imre Nagy, leader of the failed Hungarian uprising, and sent Janos Kadar back from a Moscow exile to put the country back on the straight and narrow. But Kadar was an old pro, and soon he was running the most liberal Eastern European government, known in the West as goulash communism. He taught his countrymen to be wily with their masters, and by the mid-sixties when I arrived in Hungary, he was quite popular. Matyas routinely referred to the more dogmatic members of the mathematics community as 'the enemy', as open factions in the Communist nomenclature - or establishment - jostled for influence. Those factions were not much different from parties who could have disagreed over what constituted good socialist government, or from our Democrats and Republicans who have differing views about liberal government.

Every government will at times fail to live up to their countries' constitutions, and in Hungary, socialist principles were not always translated into acts. It seemed to me that as the primary owner of the country's real estate, the government could have done more to alleviate the housing shortage by helping people build homes. We toyed with the idea of getting a group together to build a small apartment building in Buda, but were deterred by the red tape.

During the spring and summer of 1970, Michael became quite chunky, straining my always fragile back. Although I worked from home for the radio, I was glad that Matyas, now a full professor at the university, worked fewer hours than before and was able to take over much of his care. However Hungarian ideas about child rearing reflected a bicultural time warp. My mother-in-law practiced a gentle form of Victorianism, while Raul's nursery school teachers were trained in the Russian Makarenko system, or solidarity Victorianism.

Seeing my second child grow confirmed my hunch that many feeding problems come from trying to teach infants to eat properly. In Eastern Europe they trained babies not to put their finger in their

food, eat with the spoon handle, or push the plate back and forth. I agreed with N.S. Neill that totalitarianism begins in the nursery, and with Gsell, who passionately attacked clockwork up-bringing. Raul and Michael conformed to most modern observations about child rearing, but I could not convince their caregivers to modify their ways. I stuck to Dr. Spock, meanwhile carrying on a running monologue with myself about the whole issue of women's liberation and education.

Hungarian women were fantastically liberated compared to pre-war times, and even compared to other sixties countries: they were paid 600 forints a month (about one fifth of an average salary) to stay at home with their children for three years. Unfortunately, because of a cultural lag, returning to work meant putting in two shifts, even if some husbands helped. I thought part-time nurseries should be available to mothers who stayed home as well as to working mothers. Today I still believe that nurseries and household machines are where women's lib begins. Even in a Kibbutz, why should only men drive tractors and why should anyone wash dishes?

A woman for whom math is the most fascinating thing in the world will be a mathematician. When she wants to have children she'll take time off, keeping up with developments in her field, even if, with vital energy channeled elsewhere, her creative capacities are temporarily diminished; and eventually she'll go back to math. But a girl won't have a career just to prove she isn't inferior. If the relationship between the boss and the secretary isn't sexually exploitive, being a secretary is no worse than being a bank teller, or a meat packer. Men are as likely to be bored with carrying, pulling levers, pushing buttons, as most home-makers with machines and a broader scope of activity (including basic doctoring, teaching, psychology, art).

Even in socialist Hungary, women's chores appeared less rewarding because they merely made it possible for men and children to go on existing. Previously, people brought in the food and produced items of immediate utility. In modern societies, women still fed, clothed, nursed and produced food, but society also produced unnecessary products that turned people into mindless

consumers. (Some products are the result of creativity; still, creators are a minority.) What else did primitive people do? They defended and taught, governed and made war, but I was convinced that neither men nor women should make war, and that both should govern.

In primitive societies women talked about the news of the tribe, even if they were not voting members of the council. Now the clan's business had grown into highly complex affairs of state, and what was initially a more or less subordinate position due to women's biological function and comparative weakness, had grown into complete subordination, as work migrated from home, and the clout associated with money grew.

I was convinced that only a network of nurseries, equal education and job opportunities would liberate women, and that they should be considered as equal but different. Trying to be like men would imply that to be a man, or to have masculine attributes, was better; therefore, to be a woman was to be inferior, therefore men were right to consider women as inferior!

A series on women's lib in the British *Guardian*, to which I had access at the radio, showed a demonstrator pointing to a picture of a Vietnamese woman with a rifle, over the caption: "There's a really liberated woman". Irritated, I wrote: "A liberated woman should not be stereotyped as one who can use a gun, because that's adopting the male preference for force over dialogue. A liberated woman should be one who can use a gun, but prefers diplomacy." I still think the reason why women in power have not changed things is because they are acting on the culturally acquired assumption that they have to be like men. The socialist countries were definitely ahead of the capitalist world in terms of women's rights, and I hope they did not allow things to change after the Wall fell.

Currently, in the West there is a trend among highly educated women to quit their well-paying jobs and stay home to raise their kids. I told-you-so-ers say it proves that women's lib was all wrong. But barring a severe economic downturn, I am certain these women will go back to their careers when their children are older. They have not suddenly become like their grandmothers, they are simply realizing that life is long enough for them to have it all, in phases.

Why shouldn't women have a period in which they raise children and then go back to work? Why is getting to the top - which only leads to more stress, in order to have more stuff - so important?

Herbert Marcuse pointed out that sex is constrained in order that people work, but post-scarcity society requires less work. Why is full-time work so important in a society that has the means for everyone to work four hours a day and is under the ecological imperative to consume less? When we cut work time in half, fathers will again be models for their children, and both parents will live more balanced lives, as they did in primitive societies. It's not a question of going back to the past, but of seeing how modern needs can be fulfilled in simpler ways.

In Budapest, my adolescent desire to be a pre-school teacher became a conviction that freedom, autonomy, personal development and self-government could not exist unless children learned these things by living them. In my teens I had read weighty tomes on education in a language that was still new to me. Now my childhood friend Judy sent me books on education, among them a work by the New Zealand teacher Sylvia Townsend, who observed native Maoris learning things through real life, and realized they could learn to read better if they chose the words. I had already been practicing her method by letting Raul learn as early as he wanted, when and what he wanted. By the age of four he read, wrote and did arithmetic as part of playing. Reich says adults have to learn to be happy again like children, and at two, Michael was happiness personified. Only specific situations made him unhappy. Once they were resolved, his smile returned, a wail literally metamorphosing into a smile.

The books on open classrooms sent by Judy confirmed my young children's behavior. But I also thought that high schools should become part of productive units, as was the case in Cuba. Today I believe the crisis in high schools is as much a revolt against learning-as-obligation-rather-than-as-pleasure, as it is against the irrelevancy of most academic learning to most adolescents. In other times, people were taught what served religion, now they are taught what serves the economy. They are taught a lot about what was, instead of what is and could be. I continue to believe that the past

should be telescoped, with fewer dates and more interpretation, to understand how we got where we are, retaining concepts or methods that might be useful for solving present problems. Here are some of the ideas I sketched out:

Schools need to be entirely reconceived. Adults endorse regulated schools because life is work and school is a preparation for life. But perhaps they're also unconsciously jealous of children's happiness. If children raised on demand schedules are happy, but adults are not, it must be school that ruins things. Adults know that to be happy they have to do what they want, more or less when they want, so why should schools not offer 'demand learning'?

Just as adults want to do a job well if they like it, children will by and large want to learn if not forced and scheduled. John Holt says schools should be places where the teacher guides rather than instructs. Kids should go when they want, and decide together that on a certain day at a certain time that they will do something as a group, individuals attending or not, according to their inclination.

Only when the child is ready, at 10 or 12, and maybe as late as 18-20 (or even 30!), should he study in a more formal way. Programs should include economics, psychology, ecology.

During the summer of 1970, we spent a week in a mountain resort that belonged to Matyas' employer, the Academy of Sciences. The atmosphere of a place where sixteen or so families, strangers but belonging to the same milieu, shared a roof, was warm and stimulating. The glass eyed monster seemed almost civilized in a

sort of projection room; radio, cards, chess, etc. were played in another room; a huge, well equipped kitchen had a staff of five, a hostess-like matron and waitresses; grounds had many nooks, tables and chairs, a deer, playground, lawns encased with trees to sun bathe or play badminton, a pergola with ping pong. The only thing missing was a swimming pool.

It occurred to me that when organizing a community, people should consider under what circumstances they prefer to be alone or in company, in mixed or segregated company. It's fun to have separate but communicating stalls for showering, mixed company to swim, segregated company to soak in a pool of water (something the Hungarians were particularly fond of, since the capital boasted several ancient baths fed with hot springs). I didn't exactly know what had given rise to the commune movement in America, but I guessed that one of the reasons was to counter the solitude engendered by our artificial way of life. In modern cultures, solitude begins in childhood: when Michael resisted sleeping without us, I wondered whether it might in fact be better for children to sleep with parents. The family had traditionally been a mini commune; now it is no more than a 'nucleus', and technology has isolated neighbors even when they share walls.

Already in 1970 Budapest, I felt that a big city, with its overpasses and apartment buildings, was the epitome of alienation, isolation, neurosis and aggressiveness. People were beginning to complain that man was a slave to the automobile, yet bigger and bigger cities were being built precisely because we had better ways to get around, and this forced us to spend more time, money and energy getting around. Automobiles are convenient, but we have to rethink urbanism in such a way that they don't make life more difficult. In small cities one would never be far from work, school, shops, amusements; a small automobile might still be used for distances.

Hungary really was the merriest barracks in the communist camp, as the saying went, but when any situation made 'the party' look bad in my eyes, Matyas resented my criticism. As with most basic issues, we agreed that large industries should be state owned to

ensure that profits were not exported, and that men should not exploit other men, whether they were capitalists or bureaucrats. But I was also convinced that technology had become dangerous, whether in the hands of bureaucrats or capitalists. And I would point out that although Marx rightly saw the need for workers to take power from owners, how would they take power from bureaucrats and technocrats?

I lamented the fact that as more of people's material needs were met, revolutionary ideas, as they had existed ten or twenty years earlier, were fading, and no others were taking its place. I saw a parallel between political evolution and that of the human race. Slavery corresponds to a people's childhood, revolutionary government to its adolescence, while anarchism could come with full-blown maturity. Alas, it seemed that technology and organization had eliminated independent thinking. Living in Eastern Europe twenty years after the advent of socialist power, at first I thought it should be like Cuba, then I realized that socialism has to evolve with the situation, and that it had failed to do so.

I remained convinced that what the Cubans did was right when they began, however the creativity, energy and humanism of the early years seemed to have been overtaken by the requirement that everything be related to the revolution, which was rather boring. I thought the next few years would show whether humans had merely acquired bad habits over the millennia, or whether man is inherently selfish. If Che's ideas couldn't make a new man, it couldn't be done.

I agreed with Wilhelm Reich that although Marx was right a hundred years ago about men's material situation determining everything, this was no longer the case when affluence gave almost everybody an acceptable standard of living. Reich claimed that everything derives from culture, or rather consciousness, which is what was now being exploited. Maytas and his friends didn't realize that their growing affluence had convinced them that Marx wanted them to live in a consumer society. Hungarian socialism was more interested in emulating the consumer society than in hastening the advent of a post-consumer world. I felt that superfluous consumer

products could be more readily eliminated if it became clear that by creating a need for these objects, individuals were increasingly alienated in comparison with primitive people. (Roger Garaudy had said that alienation was about the relationship between human activity and the objects and institutions it had created.) Instead of only being understood theoretically, by psychologists and philosophers, everyone would have to experience alienation, and seeing how it happens, refuse to do superfluous things.

I had noticed that children spontaneously preferred white to black; they didn't think work was noble and/or nice and/or fun, but they would work for lollypops. I wondered whether workers wanted to be rich, or simply not be taken advantage of? Now the rise of Chinese authoritarian capitalism shows that people do accept to be abused in order to become more affluent, but only up to a certain point. The worldwide revolt of the 99% confirms that.

After a year in Holland and a year and a half reading and thinking about education, I contemplated with horror the prospect of Raul going into first grade in a school where six year-olds were not even supposed to know the alphabet, and where rote learning was prized. I feared such a rigid system would quash his love of learning. We led privileged lives, including frequent travel, yet I was loathe to see my children grow up in a country that had a lid on it. The talented way the Hungarians navigated the shoals of incipient democracy was what made their country an exception within the socialist camp, but they knew the limits beyond which they could not go, and so did I.

Perhaps because of my discontent, Matyas became attracted to one of his students. I knew that if it came to a divorce, I would be stuck in Hungary with a Hungarian child. We decided to take a trip to the States, it being understood that I might not return. I hoped that when push came to shove, Matyas would not either.

The Ministry of the Interior's Office for foreigners was only a convenient block away from our flat in Embassy row. The lady assigned to me was forty-fivish, slightly overweight and unattractive, and we had a testily cordial relationship. Dealing with her required all the canny calm I had acquired over the years as a veteran of

foreign bureaucracies. Beginning when I had to get working papers in France, then being a foreigner in Italy, where the bureaucrats didn't bother you often, but were particularly infuriating when they did, to my child's future at stake in Poland, dealing with bureaucracies in charge of aliens had become a habit, like brushing my teeth.

Even so, the prospect of having to hide the fact that I was probably going to stay in the States with a Hungarian citizen made me nervous. Every time I went to see my keeper, she made me repeat our plans in detail. Raul was on my passport, and Michael would be on his father's passport, since he was a Hungarian citizen. The woman obviously feared there was a loophole somewhere; perhaps before leaving I would have Michael too put on my passport. Apparently, she didn't realize that once Michael was in the States with an American mother, what would the Hungarians be able do about it? During questioning, I never departed from my perfectly bland attitude, inwardly waiting for the ax to fall.

Matyas of course had to answer the same questions from the Interior Ministry person in charge of travel for party members, and there was always the possibility that we would be caught in some contradiction. Finally, on a glorious day in June we were off in the Renault 16, which had been baptized 'Couscous' in honor of a Richard Scarry character that Raul loved. We had crossed into Austria at Heggyeshalom many times, seen the facilities enlarged and modernized when the flow of Austrian tourists became unmanageable, and celebrated when the bit of highway on the Hungarian side opened as part of a grandiose UNDP plan for a European-wide network that would connect with Asia and Africa, never thinking twice about the watch towers and barriers. Now, as we approached them, several hours out of Budapest, they seemed so much thicker than before! I held my breath, fearing we would be turned back due to some detail we had overlooked.

We were let out, but our anxieties took their toll on the children. The night before, Raul had cried hysterically that he didn't want to travel, and now, at the motel in Linz he developed a terrible attack of croup. He had never been sick on a trip before. I called his

doctor in Budapest, she prescribed an Austrian medication, and told us to stand him by the shower with the hot water running to make steam.

A few days later when we arrived at Uncle Pal's in Amsterdam, Michael came down with pneumonia. The doctor prescribed antibiotics, but did not expect him to recover for a week or so. To everyone's amazement, he recovered totally in three days, just in time for us to catch our plane to New York. He has had, ever since, an exceptionally robust constitution, perhaps thanks to those long hours spent sleeping in the Amsterdam cold.

I had left behind all my winter clothes, my several hundred books, and saddest of all because I knew I would never see it again, the Viennese piano bought with the money Jake had left me. Yet even in my despair at leaving behind an object so important to the right side of my brain, my left brain never looked back. Regina's apricot noodles had awakened my sensuality and given me the patience and tenderness with my children that I had found in her home. But by the time I left her land, I had abandoned the conviction that she had also made me a hedonist. It was Ludovico who had given me that, never dreaming it would take me so far. But even my return to the United States, however carefully planned, was not to be definitive. There would be more back and forths before I was able to become more what the man of my life hoped I would be, yet truly my own person.

[Left behind, Viennese piano]

Chapter XVI - Time in our Lives

[Welcoming picnic, Philadelphia 1971]

Twenty-four years after leaving the United States at the age of fourteen, I returned with a husband and two children. Breaking with my habit of seeing Howard before the ordeal of seeing May, I arranged for us to fly to Philadelphia, where Rachel and Walter laid on a picnic attended by my mother, her new husband Alfred, and the three cousins I had baby-sat, who now had offspring of their own. Beneath the jocular welcome was unspoken disapproval of my having chosen to live in communist countries for the past seven years. As with previous visits, no one was curious about the places I had known. A few days later, we traveled to the rambling old house in Long Island where Howard now lived with Elaine, eleven years younger than me.

There we had cocktails by the pool and sumptuous meals at odd hours. Elaine worked in town, while Howard published a newsletter and reigned in the kitchen. He made oatmeal and coffee in the morning, brought home what seemed to us an exaggerated number of grocery bags, and the fresh bread his mother had taught all her children to love. He fixed lunch while family members sat

round the breakfast bar on high stools, and generally dinner too while, perched over drinks, frequent guests looked on. My father was an excellent and passionate cook who, like his mother, needed to be complimented.

In Hungary, the living had been comfortable but not luxurious. At Howard's, lunch consisted of leftovers from elaborate dinners, compulsively covered and saved in the refrigerator. One day, after Howard had tended to us for about half an hour, he declared: "Now I'm going to feed myself!" He went to the refrigerator for the nth time, took out a peach, put it on a plate, brought out a knife, and set it all on the table. Raul, who was then six, had never seen a peach so big: "Yoy!" he exclaimed, in the Hungarian equivalent of "gee", but with a whine. "I want the peach!"

[Raul in Andover, 1972]

Without a word, my father pushed the plate over to him and went back to the refrigerator, whence he extracted a piece of cantaloup. "Yoy!" cried Raul, "I want the cantaloup!" In silence as before, Howard pushed the plate over to his grandson and stalked back to the refrigerator. This time, out came the last triangular piece of what had been a huge watermelon. It had scarcely reached the

table when up went Raul's whiney demand: "Yoy, I want the watermelon!" In silence once again, but this time with an enormous grin, my father seized the watermelon in his huge palm and smashed it over Raul's head, proclaiming: "I've always wanted to do that!" With Howard, even authority had to be flamboyant.

Although Matyas seemed perfectly at home in the States, and could have easily gotten an academic position thanks to assiduous attendance at mathematical conferences, he could not bring himself to abandon parents and country. For my part, I was still far from experiencing a real sense of belonging in the land of my birth, but I believed that momentous changes were in the making in the country I had always fled. Reading Cohn-Bendit's *The Left Wing Alternative* and also, the conservative French essayist Jean-François Revel's *Without Marx or Jesus*, I was flattered that each in his own way echoed my thoughts. Above all, I wanted my children to benefit from the open classrooms that flourished at the time. The thought of returning to a country with a Victorian school system, with Matyas probably wanting a divorce, put lead in my feet.

With our six-week tickets due to expire, we compromised: Matyas would continue to weigh his decision while at a conference in England. Tense with anxiety, I waited at my friend Judy's in North Andover, Massachusetts. Michael was enrolled in a brand-new nursery school, and his picture, stroking a goat, appeared in the local paper. One day he was put on the wrong bus home, and the hour until he was located was the longest of my life. Adding to what would have been any parent's anxiety was the fear that Matyas senior, with his 'long (party) arm', had arranged to have him kidnapped. Afterward, whenever we saw a plane flying over Judy's garden, we would joke with just a hint of superstition that it was Michael's grandfather.

When Matyas called long distance to say he had decided to go home, I could hardly believe it. This child had been so important to him, and we had a convivial if not passionate relationship. The full force of Matyas's commitment to his parents, as well as his attachment to country, gradually sank in.

When I married Matyas, Howard had been happy to have a proper son-in-law. He'd visited us in Budapest, then received us with open arms as a seemly family unit. But when I refused to follow my husband back to Hungary, his good will vanished. I was on my own. I moved into a rental apartment in Andover, which had a brand new open elementary school, taught a little French at Abbot Academy and did free lance editing and translating. New England was not as beautiful as Europe, but since my first trip to Cuba, the attachment to beauty born with my arrival in Europe had taken a back seat to my passion for politics: my country's behavior had become more important than the way it looked.

Reveling in the pleasures of small town intimacy, my first political act was to join a women's group, whence I was soon expelled for insisting that women were equal but different from men. Luckily, I made durable friendships with the more relaxed women in a second group, who perhaps not coincidentally drank wine rather than coffee.

[Michael in Andover, 1972]

After not hearing from Matyas for about a year, I was shocked to receive a divorce decree mailed from Austria. Since he couldn't be expected to pay child support not knowing where his child was (hence the letter mailed from elsewhere), I would have to

rely on his good will, which would turn out to consist of a year's worth of support every five years, when he was entitled to spend a semester or two in the West.

Had May been willing to put up the money for a handyman special, I probably would have stayed in Andover. Ever more convinced that school had to evolve as part of a change to a less alienating and more ecological lifestyle, I participated in efforts to keep the school system responsive to that philosophy. In 1972 I met John Kerry who was looking for people to work on his Senate campaign, but was only mildly impressed.

It was colder in Massachusetts than anywhere I had ever lived except for Poland, and my back acted up throughout the winter. After two years in that bitter climate - and two years of near celibacy - I was toying with the idea of moving to Arizona or New Mexico, when I met Jay Strand at a countercultural conference. He had spent time in Africa for the Peace Corps, and married an English woman. Africa had made drum parties important, while moving up the social ladder was not, eventually causing upper class Priscilla to move back to England with their two daughters. An expert in radiation at the University of Massachusetts at Amherst and an anti-nuclear activist, Jay seemed to fit right in to the ongoing saga of my life.

Nineteen seventy-four was the year of Watergate, and throughout the summer, my ear was glued to the hearings on the car radio as we plied back and forth across Massachusetts. In the fall we left Andover for Amherst and Jay gave up his bachelor flat to take a garden apartment with us, installing his precious metal working shop in part of the kitchen. At one point we had nine cats.

In addition to his work in radiation safety, Jay was teaching several courses in the new field of Global Survival. He introduced me to systems thinking and convinced me to take advantage of the University. I got a BA in six months, based on my French baccalaureat, my work as a journalist, and my book on *8 1/2*, and was accepted into the Global Survival program of the graduate school of education.

210

[With Raul, Jay and daughter, Amherst 1974]

By then, in addition to several books by John Holt, I had read Ivan Illich's *De-schooling Society* and *Tools for Conviviality* I had digested the voluminous contents of *Patterns of Anarchy*, a collection of writings in the anarchist tradition, edited by Leonard Krimerman and Lewis Perry, who considered education as the key to a society of responsible people. Probably because of the ten year long Vietnam War and Rachel Carson's *Silent Spring*, there had begun to exist in America something I called 'intelligence sophistication', meaning intelligence plus awareness of the new ideas being propounded in books that reached the growing strata of college graduates. Alas, this window onto the outside world closed again when George McGovern lost the presidency to Richard Nixon. During the campaign, I had noticed how the press, still in thrall to the spirit of McCarthy, systematically nit-picked everything McGovern did or said, while passing over Nixon's greater faults.

It was during this period that I first began to suspect that the important ideas of our time have a much greater unity than we think. Entering the graduate program after years spent observing various brands of socialism, I knew there were no definitive answers, and no real separations between women's lib, education, the north/south conflict and distribution of resources. Interdependence and carrying

capacity, which were major areas of global survival research, were as relevant as social systems.

As an assistant, I had the satisfaction of turning a few teachers on to futures thinking, starting with the findings of the *Club of Rome*, a group of a hundred industrialists and academics that funded research into systems thinking as it applied to world problems. I sensed that the concept illustrated in *Limits to Growth's* opening graph, that people relate mostly to what is near in time and space was crucial, and today, notwithstanding the thousands of books that have followed, it still applies.

My students were also stimulated by the *World Order Models Project* spearheaded by Princeton Professor of International Law Richard Falk, who is currently the U.N. rapporteur on Palestine. WOMP, as it was known, placed itself above the ideological fray, gathering a clutch of outstanding researchers to study ways in which a world defined by *The Limits to Growth* and the Cold War could evolve a structure for world governance based on law and sustainability. WOMP values were: the minimization of large scale collective violence; the maximization of social and economic well-being; the realization of fundamental human rights and conditions of political justice, and the rehabilitation and maintenance of environmental quality, including the conservation of resources. The books I read on these subjects during those years became the foundation of my subsequent writing.

Jay and I taught a class together, but once in front of an audience, Jay had a hard time respecting the planned division of labor. And for me, being a student was even less rewarding. As Jay said, it meant running to the library to read stuff other people had written and pulling it together. I was not doing the research, conducting experiments, or even reading what other people had written to determine whether it was relevant. And 'choosing a subject', I felt, was no substitute for having an original idea.

[The Stryker children, 1975]

On the bright side, the children were enrolled in the Department of Education's Elementary School, which had mixed grade classrooms. I campaigned to get Michael into kindergarden ahead of schedule because he kept bombarding me with questions. He thoroughly enjoyed being in a classroom with first and second graders and was very popular. Raul's adjustment to a new school was facilitated by our friendship with another faculty family and their children, and in summer we hired someone to take care of all the children together at our friends' rural house.

After a year, Jay and I bought a two-family house that needed insulating and repainting, and I did most of the latter as well as the floor sanding. In the garden contiguous with farmland, we planted vegetables and had a compost pile, to which Jay added Muscovy ducks. Raul was given a pet sheep, then a dog that insisted on jumping through the electric fence and running off in defiance of leash laws.

Though this was an idyllic time for the children, it was increasingly difficult for me. In summer Jay's two girls came to visit, but the pranks the three older children played on Michael were the least of my worries: fearing we might jeopardize her child support, Priscilla turned the divorce into a protracted battle. Having been betrayed by my own stepmother, I was determined not to be a wicked second wife. And while there was a striking similarity

between Priscilla and Casimira, there was also a crucial difference between my children's situation and Jay's: Raul and Michael couldn't travel back and forth to see their fathers in Eastern Europe, and I worried that if anything should happen to me, fathers and caring stepmothers would not be there for them. When we were finally able to marry, Jay gallantly offered to adopt Raul and Michael to make sure they would never be shipped off to separate countries behind the Iron Curtain. Yet even as I tried to put my situation in perspective, I gained weight and began to have psychosomatic symptoms. It occurred to me that women need a mixture of outside challenge and quiet homemaking or studying, while men find a haven from the outside world in the home women make for them, with marriage consequently found to be more beneficial to them.

Something I had first sensed in Rome as a bachelor now became clear: when men had undisputed authority over women, they appeared stronger. Now they try to exploit that past authority, without developing new strengths. A breadwinner husband will allow his wife to handle matters that appear as extensions of care-taking, but which in fact are as complex as his job. When he realizes that she is as good at her tasks as he is at his, he loses part of his authority. Simultaneously, when women who work also have to take on life support and problem-solving, they become frustrated by the fact that authority continues to be vested in men.

I wanted to unravel the ball of yarn to the industrial revolution, the automobile, etc., to where we turned progress against ourselves. For example the way men accepted to work for money to buy a car, which led them to live far from their workplace. I thought computers might partly counterbalance the increase in population, and give us more time. I was wrong: the tyranny of time has sped up. As I saw it then:

'Time' is directly related to 'people' and 'distance'.

$(+P)+(+D)=(-T)$

As population increases, transportation is modernized, distances decrease, but we have less time.

(+P) +(+Tr)=(-D).
But: (+P)+(+Tr) = (-T)

One day I had kept an exhaustive - and exhausting - list of everything I did that showed how ridiculous our lives were. Forty years later, the total number of activities has not diminished, because many of them involve the apprenticeship of ever-changing technologies. Having previously been increased by speed, time is now vanquished by information overload.

Among my readings as I learned and taught about interdependence, was Ram Dass's *Here and Now*. I was struck by the saying "If it can't be said it can't be whispered either". I went on to Huxley's *Perennial Philosophy*, finding more proof that while religion was a non-starter for me, mysticism, especially as expressed by Hinduism and Taoism, seemed irrefutable. This epiphany would eventually meld with the new physics to transform my view of the world. Meanwhile, I discovered William Irwin Thompson, a historian and poet who seemed equally at home with physics, a mystic who put it all together in a way Theodore Roszak, whose *Wasteland* had been a revelation, could not. Or was it simply a difference of generation?

Reading linguistics and educational methods, I became convinced that the school of education should not isolate itself from other disciplines, especially linguistics and sociology. I was amused that Rabelais, rejoicing in the restoration of Greek, Hebrew, Chaldean and Latin, had declared: "When I have money I will buy Greek books, then clothes". My spending priorities are similar, but whereas Rabelais considered that a learned man had to know at least four languages, given the size of today's world, which can be held on an iPhone, a universal language, alongside the ones we learn for pleasure, is indispensable and for the foreseeable future will be English. Living in Poland, I had realized that a person's psychology is partly dictated by his culture and language. For example, the

Polish language, with its clutter of consonants, seemed to reflect opaqueness and perhaps not coincidentally, the people seemed to have a penchant for conspiracies. English, though difficult to spell, will probably contribute to a lessening of formality.

My personal experience with languages, as well as my children's, obviously played a role in the strong opinions I had about their teaching. Somewhere along the line I'd learned from an authoritative source that in bilingual households, each parent has to speak to the children in his or her own language if the children are to grow up knowing both without being confused. It had been very easy for Matyas, Raul and me to maintain three languages between us. Spanish was firmly established between Raul and me; and when I met Matyas, I could hardly speak Hungarian, while Raul soon could. So Matyas and Raul spoke Hungarian together; Raul and I spoke Spanish, and Matyas and I spoke English. When we were in public, those within earshot were at a loss to figure out what was going on, but we never had to think about it. After we arrived in the States, Raul completely lost his Hungarian and his Spanish. But one day, when he was being introduced to foreign languages in junior high school, he came home quite puzzled: "We're doing Spanish and for some strange reason I seem to know it already."

Although Jay was really a warm and caring person, to whom I felt exceedingly close, he not only lived on what he called African time, he had a myriad of interests, and a way of consuming all the available oxygen. Priscilla had apparently been affected the same way I had, although she and I were very different. During my second year at the university, Massachusetts suffered a severe financial crisis that affected the availability of teaching jobs. I thought about switching to urban planning, which was linked to Future Studies and where there might have been more jobs, but did nothing to make it happen: I had to face the fact that life with Jay was making me depressed.

While I was perfectly happy immersed in challenging books or interacting with my family, Jay liked interacting with as many different people as possible. I living in relative security, with a house and good schools for the children, but I increasingly felt as though I

had only half a mate. One day it came to me in a flash: Perhaps Jay and Priscilla were equally egotistical: she wanted him for his support, he wanted her to be there but not be there.

Although I was still fond of Jay and nothing earth-shattering had happened, my anxiety symptoms were getting worse: I often felt I couldn't breathe, especially after meals, and those panic attacks would keep me indoors for days. If there was a planning board meeting, I was more likely to forget about it during the snowy winters, when the cold aggravated my back problems. I spent hours at a time in a zero-gravity chair, which luckily, was wide enough to read to a child in, wondering whether I might feel less frustrated in a congenial climate.

I knew by then that to flee is not necessarily a solution, especially for psychological problems, but I began to realize that I'm probably not made for marriage. However much I cared about the children, after three years with Jay, I decided my life was at stake. Much as I hated to break up yet another family, in the fall of seventy-six, I concluded that I had to leave. The doctoral program in Future Studies was losing funds and there were too many graduates seeking jobs in the region. New York frightened me, so I decided to look for work in Washington. A friend who had become a consultant on the Hill told us that jobs always opened up after a presidential election, and Jimmy Carter had just become President.

Chapter XVII - In the Belly of the Beast

[My State Department ID, 1977]

The children and I set out in my car on the day of the first snow, Jay obligingly driving a U-Haul with our belongings. I rented a modest townhouse in Reston, but the children had to adjust, not only to the move, but also to the southern schools, which were staffed with a lot of ex-military and very authoritarian. Raul attended a school for the gifted, but there was none in the vicinity for Michael. He was given three counts to drink water at recess.

The change gave me renewed vigor, and within three months I had been hired as speech writer to the Assistant Secretary of State for Cultural Affairs, the department which, among other things, administered the Fulbright program. Reading the stream of communications that were distributed daily to political officers, I gained precious insights into facts my life had familiarized me with, such as the way the U.S. contrived to keep the left out of power in Italy, where it represented the majority of citizens. It occurred to me

that the 'City Upon a Hill' was now determined to subdue the world below.

The Earth rotates, slides under our feet, we're still at the top but the rest of the world is on the bottom. They look to us to do something, but we don't understand them because we see them upside down.

> *We need to understand the third world, and make international structural reforms that will enable us to do the job that falls to us. No great power has ever been truly democratic. No true democracy has ever been a great power.*

I soon came to the conclusion that in order for the U.S. to pursue a more successful foreign policy, the State Department had to be reorganized. Nothing less would do. The emphasis should be on responsibility rather than politicking and lead to decisions made on the basis of information, carried out by people-to-people processes rather than people to paper to people processes.

But why stop there? Inspired by the still vivid example of Cuban solutions to problems that others would consider insurmountable, I decided that the entire U.S. government needed to be reorganized!

And yet, at bottom, I sensed that the biggest problem was the fact that power was not truly representative. Thanks to my studies, I understood that foreign and domestic policy were one, and that economics underlay all. But my introduction to systems theory suggested there was a contradiction between the open physical word in which we lived, and the essentially closed political system we had created. With everything being connected, we could not get our diplomacy on track unless we knew where we wanted the track to take us. The American people needed to be told up-front that significant changes were necessary, but that this would be an exhilarating process of renewal, taking our founding principles in the direction of the solidarity espoused by most of the developed world.

As a result of everything being linked, the world was moving toward the disintegration of the nation-state. In America, the federal government would have to cede some of its powers, while individual states unified their laws derived from the powers and responsibilities of the central government. Regions would be better able to respond to the needs of specific/geo-ethnic areas, and local entities would have more power. I had not forgotten the ideas inspired by my observations from the interpreters' booth at international conferences, and felt the new Communications Agency should send Americans to live among foreigners, especially newspaper owners/editors.

What I failed to perceive in the seventies was that before WOMP values could be adopted worldwide, corporations would replace the primacy of the nation-state. But in terms of its thrust, I'm impressed by how consistent my thinking has remained. With respect to work, I wrote at the time:

> *The notion of work has changed radically from something that was in one way or another available to all, to an occupation organized and administered by society. The very basis of man's self respect and independence is now denied him. The budding entrepreneur is dependent on the banks; the professional on publish or perish; the actor on knowing the right people, etc. Two hundred years ago a person may have had to remain within his rank, but he functioned fully where he stood.*

Twenty years later, when those notes were still in a box, *A Taoist Politics*, the book in which I outlined the link between circular thinking and the role of politics, included the following:

> *"Although tribute can now be extracted mainly from machines, men continue to demand work*

because it is the only thing they know, even though its meaning has changed radically. Work used to be part of Being, now it is something you either Have or Don't Have. If men have no work, they starve: having been persuaded to buy on credit Things which are often useless, they cannot buy their daily food. Originally, work served directly to sustain individuals; gradually, it became a mediated phenomenon: people work for someone else, to provide mediated consumption for all, receiving in return the means to sustain themselves through their own mediated consumption. From a personal necessity, work has been transformed into an entitlement dependent upon others, and we discover painfully that this system can go berserk.

Primitive man, seeing that there was nothing more to gather or hunt in a given place, moved on to another. But when the basis for work-as-survival is no longer a place but a mediated process, men can only shout their despair. Having allowed work to be transformed from a relationship with the environment, to a relationship with an Other, they have lost the internal authority that enabled them to control their means of survival. Now they must demand work of those who have decided that Being is Having, and that they can Have without others Being, in other words that they can consume without others working."

In 1977, between writing Assistant Secretary Joe Duffey's speeches and drafting the occasional policy paper, I found time to write an article on US-Soviet relations. Under the title: *A Three-*

Point Strategy for Qualitative Change in U.S.-Soviet Relations it appeared in the *The Open Forum*, the Department's in-house journal, in November, 1977. Several congressmen and senators responded favorably to it, including Lee Hamilton and William Fulbright. However, I was less successful in promoting my ideas with Secretary Vance's Soviet advisor, Marshall Schulman. Spirited discussions with him revealed why Vance was no match for the National Security Advisor, Zbignieuw Brzezinski, much more hawkish than now. My article called for the United States to engage the Soviet leaders in a dialogue to identify goals and beliefs we held in common in order to diffuse the Cold War. Today, rather than trying to defeat each Muslim rebellion against the world we have created, we need to talk through our differences with Islamic fundamentalists, who in fact share many ideas with Christian and Jewish fundamentalists. After reading Gary Will's *Inventing America*, which showed the significant influence of the communitarian Scottish philosophers on Jefferson's political thought, as opposed to Locke, to whom that honor is attributed, I realized there were striking differences between the American concept of democracy and the Western European one. An unfinished project began with a quote by John Kenneth Galbraith, whom I admired for his unique combination of wit and intelligence:

> *"...no design for social reform is so completely excluded from reputable discussion as socialism in the United States... So high is this moral purpose that men of exceptional zeal do not hesitate to urge that advocacy, even discussion, of socialism be outlawed in order that freedom may be preserved."*

Today, pundits invariably refer to the seventies as a time of relative grace in America, the middle class earning well, having medical coverage, the press reporting without bias. My notes show that I saw that decade as a time of profound, debilitating crisis, with the media purveying "the best kept secret in history, secluded like a

highly classified government document that has maintained Americans in the belief that our defense policies are required by a righteous ideological confrontation with the Soviet Union; that not only communism, but also socialism is undemocratic, even though our most democratic, prosperous and peaceful allies have lived under social democratic governments for decades." Most irresponsibly of all, the media had "led Americans to believe that we would survive a nuclear war, even though our industrial plant would be decimated, our soil, air and water contaminated for decades, and long-term radiation deaths would be inescapable." At the time, the Third World was loudly demanding a New International Information Order, through the U.N. This didn't happen, because the major U.N. contributor requires the media to be cleansed of ideological content.

A book published in 1977 by Friends of the Earth called *Progress as if Survival Mattered* devoted a long, well-documented chapter to the failings of the American press, and several academics published books on the subject, yet today pundits claim the press was really free at that time, its failings mere aberrations. In my unfinished project I wrote that secrets could be successfully kept from the American people because the press's freedom from government intervention protected the publisher rather than the journalist.

> *"Although the press benefits from a constitutionally guaranteed freedom, the journalist works for the publisher, an entrepreneur who chooses what news the public will read according to his own political inclinations and the sensitivities of his advertisers. A journalist who reports facts that displease either the publisher or his advertisers, is summarily dismissed. Constrained within self-imposed limits, the daily ration of commentaries offered up even in our most prestigious news-papers is of little help in*

understanding current problems, and offers few
ideas for their solution."

During my years at State I read *The Washington Post*, which I preferred to *The New York Times*, and discovered the British weekly *The Economist*, to which I have subscribed ever since. *The Economist's* professionalism more than compensates for its openly conservative point of view. (That point of view eventually led *The Economist* to dismiss Gorbachev as a possible Soviet leader, while based on op-eds by Jeffry Hough and Stephen Cohen, in the first draft of my 1989 book on Europe, I foresaw that Gorbachev would be chosen as the next Soviet leader.)

In Washington, I also read up on American history, and realized that McCarthyism's long shelf-life was a logical continuation of the absolutist attitudes of the first settlers, who expelled from their colonies anyone who deviated from the Puritanical principles laid down by the leaders. Given the continued reluctance of American intellectuals to deal with McCarthyism, it's not surprising that so few people today have heard of the man who gave his name to an era, and for whom a word was coined.

My unfinished project was called *America's Great Classified Idea*. In it I wrote:

> *The legacy of McCarthyism rules out any long-*
> *term solutions to our domestic problems, by*
> *maintaining an unnecessarily high level of*
> *military spending, and precluding the entire*
> *range of economic options that have anything*
> *to do with socialism. The result of both these*
> *trends is failure to provide for the basic needs*
> *of all Americans.*
>
> *This failure keeps global leadership, which*
> *would otherwise fall to us as the most*
> *sophisticated and powerful nation on earth,*

increasingly out of reach, and explains why our allies have so little patience with us. They live in the real world, where the entire spectrum of political thought, from extreme left to extreme right, has free play. We live in a Rinso White world, laundered in McCarthyism, where respectable political thought runs the narrow gamut between the Democratic and Republican extremes of centrist policies. Although we have more daily newspapers than any other country, thanks to this national frontal lobotomy, we are the only ones who do not know how little we know.

Having created a government predicated on freedom of conscience, after 200 years the American people find themselves with a government whose primary function is to ensure the freedom of business, which by definition has no conscience.

We are told what to do by advertising and what to believe by the press - all in the name of not being told what to think and what to do by the government.

I wish I had been wrong. But McCarthy's legacy survived the change of century and the electronic revolution. In the seventies, government was beginning to tell the media what to tell us. Today its directives are casually called spin, a misleadingly amusing term for government control of information. It's only in the last few years that the mainstream media (known as MSM), has been recognized as a culprit, as the internet enabled an alternative media to reach a comparably large audience. Yet publications such as *The Nation* only timidly placing themselves to the left of the Democratic Party. Even as the Occupy Movement gathers steam, most Americans turn to

sources that tell us we can win the war against terrorism by allowing our civil liberties to be severely curtailed.

Getting back to my time at State, the purpose of the Fulbright Program, which my department ran, was to bring prominent foreigners to the United States so they would come to appreciate the American way of life and return home to influence decisions accordingly. My colleagues were bitterly disappointed when Joe Duffey failed to prevent what they saw as a respected academic program from being transferred to the government's propaganda department, the newly christened International Communications Agency. (President Carter had taken this bold decision in response to Congress's longstanding opinion that this operational unit had no place in the Department of State).

By the time the transfer happened, I had just emerged from a nine month battle for clearance. At the administrative level, government agencies were manned by a predominantly Republican apparatus, which could not bring itself to clear someone who had voluntarily spent seven years behind the Iron Curtain. I told the head of security that he could tap my phone and have me followed, since I had absolutely nothing to hide. He had never dealt with anyone like that. Finally he informed me that I would be interviewed, and if all went well, I would be cleared. The interview took place in a small room (I believe it had no windows but cannot swear to that), with a table around which were several chairs. One man asked the questions, a second did nothing but observe my reactions. This went on for two days from 9-5 with an hour off for lunch.

Though the interview had seemed to proceed smoothly, several weeks went by with no decision. The security apparatus had found nothing to peg a refusal on, yet could not resign itself to clearing me. I harassed the head of security until he finally broached the idea of a lie detector. I accepted immediately, but felt I should extract an airtight promise that the clearance would be delivered quickly if I passed, since the last temporary contract the State Department could give me would expire a few days later. When I put the question to him over the phone, I got such an evasive answer that I knew this was not going to happen. Realizing I had nothing more to

lose, I let out my pent-up anger and told him I was taking the matter directly to Warren Christopher, the Secretary for Management.

By the time I got Christopher's secretary on the phone and told her what my problem was, the security officer had arrived at his door. Kindly, the secretary advised me to call back in half an hour. When I did, I was told to report that afternoon to receive my clearance. Apparently, the head of security had ignored a rule that required the Secretary for Management to sign off on any proposed lie detector test.

My victory was short-lived: soon afterward, we were moved lock stock and barrel to ICA. The Assistant Secretary jumped ship just in time, and the new person in charge of cultural exchanges didn't need a speech writer. If I stayed on, I would have to become a bureaucrat. I felt like Fajardo, the barely literate Cuban commander who'd complained: "They'd rather have me keep track of how many times a steer humps a cow, than make sure the meat gets on the table!"

Chapter XVIII - Thrashing About

After almost two years in the capital, which seemed devoid of human warmth, personal relationships invariably taking a back seat to career advancement, I felt the need for a European interlude before deciding what to do. Seeing *Julia*, the film with Jason Robards and Vanessa Redgrave about the rise of Nazism, with its European train stations, suddenly filled me with nostalgia for the Old Continent.

The children had been two and six when we left, and I thought it would be good for them to know that the U.S. was not the world. At thirteen Raul needed adventure: I sent him to New York by bus to buy Eurail passes, and he carried out his mission without a hitch. We flew to Budapest to see Matyas, then to Greece, where we spent a few days on Aegina and I renewed my love affair with the Mediterranean. Then it was on to Rome. I was so engrossed with an old friend at lunch in Piazza del Popolo that Michael got drunk on the white wine the waiter kept pouring into his empty glass. By the time we got to the Forum he was hardly able to stand, and is immortalized sitting tentatively on a broken Roman pillar. Yet from this experience was born his desire to become an architect. He fell in love with the ancient monuments, and my architect friend Roberto gave him his first slide ruler and triangle.

We had lunch with Fellini in a small studio dining room. He'd changed somewhat in the fifteen years since I'd last seen him. Beneath his easy banter and warmth was a new gravity - as if he had finally resigned himself to growing up. After a seven year absence, I considered returning to live in Rome. Fellini told me the cinema was in a sorry state and competition for jobs was fierce among those who'd stayed, but other friends encouraged me. Before we left I ascertained that there was an excellent English school for Raul, while Michael, at nine, could go to an Italian elementary school.

[The Roman Forum, 1978]

On our way back to London, Raul got off the train at the Gare du Nord to buy a magazine, and was left behind when the train changed tracks. Michael and I spent several hours in anguish until Raul finally heard himself being paged in heavily accented.

[In Trastevere, Rome 1978]

English, as he sat on the platform waiting confidently for us to come back for him. He caught up with us in the little town of Amiens where we'd got off to conduct a frantic long-distance search.

June, 1978

Downtown London is shabby. Strange foods are offered in Victoria Station, which more resembles a scene from Southern Yugoslavia or Greece than merry England, where once everything was in its place.

The tremendous influx of Commonwealth members, in particular Bangladeshi, Indian and Pakistani, has transformed the cityscape and the British way of life. These peoples bring with them a culture older than that of their hosts, that imposes itself rather than being assimilated. Britain appears to be going to the dogs, but out of it may come a better bark.

When we returned to the United States, I tried unsuccessfully to land a creative job in Washington, finally concluding there must be a secret code on my clearance indicating that I was persona non grata. Seeing that Washington really wasn't ready for me, I decided to return to Italy where I felt so much more at home.

Alas, after two or three months in Rome, I had to accept that the venture was too stressful for the children, both jobs and apartments being scarce. I decided to cut their losses, and with Howard's help (required by the embassy in Rome), we ended up in Long Island in October of 1979. Howard announced his intention to set up a trust fund for the boys, while Elaine informed me they would receive parcels of the land that made up the beautiful garden (the house would be sold to developers after my father's death). One

day sitting idly on the sofa in the living room, I noticed some documents on the coffee table among the usual newspapers and magazines. Idly, I picked them up and saw they contained Howard's will, which left everything to Elaine. The fact that his will had been left where anyone could come across it didn't prevent him from accusing me of indiscretion. Had Elaine left it there on purpose? Things were never the same after that. Indeed, reality was spelled out in an incredibly nasty letter, which accused me of using the children in a battle against my father, while 'they' (sic) were not contemplating any such thing, although they could, and would certainly wish to provide for the children's future education, were they sure I would not get hold of the money!

After a few stormy months as Howard's house guests, and another few months sharing an empty house across the street with some semi-official squatters, we moved to a cheap apartment in Riverdale. The boys had been awarded generous scholarships to Horace Mann, and Howard promised to pay the remaining tuition. Having developed a proprietary feeling toward Raul, he now behaved like an estranged husband toward me. Continuing his long-standing pattern of being incapable of treating me like a daughter, protecting and caring for me, starting with his reluctance to pay child support, his rare visits, his beating when he learned I'd had sex, the estrangement that followed my marriage, and the lack of interest that followed our reconciliation, he again failed to help me professionally, not-withstanding his many relations.

Although I was fluent in four languages, I had none of the assurance required for a successful assault on the big city media. Having spent a good part of my career working from home, I have a poor sense of hierarchy and generally evolve non-typical arrangements with bosses, ruffling colleagues. To make matters worse, I don't mind criticism, though I may disagree with it, hence tend not to wear silk gloves when criticizing co-workers. I was able to work with important people because I didn't make up to them, an attitude that causes problems with people who only think they're important.

As for free lance work, it's easier to juggle in some situations and places than others; it depends to a large extent on chance, stamina and resistance to failure. After several months of job hunting in New York, following on my grueling experience at State and the Italian fiasco, the stress of the last couple of years caught up with me. I seemed to have gone through an endless series of beginnings, constantly passing go, with 'only' my children to 'show' for it, while feeling guilty at being unable to consistently meet their needs. No longer able to cope with the wealth of episodes of my life, I had to find out where I belonged. My rejection of consumerism, to seeking financial security, was now causing me grief. I decided to suspend the heroics and go for some concentrated therapy.

When, at the intake session, I learned that the missing parent cannot do as much harm as the one who is present, I knew this was going to be a valuable experience. My exploration of the past was helped by the fact that May continued to behave as usual, helping us, but charily, as always. Even more painful was the fact that May invariably defended Rachel's decisions to exclude us from family gatherings. On the one occasion when we were invited to Philadelphia for Thanksgiving, she refused to ask her docile husband Alfred to make a small detour to pick us up in Riverdale, from their new home in upstate New York.

As for Jay, although he had adopted Raul and Michael, our marriage contract had stipulated that he would only continue to be responsible for them if we remained married for at least three years. Since that hadn't been the case, I had not asked him for support. The City of New York thought otherwise, and he wisely skipped off to Africa.

In Riverdale, I did some translating, some rewriting, and some temp work, but mostly I concentrated on my therapy. Meanwhile, Howard introduced Raul to pot, which he grew in his garden. One day, he gave him a big bouquet of the stuff to sell. I explained that this would be morally wrong, and shortly thereafter Raul landed a job bussing in a neighborhood restaurant.

Working with Mrs. A. at a local mental health center, I discovered that as a child I'd gotten different messages from my

various caretakers: Rachel's message was that things had to be perfect, and failure to meet her expectations was a personal insult. For May I was a burden, and should not expect much in the way of material goods or pleasures. For Rose, everything was a problem, and there were no pleasures. From Howard I perceived that I was incompetent and unlucky, and later, that I took after my mother in some awful way.

Frustration at powerlessness was the hallmark of my childhood. When I was re-served uneaten foods at Rachel's table, May didn't intervene, although butting in was reflexive. Rachel would get hysterical over chores; Walter was generally indifferent, refusing to be a father figure, but on the rare occasion when he became angry, he was frightening. (The good times were when he showed me how to plant nails and paint furniture in the basement shop which was his haven.)

Powerless to change my circumstances, I would run away to my best friend Judy's. When I moved to postwar France, the relative lack of material goods was nothing new to me, and I was happy solving everyday problems. I never experienced anything as foreign, yet by solving the problems inherent in constantly going to new places, I ensured that I would never belong. Mrs. A. helped me understand that I had replaced the good feelings one gets from being loved and supported, with the comfort brought by esthetic experiences. Most people like attractive surroundings, but for me they are uncommonly important. I began to doubt whether I should remain in the U.S., where I found little beauty.

It occurs to me now that being in control is also a way of not having to be afraid. May resembled a witch, with her hook nose and uncaring facial expressions. Though 'powerful', she didn't take care of me, so I knew I was not important. Her indifference could only be countered through contempt. According to Mrs. A, I found a way to control my relationship with my mother, but because there was comfort in moving back to a familiar situation, I'm attracted to people who can be expected to deny me, replicating what I experienced with her.

I didn't understand why Mrs. A said I only saw one side of people until I realized that this could be related to my not seeing the hateful side of my parents. To have done so would have been like getting rid of them, and there would no longer be a chance that they would love me. Also, I probably rationalized that hate wasn't logical: why should you hate someone because they don't love you? No hate, no grief. And since I could not admit that my parents were despicable, I sublimated my feeling of powerless by taking control. According to Mrs. A., because there were too many things I couldn't control in my childhood, I became convinced that I had to change reality, making things right through action. But by putting all my energy into things I could not control, I had relatively little energy for the things I could control - like making money!

By late 1980, I had wrested this much insight out of my psychotherapy, but knew it was not sufficient to enable me to own the world of my childhood. In the end, I wasn't really Jewish-American, a New Englander, or a New Yorker, and hardly a Philadelphian. Nor was I French or Hungarian. Although I felt comfortable among Italians, I didn't have Italian roots, and knew I could probably never be accepted into an Italian family. But then again I was pretty much a stranger in my own family. I mused that even if I were to marry a Jewish-American from Philadelphia I would always feel, and no doubt be regarded as, something of an outsider, because of all the years I'd spent abroad.

Though once again obsessed with the fear of destroying the children's sense of place, I began to feel that if I didn't fit in anywhere, I had to find out where I would be least uncomfortable in order to function well as a parent. I never thought of myself as an unhappy person: barring a specific crisis, my mood is usually upbeat. But I had begun to feel that if I remained in the States, life would become all gray. The most promising place for the children's future held no promise for me.

I had been comfortable in Andover, with its small-town intimacy and the closeness of friends. But I did not really fit into academia, anymore than in bureaucratic Washington. I looked into Philadelphia schools, but was dissuaded from moving there by both

my mother and my aunts, all of whom feared being asked to help financially. That was painful, but their fear was understandable, given that I'd often been in need of help from my mother. (In the final years with May, I learned that she had complained loudly about it to all, inflating the burden.)

I began to toy with the idea of going back to Italy. It's relatively easy to get to know people in Rome, and I felt comfortable in artistic/intellectual/political circles (though perhaps not as comfortable as in Andover, which however had the New England climate against it). After thinking of myself as French for years, when I settled easily in Italy I realized that wasn't true. Now I had the good sense to conclude that however much I loved that country, I would never feel Italian even if, with my dark eyes and ability to speak the language without an accent, Italians often took me for one of them. (The French had more often thought I was Swiss because of the relative slowness of my speech.) I was not about to be fooled a second time into thinking one could become something other than what one was, and wondered whether one of the reasons why I missed Italy for so long was because I associated it with being cared for.

The ease with which I've always left places made it as difficult for me to understand why my children found it so difficult, as it had been to identify with Matyas' attachment to country. Ever since I first left the States I've felt that the earth was my home. Some places have suited me better than others, some were preferred over others at different times in my life, but I've never experienced what people call 'roots'. Of course, one's formative years leave an indelible imprint, so I'm probably more American than anything else - as in my tendency to pick myself up and go elsewhere. But also, in the directness and openness that Europeans often find difficult to deal with, and the ability to make quick decisions and act on them.

In 1981, perhaps because I was disappointed that the process of American political renewal had been aborted, and that consequently I had not found a niche for my talents, I began to question whether the U.S. was really the best place for the boys. I realized that some of the same factors I could not accept implied

things that I didn't want for them, such as the possibility that they would be drafted to fight in Nicaragua. I realized that the alienation that pervaded this society was spreading to Europe, but here it was increasing at a dizzying pace.

Italy's cultural decline was evident in the strident TV, and the fact that single friends had created new family lives, was a deterrent. Still I loved Italy's pervasive gaiety and its embrace of modernity (unlike the French, who clung to their past). A major factor in the failure of my earlier move back to Italy had been the difficulty of finding decent housing and I felt that, with better preparation, a transfer could work. On the other hand, the children identified ever more closely with American culture - for Raul, the history, and for both the rock stars, sports, TV, magazines, etc. Was it fair to take them away?

In the end, it was the painful fact that Howard used the children's visits to try to turn them against me that made me decide to take them back to Europe. But mindful of the debacle of '78, I decided to check things out in Paris before making another attempt to settle in Rome.

Chapter XIX - Passing Go

[Paris, 1981]

Again after an absence of twenty-four years, I returned to a country I had long called my own. As soon as school was out, in June of 1981, Michael was put on a plane to Budapest for a visit with Matyas, while Raul and I flew to Paris to reconnoiter. Moving to Europe was the last thing Raul wanted. He was going to be a senior at Horace Mann, and he had made good friends. Frustrated that he didn't feel quite old enough to manage on his own, he brooded as we stood on the platforms of the wonderfully clean and well organized Paris metro, while I tried to memorize the instructions on the yellow alarm box "in case someone falls, is pushed or jumps onto the tracks".

My only hope was food. My oldest French friend Evelyn Mounier, had agreed to put us up. She was an excellent cook, her

husband was a connoisseur of fine wines, and their street was lined with food shops. Every day before returning to the apartment for dinner, I would study the creations displayed in the neighborhood charcuteries and pick out something I thought Raul would like. One day Evelyn sent him to the bakery to pick up a chocolate cake she had ordered for dinner. He had acquired just enough French to say, with feigned Bourbon assurance: "Le gateau, c'est moi." He studied the ten commandments on Evelyn's apron, his favorite being "Le chef a raison, le chef a toujours raison," and after a week came up with his first bilingual play on words: "I Camembert it anymore."

I realized almost immediately that we had a better chance of making a go of it in France than in Italy. Schools had retained their classical rigor, and the country seemed to have completed its transition to modernity: things worked. But keeping in mind Mrs. A.'s advice, I wanted a little more time to be sure the environment would provide sufficient support. Luckily, the "d" system was still in effect: a doctor obligingly certified to the airline that Raul had to have his appendix out, giving us two more weeks to reconnoitre. Finally, having looked into schools both French and bilingual, we arranged to arrive back at Kennedy a few hours before Michael's touch-down from Budapest. He announced triumphantly that he'd brought a Hungarian salami, wrapped in a dirty sock to foil the nose of customs, and an equally carefully packed antique Venetian mirror that Ludovico had given me, and that Matyas had been reluctant to trust to a shipper.

We disposed of most of our things in three weeks, and carefully packed those we wanted to keep, including a second hand piano, a fifteen year old washing machine and several hundred books. We flew to London because it was cheaper, then took the train to Paris, with Raul holding the pink Selectric with which I planned to earn a living on his knees. At the Paris train station, Michael insisted on pushing the baggage carriage, and the Selectric fell off. In a moment of panic, I wondered if modernity included IBM repairs.

Evelyn had arranged for us to stay in the apartment of a friend who was on vacation. We had been traveling for 36 hours, but

I had promised Michael we would see the Bastille Day fireworks in Paris, since we'd had to pass on the 4th of July celebrations to pack. We walked home from the Palais de Chaillot to the Porte d'Italie among the crowds thronging the streets at two in the morning. That very afternoon the boys were enrolled at the Alliance Francaise, in the same Boulevard Raspail building I had attended. The place still catered to students from all over the world, but now they could sip espresso in the garden.

It was like being born again. I wondered how I had managed to spend ten years in the United States, when Europe was where I felt at home. For once sensible in my folly I had made a decision preceded by careful planning. And every morning I woke up exhilarated by the fact that I was in Paris rather than Riverdale, Andover or Washington. I exulted in the beauty that surrounded me, able to tolerate the third rate building we lived in because from the window of the living room we looked straight onto the upper third of the Eiffel tower, which no longer looked like an oil rig.

Paris flooded my senses in a way it never had before, and I was glad when, from time to time, its beauty penetrated my children's adolescent sensitivities. Francois Mitterrand had just been elected President, bringing the socialists back to power for the first time since 1959. The atmosphere in those first heady days following the 'victory of the rose' was remindful, all things being equal, of that which prevailed in Havana in the early years of the Cuban revolution. People gathered on rue St. Honore to watch official limousines coming and going to the presidential palace, and when I took a note to Regis Debray, Mitterand's special advisor, a very un-French relaxation of protocol was evident at the gatehouse.

The Selectric was quickly fixed, and I signed up for temp jobs and translating. After the boys had spent six weeks in an intensive class at the Alliance Francaise, the question arose whether they would be able to function in a French school. Their teacher was confident they would, and it turned out he was the son of the director, who had formerly headed a prestigious lycee. Although registration had ended in April, both boys were enrolled in schools reasonably near our apartment. After the first week in a middle

school, Michael threw a fit, claiming he would never be able to cope, but by the end of the year, he was first in his class.

Things weren't as easy for Raul. On the basis of his grades at Horace Mann, he had been placed in the lycee's top section, where students were tracking to the elite engineering school known as Polytechnique. By the end of the first quarter, it was clear he was failing math, which was more advanced than in the U.S. and taught differently. Fortunately, his literary bent was discernible from the papers he wrote looking up almost every word in the dictionary, and his French teacher was able to persuade the principle to move him to a section with a less demanding math program.

One day, while I was at work, Howard made a surprise visit on his way back from a trip to Samarcand. Having obtained our address from the Alliance Francaise, he rang the bell and took the boys to dinner at the famous *Brasserie Lipp*. As the notoriously snotty maitre d' ushered them to the door, Howard complained about the puny size of the sole meuniere, and bending his tall frame over the little man, stuck the bone in his breast pocket. He died the following year from a massive heart attack brought on by emphysema. May obligingly sent me the obituary, and a letter from Howard's lawyer informed me that neither I nor my children would inherit anything.

During our second year back in France, two political figures had come to my attention. One was Nicholas Sarkozy, the young mayor of the posh Neuilly suburb whose father was Hungarian. From his style I sensed that he would be someone to contend with. He rose with unrelenting energy to become the president of France in 2007. The other politician was Jean-Marie Le Pen. In 1983 a surprise win gave his nationalist party control of the city council in a town near Paris that had a significant Muslim population. Most people discounted him, but it was clear to me that his bullying, xenophobic style would make him a long-term threat. Twenty-four years later he knocked the socialist presidential candidate out of the 2007 election, and has since passed the torch to his daughter Marine, who came in third in 2012.

With tutoring, Raul was able to pass the math requirement, but rules set in stone prevented him from postponing the French part of the Baccalaureat exam. With barely a year of French under his belt, he managed a B, a truly remarkable feat. This confirmed his determination not to stay in the math track, as gifted students were expected to do. He no longer wanted to be a doctor, he wanted to do literature. Against the advice of all my friends, who told us the humanities were the refuge of mediocrity, I supported Raul's choice.

He had complained that his French classmates were totally lacking in complexes or craziness, but now he met Fleur; he was seventeen, she sixteen, and she was his woman. I had no objection to this, but Fleur's parents had recently divorced, and she claimed that when she wasn't with Raul she felt like an old sock, making him responsible for her well-being. After spending hours with her after school, the minute he entered the door the phone would ring and it would be Fleur, and they would be off on an endless conversation. I was worried he would fail the second part of the Baccalaureat, but he did so well that the principal encouraged him to take the two-year preparatory classes for the competitive exams to the prestigious Ecole Normale Superieure. For that he had to make up two years of Greek and ten of Latin. After doing so, he passed the daunting Normale exam on the first of three permitted tries. Because he was the only Franco-American to have sat for the exam in twenty years, other students sat in on his orals. Modestly, he claimed they had put easy Caesar in all three envelopes of the Latin draw.

By then we had moved from an old walkup to a comfortable modern flat, and Michael was also in a prestigious high school, where he continued to get top grades while spending most of his time goofing off with the friends made in middle school. Both boys were tall and handsome and Michael managed to have blond hair to go with his blue eyes while being the image of his black haired father. One of my favorite times was strolling home across the river with my two sons after a movie on the Champs-Elysees.

[View from Rue de Grenelle, Paris, 1984]

Michael visited Matyas for a month in summer, but it was not a happy experience. Matyas had divorced his second wife because she could not bring a pregnancy to term, and now he was married to a woman who was determined that Michael not be part of the family she had created. The similarity with Andrei's wife made me wonder whether this was a typically Eastern European attitude, but the two women were so different that it seemed unlikely. Matyas took no vacation while Michael was visiting, he was left home with his stepmother, and behaved badly. Finally, he was packed off to Lake Balaton with his grandparents, who saw nothing wrong with the arrangement. Their genuine affection could not make up for Matyas' lack.

March, 1982

Get this on paper before it dissolves.

Raul talked about repressing things we want to forget, but which affect our behavior. In the middle of the night everything seemed to come together: maybe I didn't know I had a score to

settle. Maybe I've repressed the fact that I have every reason to be angry with Howard.

Maybe it's because I've suppressed rightful anger instead of owning it, that I'm usually nicer than other women. When I finally react to bad behavior, men are surprised and think I have a score to settle.

I avoid authoritarian men because they're like the Goldberg women. I imagine that gentle men won't hurt me, just as I had to believe that Howard wasn't.

As if to confirm this insight, I soon became involved with a man who, while fitting the psychological pattern of so many others, brought a new dimension to my sex life. Francois had been married to a woman who was not interested in sex, and had fantasized about love-making until his children were grown and he felt free to get a divorce. Before meeting me he had been involved with a woman who embodied his sexual ideal, but was married and determined to raise her young children. Francois had vowed to wait for her, but recently, she had been transferred to a distant part of the country, and didn't seem eager to continue the relationship.

We met at a single's club. It was one of those times where you see someone on the other side of the room and you know there can be something. That much was banal, but the rest was not. The first time we made love, I had gone to Francois' apartment on a sunny Sunday afternoon. We had planned to go for a ride in the country, but the tennis finals were still on, so he offered me a drink. Fond as I was of rides in the country on a lovely spring day, I was in no hurry. The match over, Francois began to believe in his luck, and made tentative advances. Finding no resistance, he led me into the bedroom. As I lay naked on the bed, he knelt beside me and said something which translates roughly as: "Get ready for something nice."

I suppressed a giggle, but for all the many pleasures I had experienced, nothing like this had ever happened to me. Francois caressed me as if time had ceased to exist; the tribute he paid to my body was its own end, as each part of me received leisurely attention. I had never appreciated foreplay, but now discovered it was another, vast area of pleasure.

Francois, who ran a drafting office for the railroad, was a few years younger than me, and hailed from Lorraine, the part of France that had constantly passed between France and Germany. This made him fair, blue-eyed, and rather more phlegmatic than your average Latin lover. He hadn't had a lot of formal schooling, but was intelligent and interested in the world, and I invariably found him more stimulating than the men I encountered in the course of my writing or translating. And our love-making grew to be like good bread.

During those years, my life had four parts: my children, my work, Francois, and what was happening in the world. Perhaps the children got short shrift, although they didn't seem to feel neglected: school was demanding, they both had friends, and because I worked at home, I felt that I was available. I later learned that they were affected by my constant struggle to make ends meet, and the reflected stress of my caring for someone who loved another person. Francois dined with us several times a week, and we took two vacations in Italy with the boys, with whom he got on well. He drove me to Hungary in his little Alfa Romeo to pick up the hand-painted Italian chests that Ludovico had given me, and corrected the drafts of the book I was writing about Europe.

Although my French had suffered considerably from twenty-four years of neglect, I felt compelled to tell the French some important things they didn't know. Unexpectedly, under the new socialist government, the left had become positively lyrical over America's modernity. Jean Daniel, the widely known journalist and founder of the weekly *l'Observateur*, who had gone to Cuba in 1963 with a message for Castro from Kennedy, days before Kennedy was assassinated, agreed to see me, but we never did discuss what Americans could expect from France's socialist government, because

we got into a heated argument about the United States. The incident convinced me there was a fundamental difference between the American idea of democracy and that of Europe.

[Francois with Budapest bounty, 1984]

The Declaration of Independence, with its formula: "...all men are endowed by their Creator with certain inalienable rights; among these are life, liberty and the pursuit of happiness," put rights at the top of a values pyramid, leaving responsibility out in the cold. That was all right during the first hundred or so years of American history, because religious practice included a strong sense of social responsibility. But when religion was marginalized by science, the concept of responsibility disappeared from public discourse. Later efforts to bring solidarity into the political arena were condemned as socialist and therefore un-American.

In the euphoric days of the 18th century, the American and French mottos were seen as synonymous. But the French Revolution's trinity was: *liberté, égalité, fraternité*, and there is a

basic contradiction between 'fraternity' and 'the pursuit of happiness'. Fraternity implies the solidarity of the community toward the individual, while, taken literally, (as Fidel pointed out the first time we met), liberty implies that it doesn't matter if some go hungry.

I realized that the gap between American and European attitudes toward the Soviet Union was due to these differing definitions of freedom. As for the Soviets, they also failed to place the overarching principle of equality where it belonged; they did not subordinate it to individual rights, they did subordinate it to political participation. Where Americans say: "Since the State has no rights over me, it has no responsibilities toward me", the Soviets said: "Since the State takes responsibility for the needs of all, the citizen has no need to take any, and therefore, no need to participate in government."

Americans and Europeans both defend the idea of democracy, but because they do not define it in the same way, they practice it differently, then wonder why they are at odds. The difficulties encountered through centuries of transatlantic diplomacy could well be due to the fact that their definitions of freedom are fundamentally different. In the nineteen-eighties, because France accepted the false premise of shared values, it could not play the role it should have at a crucial time in the Cold War, when the United States wanted to station Pershing missiles right next door in Germany.

1983

The only thing that's really important is that we shouldn't blow ourselves up. Realpolitik, but not in the Kissingerian sense. A measure of socialism, but not dogmatism. To allow the world, with its inevitable patchwork of better and worse, to eventually develop its inherent possibilities. It's not so much a question of political system, but a broader one of learning

to live and share. Muddling through is about
the best we can do, and if we succeed, we
won't be doing too badly.

I had been allergic to dogma ever since I first went to synagogue with Regina, and I also knew from living in Cuba and Eastern Europe that you couldn't force good things on people against their will. But I rejected the idea that freedom was more important than a full stomach. I felt comfortable in Europe, where each country has a multi-party system, and governments accept the idea of public responsibility. The party in power doesn't have to resort to spin because it has its own press, while differing views are presented in those of the various opposition parties.

The book I was writing on Europe included an annex that dealt with the Greek-Turkish standoff, an important issue at the time, given that Turkey was touted as the southern bulwark against the Soviet Union. In 1986 I persuaded a Turkish researcher to take me in his bags to a meeting of diplomats and academics debating Mediterranean issues. I came away from that conference on the lovely island of Spetsoes more convinced than ever of the difficulty of listening to others. One of the attendees was Schlomo Avineri, a professor at Hebrew University and a close advisor to Simon Perez. Having read one of his books, I was so in awe of his intellect that I scarcely dared speak to him. Amre Mussa, who went on to become Egypt's Foreign Minister, then Secretary General of the Arab League, was friendly almost Italian-style. In a spirited discussion he claimed that India was a tool of the United States, and that it would never be a major player.

[German youth have renounced nationalism to welcome the Other.
Scala Review, Jan/Feb, 1986)]

As a result of these encounters, and much as with my decision to go to Cuba, the following spring I decided that I had to see the Israeli-Palestinian standoff for myself. I spent a week in Jerusalem/Tel Aviv and another on a beach in Eilat, surprised at how materialistic the Israelis seemed to be, and also, how traditional: a young soldier who sat next to me on a bus asked if he could visit me in my hotel, and from his surprise at my negative response, I guessed that it was common for single Israeli men to visit older women, while young women remained celibate until marriage. I had no feeling of being among 'my people', and notwithstanding the Mediterranean, didn't think I would want to live there. (Many years later a rerun of Visconti's film The Garden of the Finzi Contini, in which a Jewish family sings a Hannukah song similar to The Twelve Days of Christmas, drinking wine between each verse, made me think that Rome was the only place where I could imagine being Jewish.)

[Amre Mussa at Spetsoes, 1986]

I interviewed Moshe Peled and several other Knesset members of varying political persuasions, and although the trip to Eilat in a tiny plane brought home how extraordinarily narrow Israel's east/west dimension was, my sympathies remained with the peace camp. With France's large Jewish population fanatically pro-Israel, my article for a Jewish weekly was rejected. It suggested joining the West Bank and Gaza by sacrificing a slice of the Negev, and proposed that Jerusalem become not only an international city, but a U.N. center for the resolution of border disputes. I outlined the idea in an article to the *International Herald Tribune* which was not published, but was plagiarized by a well-known French commentator to whom I had shown it.

In an interview in Paris after my return, the Israeli scholar Itzak Dror predicted decades of violence before the problems between Israelis and Palestinians would be settled. He also foresaw that the dispute would morph into part of a broader conflict between the West and Islam. At the time I considered the Jewish people too intelligent to allow that to happen, but Dror is proving tragically right.

Chapter XX - Europe Personal and Political

In addition to diplomatic and economic papers from the foreign ministry and the Elysee, I translated scenarios. At one point, I needed to find out something for a film script that only someone who had covered the war in Lebanon would know. Remembering a recent article on Iran that quoted a newsman whose name sounded vaguely familiar, I wondered if it might belong to that tall blue eyed cameraman I'd had a fling with in Cuba. I assumed he had probably covered Lebanon, and called his network in Paris to find out if Claus Strumling ever passed through. "He lives here", was the reply, followed by a phone number.

A voice with an eerily familiar accent answered. I identified myself, asked if he'd been in Cuba in July, 1963. He seemed to vaguely remember me, and yes he'd covered all the wars everywhere since, including Beyrouth, and I could come over with my dialogue problem.

It wasn't the first time I had seen an old acquaintance, friend, or lover after a long interval, and I did not expect the zing to happen the minute the door opened. But balding and wearing glasses, Claus had the same smile that had arrested me in the Mexican airport, and it produced the same effect. After an hour's conversation I concluded he had aged gracefully, mellowed, and used his brain well. He had lived in Paris for the past 28 years, married to a beautiful woman who'd brought him two daughters. The apartment was full of beams, music and general gemutlichkeit. The kitchen was as big as some flats I've lived in. Tall and slender, Helga spent most of her waking hours there, and excelled in the art of homemaking.

As we stood by the elevator, Claus kissed my hand and suggested we meet for lunch. A week later, he took me to an old Parisian standby, and no sooner had we sat down then he said: "The day we fall into bed together you'd better know that I love my wife and will never leave her." I recognized the Claus of yore, mildly annoyed that he should assume. After lunch, we walked, and the talk

flowed as if it had never been interrupted. Suddenly, he was late: a quick kiss, and he turned on his heels.

Several months went by. My lover, Francois, was still dreaming of another woman, we had split up and made up several times. Occasionally we saw Claus and Helga for family dinners, the zing lurking in the background. One day in the middle of winter, when I didn't have any work and wasn't seeing François, Claus called: "I've been home for three months, Helga is about to throw dishes at me, I gotta get outta here. Would you like to come to Chamonix for a few days?"

Claus had never accepted the gilded contracts the networks had offered him, but remained a free lancer working exclusively for one. They would call in the middle of the night and tell him to be off somewhere, he had his own equipment and crew and that's how it had been from Emmy to Emmy. Now they weren't calling him as often, and he was restless.

Michael and Raul were sixteen and twenty, and could manage. I packed a few clothes and my manuscript: I hated the snow and didn't know how to ski. The next morning on my way down to meet Claus, I realized I had never driven with him. Almost every Frenchman I knew gave me a heart attack at the wheel, including François. I got in and said: "I hope you don't drive like a madman."

"I used to race", he quipped.

Not to be intimidated by the mere possibility of disaster, I told myself that an old Diesel station wagon was not a racing car. Claus turned out to be a masterful and careful driver, turning fear into pleasure. We checked into a small hotel in Chamonix, had an early dinner, and popped into bed. As if nothing.

At 57, with the equipment of a twenty-five year old, Claus was tender, caring about my pleasure as he had not before, but still totally uncontrolled. We spent two more days together, but only one night; the drive back was glorious, with great music and talk, but at the motel, Claus declared he was too tired to frolic, and insisted on watching television in bed. In the morning, brief and to the point as usual, he confessed that his war torn childhood had prevented him from ever being able to love anyone.

I knew Claus would not leave his wife, who daily recreated the family warmth the war had destroyed. Once in a while he'd call, come to lunch, lunge into me, and take off on some urgent business. One afternoon in bed he told me there had been three important women in his life, his first wife, his second, and me. He asked me if I was free to go away soon, but then went away with his family. I knew he cared, but decided that he was not a dog and I was not a lamppost.

Shortly thereafter, my relationship with Francois ended, not because of his hopeless love but because of Scientology. I campaigned in the name of reason, but brainwashing eventually won out. Our love-making had become a sort of drug, and I was devastated, knowing it was unlikely I would have another relationship.

I remembered turning twenty-seven in Rome, having lunch at the beach with my boss at the French news agency, and thinking: "How is it possible that I am twenty-seven and I still feel the same as when I was twenty-one? As one gets older, one should feel different." Periodically I had remembered that day, and thought approximately the same thing. Not that I continued to feel twenty at forty or fifty, but there was a sense of still being essentially the same person. Now I was caught between that view of myself and the evidence that, since others were no longer likely to see me as a partner, it must not be true.

At the time I was living on the back of the 'butte' (or hill) of Montmartre, at exactly the intersection where the neighborhood turns from bourgeois to lower class interracial. Not being on the tourist circuit, it had retained a sense of neighborliness that even included the shopkeepers. There were many bakeries, and two good butchers: one had a bench for waiting, and indulged in a sort of snobbish intimacy with established customers, the other was stout and friendly. There was a wonderful Italian food store, which I suspected was a Mafia front, and across the street was an eighty-four year old shoemaker who would do your work in a matter of months if sufficiently prodded.

Most of the inhabitants were pensioners who spent their days chatting and playing cards in the cafés. Although I had some misgivings in terms of security, I soon got over my fear of walking to the metro in the nearby African quarter, enjoying the feeling of being in the middle of the world. A Lebanese family restaurant marked a milestone in my culinary education, its amazingly fresh dishes different from anything I had ever tasted, and at the opposite end of my street, on the northern outskirts of the city, was the flea market. A bus to the center of town stopped in front of my door.

After finishing at *Normale*, Raul had opted for the French equivalent of the Peace Corps and was teaching in Botswana, while Michael had gone to Berkeley with near perfect SAT scores. I continued to update my book on Europe, as events that I had foreseen invariably came to pass. My insights about the Soviet Union may seem obvious today, but in the eighties, before someone coined the title independent scholar, I could not find a publisher.

We have been taught to believe that only action can bring change, but it seemed that the U.S. was trying to confront the problems of the present according to yesterday's paradigms. I was beginning to suspect that change happens regardless of what individuals or governments do, swinging first one way, then the other, and I rejected the conventional wisdom that the conflict with the Soviet Union could only be resolved through nuclear war. Although the United States was convinced it was inevitable, the Europeans were not, and I could not understand why they accepted America's leadership.

When reminded that in the event of war, they would be on the front lines, influential French intellectuals such as Bernard Henri-Levy, today one of Fareed Zakaria's favorite guests, claimed that people should be ready to die for their convictions, in other words, 'better dead than red'. They argued that even if Europeans were to accept Soviet domination, they would ultimately perish in a nuclear war between the Soviets and the Chinese. They claimed that American missiles would prevent a Soviet takeover of Europe, adding that if they failed 'at least we'll die for a noble cause. In a Sino-Soviet conflict, we would be dying for the wrong reasons.'

I was and still am convinced that to prefer peace to war, life to death, is unworthy of humans. In a civilization dominated by the immediate fulfillment of ever increasing demands, otherwise intelligent people had arrived at the absurd notion that we should prefer death - and even a global holocaust - to patient and tenacious efforts to avoid or change an unwanted outcome.

For me, a moral attitude toward nuclear war meant not sacrificing future generations on the altar of our needs. Each generation must solve the problems that confront it, without holding hostage those not yet born. However difficult our problems may be, we have no right to risk eliminating humanity - not only our contemporaries, but children to whom we will have denied the right to be born - in order to solve them. Our problems will not be their problems, for the simple reason that nothing lasts forever. No dictatorship, however cruel, has ever been eternal. Only death is final.

Since nothing lasts forever, it was clear to me that the division of Europe would not be permanent. My childhood hunch about the African and Latin American coastlines having long since been confirmed, where everyone else saw a Russian giant threatening the world, with Europe an easy prey, I saw a system whose components were of comparable potential strength. The two super-powers had chosen a tit for tat relationship, but Europe could choose a circular relationship with the Soviet Union, China, India, and the Middle East, recognizing that their policies and economies were interdependent.

I wanted the French to stop thinking only in military terms, but after suffering three German aggressions in a century, American missiles gave them a sense of security. Ironically, when it came to the Soviet threat, nothing irritated the French more than German pacifism, yet they were openly opposed to any idea of eventual German unification. They did not seem to realize that by insisting on having two enemies at once, Europe could not unite, and, therefore could not really defend itself against the supposed Soviet threat. As I wrote in my book:

> *"A few French politicians are beginning to admit that Germany could eventually be entrusted with its own defense. But this will have no effect on Western security, for with or without nuclear arms, the Germans will never fight each other. What reality can a political or economic entity have if its borders are guarded on either side by brothers?"*

'Finlandization' was the American idea that Communism could take over Europe peacefully. From years spent living in its heart, I knew there was no real ideological impediment to another idea: 'convergence' between capitalism and communism. Western Europe, after all, consisted of welfare states committed to balancing solidarity and free enterprise.

In April of 1989, after six years of up-dating, *Une autre Europe, un autre Monde* was accepted by a small academic publisher. It foresaw a time when solutions would no longer be found in Washington but in Peking, New Delhi and Tokyo, "meaning that there will no longer be a core and a periphery - or that everyone is someone else's periphery." That time is upon us now.

After the Ti'en an Men massacre, in June, I wrongly believed China would democratize before Post-Solidarnoscz Poland, but I did foresee its economic rise:

> *"It's useless to see things in Manichean, linear terms when a regime is facing an existential threat. But as part of an interdependent, modernizing future, China will probably deal differently with similar situations."*

At a conference at the European Union's Brussels headquarters organized by its then head, Jacques Delors, to speculate about Gorbachev, I seemed to be the only person who realized that

he was for real. In the first draft of my book I had foreseen that he would be chosen over his rivals to lead the Soviet Union. Later, when Gorbachev appointed Schevarnadze to be his Foreign Minister, and the Soviet watchers at The Economist were saying "Schevar-who?" I was certain that they had been old friends and colleagues waiting in the wings for an opportunity to do great things, and this turned out to be true.

During that summer of 1989, I assured a Czech high school senior whom Michael had met at a party that things would soon change for her. She invited Michael to Prague, where he witnessed the ferment when Hungary opened its border with Austria, setting off the series of events that would culminate in the fall of the Berlin Wall a few months later.

August, 1989

The other day as I was falling asleep, lamenting the fact that there was nobody beside me, I wondered why it is so difficult for men to understand that a woman who is generally strong has her weaknesses. I had reached unknown heights in sensuality with François, but arguments over his driving proved that a 'strong' woman is never allowed to be weak. Leo had leaned on me, Ludovico loved me 'active and intelligent', Andrei had considered I would be better able to take care of his child alone than his wife would hers, and now most men refused to believe that I could be afraid of reckless driving. They want to decide what I am allowed to be afraid of - thereby denying the very strength they claim I have. When I get angry, they react as though the product has been misrepresented. A strong woman is a convenience for men as long as they can decide what she is allowed to be strong about.

Michael returned to Berkeley after summer break, and Raul, returning from Botswana, decided to take over the maid's room that came with my apartment. He brought with him a dog that had come to him in the village where he lived, the day after Samuel Beckett, his literary hero, died, and who consequently bore the name of Bebeck. When Raul forgot to close his door, Bebeck would commute between the 6th and 4th floor, slip-sliding on the wooden stairs, to whine in front of mine.

[Michael, on a visit from Berkeley, 1987]

At one point, Raul decided he would never find himself unless he could put a face on his father. My only advice was that he should curb his violent impulses ("part of me wants to kill him, the other part wants to be recognized"), and know that his whole life did not depend on finding him, even if it was important. He was to stay a week in Warsaw in order to get a discount fare. I'd given him all the information I had, which was old, reminded him there was a French consulate, and the Red Cross.

A few days after he left, the phone rang and a woman's voice with a heavy accent said peremptorily "noomber fax". I asked who she was and she said only "Varshava". I didn't remember enough Polish to ask her to put Raul on, but gave her the fax number. A

scribbled note immediately scrolled out of the machine indicating he had seen his father and wanted a plane ticket to come home that night. I was to fax the answer back to the post office where he was waiting. An hour and a half later I was still on the phone, having been told by the airline that there were no seats for a one-way ticket, and unable to reach the post office either by fax or by phone. Finally, the French consulate in Warsaw, after leaving me dangling for fifteen minutes, called Air France and found out that Raul was there with a reservation, waiting for the fare to be paid. It was four o'clock and the plane was due to leave at six- thirty. I dashed off to Air France.

That night, while sipping Polish Zubrovka, I learned that Raul had been reasonably well received, but that his father was about to leave on a trip. Raul was chary with details at first, but as the vodka got to him, or the first moment of sanctity passed, he distilled them drop by drop.

He had gone to his father's previous place of employment, and the receptionist had handed him the address of his new office. Andrei's name was at the top of the directory of a big modern building: he was president of some Polish national bureau. Raul went to his office identifying himself as Strand, and asked to see him. Andrei took him into his office and Raul greeted him in Spanish, the only language they had in common. Oblivious to the strong family resemblance, his father asked where he knew him from. "Cuba", replied Raul, stingily. Getting a blank look, he ordered: "Look at me, I'm your son." They embraced, somewhat formally. The following evening Andrei took Raul to dinner in a good restaurant, constantly glancing over his shoulder at the door.

"Why are you always looking at the door?"

"I'm not a tranquil man," his father answered quietly.

I had always thought the reason for Andrei's silence was political, but it turned out to have been Casimira. She had never forgiven his adventure; he had taken refuge in his work.

He told the typical Polish yarn of having thought Raul was dead when I sent a photo with the request for him to authorize Raul's adoption by Jay, yet claimed not to have received the authorization. He had made several more trips to Cuba, spoke flawless Spanish,

said he would be in Paris in a few months, and would like to see me. I was dumbstruck when Raul added casually: "He said: 'tengo muchos sentimientos para ella'". Here was a man whose lack of courage had determined the way my two children had grown up, and he claimed to have deep feelings for me! In fact, we never heard from him again.

Meanwhile, my small publisher, a professor of information technology, was more interested in my systems approach to politics than in politics itself, and didn't really have a distribution network. The book had been plagiarized by several political figures, one of whom, a well-known dissident communist, was ordered by a judge to acknowledge it. When I told the story to the press agent the publisher had contacted, thinking it would be a plus, she backed off, fearing a political backlash. The book was ready for distribution on the day the Wall fell, and Europe started on the road to reunification, though by a different route than the one I had imagined. Hearing the news on the taxi radio as I carried the first copies fresh from the press, I picked up a bottle of cheap champagne and broke the news to my German neighbors, predicting that within a year Germany would be united. Though highly political, they were skeptical; Germany was reunited eleven months later.

In December, like the icing on the cake, one of my heroes, Vaclav Havel, was elected President of Czechoslovakia. The French eight o'clock news showed him marching in a solemn procession at the ancient Charles University, draped in a heavy black toga, then receiving an honorary degree. With the usual twinkle in his eye, he said he was happy for his mother, who had always wanted her son the dunce to get a doctorate. The celebration continued in the theater where Havel's plays had been performed when they weren't banned. He sat on the stage on a straight-backed chair, in a row with other former dissidents, who took turns talking to the audience while off to the side musicians tinkered on their instruments. When one speaker said that power always ended up limiting the freedom of intellectuals Havel made the comedian's classical gesture of half getting up as if to leave, then sitting down again. When his friend finished, he turned to him and said: "When I was giving my speech to the American

Congress and I referred to that, I spotted you in the audience - and you were asleep!" I couldn't imagine any other country where the President would celebrate his election that way, proof that *The Good Soldeier Svejk's* legacy would never die. I thought of the Czech Vice Minister Milan Tabor who had died on an operating table during an Italian exile, and of the lovely Susan who had committed suicide in Verona a few months later.

Soon after the book's publication, I was again invited to Brussels, this time for a conference with participants from all over Western Europe, where I was the only one to lobby for rapid integration of the Eastern European countries into the European Union. I knew from papers I had translated for the French Foreign Ministry and the Elysee how reluctant Mitterrand was to see Germany reunited, fearing a loss of influence for France. None of us foresaw that, grateful for America's unrelenting condemnation of their captive status, the Eastern countries, once free, would be more pro-U.S. than Mitterrand's old Europe. Now the situation is changing again, because the U.S. wants to install defensive missiles in Poland to guard against Iran, and the East Europeans know that means trouble with Russia.

When in 1990 Presidents Mitterrand and Havel called a conference to discuss Mitterrand's plans for a Confederation, I sent a paper on the future architecture of what I called the peninsula of the Eurasian continent to Catherine Lalumiere, the Secretary General of the Council of Europe, with a copy of my book. I received a polite letter, but from her talk and what I read in the press, it was clear that no thought was being given to a European framework. One camp, led by the French and the Germans, wanted to build a defense system; the other, especially after the 1991 Gulf War, wanted to remain dependent on American military strength, confirming America's position as the lone superpower at a time when the U.N. could have become the embryo of a world government.

After several years with both my sons away, we had a mellow Christmas. As is the case for most non-religious, non-identified Jews, the holiday means nothing to us except as an occasion to be together for better or for worse, but this Christmas

turned out to be one of our best. I invited two of Raul's close friends who were not going home for the holidays, and decided to innovate with pheasant. The neighborhood butcher instructed me on how to roast it, his wife sold me a jar of cooked chestnuts to go with it, and the guests brought fresh foie gras, chocolate fudge cake (both made in a Normale Sup dorm kitchen), and a rich assortment of high quality cheese. Raul's then girlfriend Melanie brought several bottles of a well aged Bordeaux. Having begun with foie gras at about ten thirty, we finished around two. It wasn't until four that everyone left, after listening to Indian rajas (a nod to Jay Stryker who had introduced them to us), slouched on the couch and the floor, Michael and Melanie indulging in their usual flirtation under Raul's benevolent gaze.

It's difficult to describe these moments, but as I lay in bed I tried to get to the essence. I think it has something to do with a momentary release of the tension that exists between parents and children from the moment a child is born. Even euphoria is never far removed from anxiety or preoccupation, whether it be with the child, or an aspect of one's life that affects him. As children grow up, more specific tensions arise, and battles are more on than off. During the rare moments when problems and antagonism are absent, each person experiences the mellowness felt by the others, and I think that's what makes these moments special: it's not the sense of relief after long years of battle, it's the mutual awareness of that relief, the palpable pleasure each one takes in that moment, knowing its fragility. Underlying all the other feelings is the knowledge of a bond that survives the worst trials.

I remembered a picture I had taken of of Regina and her five children in her living room, when Howard and I spent a weekend on 13th street. The evening seemed to never want to end, everybody eating Regina's wonderful homemade cakes, brewing pot after pot of tea or coffee, washing the dishes and cups, ambling to and from the kitchen, talking in twos and threes or all together. That evening clamored loudly that the moment was ours, and there would always be time to sleep. The special status that Howard enjoyed in his family allowed him to gently impose his rhythm. As the only male

child, he had left home at fourteen, then traveled the world pursuing a glamorous profession. In the same way, when Raul and Michael were at my place - which, to the extent that it suited them, they considered home - they imposed their rhythm of life on me. And like Regina, I basked in the plenitude of my children's fleeting presence.

[Regina and her children, 1957]

Chapter XXI - Last Fling in a Not so Douce France

February 10, 1991

After waking up late as usual and having breakfast, I settled in the cockpit, which is how one of my clients called the desk where I always seem to be doing three things at once, and worked straight through to meet a deadline. Just as I had finished putting my translation on a floppy disc and decided to make myself a protein drink, I remembered that I had an appointment for a neck massage at six. Realizing it was six fifteen, I called the physiotherapist, who kindly proposed to fetch her daughter at the nursery and see me at six thirty. I wasn't the only person in Paris juggling a life.

On the way to the physiotherapist, I thought to myself: "With a life like mine, who has time for a husband?" Then, for no apparent reason: "If you stick your neck out, you get in trouble. And that's what I do."

I wondered how I had gone from a shy, worried, introverted child, to this. But only for a moment. I knew that fundamentally, one doesn't change, rather one becomes ever more what one is. The original child, after all, was the one belly-flopping on the sled.

I continued to feel the lack of a male presence, knowing that with each day that passed, it was all the more likely to be permanent. I had been able to talk to François about anything, his curiosity and native intelligence made up for his lack of education. And on a

physical level, I had reached the peak of my sensitivity. After we broke up, I went to bed with a lot of men, seeking in vain the quality of love-making I had known with him, acquiring instead a statistic: only one in four men appear to know what love-making is about.

Men in their fifties wanted women in their early forties, who considered them too old. Divorced men had no desire to remarry until they were over sixty, when they began to fear for a lonely old age. It was not difficult to find someone to fall into bed with of an evening, or more likely of an afternoon - extremely inconvenient if one had to use one's head afterward - but that person was likely to be married or in one of the above categories, moving quickly from one bed to another to avoid getting stuck between the sheets. I came to the conclusion that single women have too often taken the place of prostitutes. Before women's lib, non-marital sex took place mainly in brothels. Now, men have their pick of beautiful, intelligent women with whom they can access pleasure for the price of a lunch or dinner. And a 'liberated' woman does not necessarily encounter the confidence, complicity and consideration necessary for shared, purely hedonistic pleasure.

After four years in the apartment on the 'Butte', the Paris climate caught up with my chronic back problem. I knew it would improve if I went south, and as usual, once I started to think about a change, I began to make it happen. By December 1993, I had decided to move to Hyeres, a southern town visited briefly with Francois eight years before, and which had enchanted me. Before the month was over, I had found a cheap apartment that met my needs. It wasn't until I was back on the train to Paris staring at the parasol pines moving by, that I allowed the emotion tied up in the Mediterranean landscape to overwhelm me. No place on earth has meant so much for so long as the one that came with Ludovico's love.

[L'Almanarre beach, Hyeres, 1996]

The hot dry sun of the Mediterranean, where the air is incredibly light, is a contrast both to humid Philadelphia and teasingly tepid Paris summers. A Mediterranean landscape is sparse, yet the colors sing. Rome had shown me that scorched earth and stone against vibrant blues and greens could be more beautiful than the gushing green of the north bound up with the despair of my childhood. Cypresses and parasol pines punctuate the landscape, the latter a giant standing alone, its thick straight trunk supporting a dark, umbrella-shaped crest that makes a massive statement against the sky, but is also like a protective quilt. I too am taller than most women and have a decisive personality that reassures others. Perhaps that explains my affinity with parasol pines.

[Medieval Castle, Hyeres]

The town of Hyeres is set back about three kilometers from the Mediterranean, on a hill graced by the ruins of a medieval castle.

I relished being able to do most of my errands on foot, however it was not possible to survive without a car, so I bought an old, but little used Peugeot 203. It allowed me to enjoy the countryside, where I made several friends.

[Hyeres market street, 1997]

And yet my pleasure at being back on the Mediterranean had been compromised from the start. On the day I arrived, the local parliamentarian, an outspoken woman, was murdered by political opponents. I refused to extrapolate from that incident, but gradually realized how severely tainted the south of France was by right-wing politics. The easternmost part of the Cote d'Azur having once been part of Italy, most of the population were of Italian stock, yet they had neither Italian warmth nor Parisian sophistication. Just trying to live peacefully was a challenge, as small mishaps became full-fledged dramas. I soon realized that far from being influenced by the beauty that surrounded them, the inhabitants of this paradise, many of whom had reluctantly left former French North African colonies, were always ready for a fight. The atmosphere brought the frustrations outsiders usually experience in France to a pitch.

To make matters worse, and contrary to assurances, most of my clients did not follow me, finding the cost of faxes prohibitive.

(In my calculations I had overlooked the fact that France Telecom was a rapacious government monopoly.) I fell increasingly behind in my social security payments, which, combined with other taxes for the self-employed, took more than half my income. Local assignments were scarce, and usually involved payoffs, which I couldn't bring myself to accept, anymore than I had been able to take a percentage of Paris colleagues' gains when I shared work.

By 1996 I was being threatened with legal action by social security, seeing no end to the accumulation of penalties for back taxes. I appealed my case to the social security court, but knew it would take several years for it to be called, and that the Napoleonic Code had been repeatedly amended by civil servants who had never studied law. The only solution was to take an early retirement. The thought that in the United States much of the safety net would have been missing altogether was a consolation.

In France, the threat of legal action is incarnated in the ubiquitous collection officer or 'huissier'. He's usually the first person you encounter when you have a brush with the law, or when you owe money, in particular to the State. He'll send you a blue paper threatening to take legal action if you don't pay up. Then he'll send you a green paper threatening to confiscate your belongings. Should the whole thing be a mistake, there will nonetheless be charges. If a huissier comes to deliver a summons and you're not home, he'll leave a note with your concierge or in your mail box, instructing you to pick up the summons at the town hall. If you fail to do so, you're in trouble.

Early on, President Mitterrand had decreed that every government employee should make known his or her name to petitioners, but that innovation lasted no longer than the socialists' rose. The French bureaucrat stubbornly refused to become a person. He did not like you to ask his name, or to comment on the weather. After the first year of euphoria, bureaucracy had become so pervasive that children learned Ministry of Education acronyms in school.

The socialist administration soon became known as the caviar left, as the perks that came with power got the better of

socialist morality. Although prosperous, the country lurched from one economic and social crisis to another, just as it had when I first arrived in France half a century earlier. Anyone familiar with the language knows that the French are inordinately fond of the negative, even when they're saying something positive, as in "It doesn't displease me." It comes naturally for a bureaucrat to respond "No." Or: "It can't be done." Or: "It will take a long time." Or: "It's very difficult." Or: "I wouldn't count on it." The first response is often: "I don't know".

If you call someone at an office, you're likely to be told he/she is on vacation, taking a training course, on a business trip, on sick leave, or doesn't work on Wednesday afternoons because school is closed and he/she stays home with the children. If you're immensely lucky and the person answers, he's likely to tell you at two o'clock in the afternoon that he hasn't yet opened the morning mail, or that your check is signed and will go out the next day (barring vacations, business trip, sick leave, or it being a Wednesday). Ignorant of the Protestant work ethic, the French never do today what they can plan to do tomorrow. You'll never hear the words "I'll get right to it", and it would be politically incorrect for a boss to demand such a thing.

Away from Paris, I realized that many French behaviors are due to a failure to grasp the key capitalist idea that the customer is always right. After years of haggling to get my money back in France, I hesitate, even now, to make a purchase that I think I may want to return. Although I hate consumerism, in the nineties, France had still failed to grab it by the horns and turn it into a permanent milk cow.

French democracy is based on *The Declaration of the Rights of Man*, and with a dozen parties, the legislature is more representative of the population's ideological diversity than is our Congress. However, as in the U.S., but in different ways, free speech prevents the public from realizing the lack of a truly democratic process, and also as here, analyses of media pundits and academics, though often grounded in political theory, have little effect on government policy. Not surprisingly, powerful demonstrations over

issues of work, education and war counterbalance the endless rules and regulations that govern French lives.

While in the U.S. the media emphasizes fear, in France the black box is a constant reassuring hum: when in 1986 the fallout from Chernobyl blew across Europe, France was said to be untouched; when a camping site in Spain was flooded, killing almost a hundred people, safety regulations in France were claimed to be much tighter; when a pedophile ring was uncovered in Belgium, French law was touted as more protective. The two state-owned television channels took the lead, followed by the private channels that dared not upset the national apple cart. All of this tended to lull the public into believing that even if the world was going to hell in a breadbasket, somehow, chez nous everything was all right.

If there is one thing twenty-seven years in France brought home to me, it is that however glorious their past, the French had failed to realize that nothing is forever. The very things that made France so attractive for those of us who became expatriates prevented France from accepting that its time in the limelight was over. All that History! All that Gloire! All those great artists! Napoleon and the Impressionists, the cancan and Edith Piaf, Debussy and Ravel. Yes, there was still Dior and Airbus.... But if it weren't for the European Union, France would still be afraid of Germany!

One day, listening with my usual annoyance to a French orchestra playing Beethoven as if it was Debussy, I was reminded of the trip to Chamonix with Claus, when the music exhilarated us both. On an impulse I sent him a note for Christmas. About a month later he called to say he'd just opened his mail (sic) and how nice it was to hear from me. He would soon be spending a few days at his place in the fashionable mountains nearby. Would I like to drive over?

Claus's fashionable mountains being one of the few places in France I had never visited, I said of course. Another few weeks passed, then a call came on my answering machine. The next day it was Claus in person, saying he'd arrived at his mountain retreat and how about dinner the next day.

The weather was especially fine for February, and I looked forward to the drive. Claus had told me to call him when I got to the nearest village. "There's only one phone. You can't miss it." The village wasn't the usual spattering of houses along the road, but wound up a hill. Finally I came to a belvedere parking lot with a pay phone. I looked at my watch as I inserted the phone card: it was just four o'clock. After driving almost 180 kilometers, I hoped Claus would be impressed by my improbable punctuality. He told me to wait for him at the crossroads at the bottom of the hill.

After about ten minutes, a station wagon appeared across the road and a man's arm gestured 'follow'. I assumed it was Claus. We turned into a dirt road which threaded its way between woods, fields, and an occasional house. I tried to guess which one might be his, but when we arrived, what I saw was different from all the others: A one-story white stone house with orange tiled roof and large plate glass windows.

"Everything you see is mine", he said grandly, as we eyed each other getting out of our respective vehicles, he with his new beard and me with my new glasses.

I had suspected from Claus's few words over the phone that he would be alone. One of his stepdaughters was working in Copenhagen. Now, in answer to my question as to whether his wife was commuting, he said merely: "She spends a lot of time there." The low tone was new, and barred further questioning.

He offered me a drink and proposed a walk. I remembered he was a big walker. Stomping over rustling leaves with his shaggy dog, now grown old, we argued about Cuba. Claus had been back a number of times to see Fidel, and had him to dinner during his last visit to Paris, finding him in very bad health. We chatted about the Pope's trip to Cuba, and Claus poked fun at "the two old men holding each other up".

I was convinced Fidel had invited the Pope in order to prevent Raul from installing a harsher regime once he was gone. Claus countered with his usual cynicism: "Raul's not going to take over."

"What's to prevent him.?"

"The Americans."

"But if there are human rights reforms, they won't."

"Of course they will, the minute Fidel goes."

"What makes you think that?"

"I went to Cuba a few months ago with a banker who wanted to invest some money there. The Americans have passed a law that would allow the Cuban exiles to reclaim their property."

I couldn't convince Claus that not even the United States can make a law for another country. With his staunch belief in universal megalomania, he brushed reason aside and launched into an account of his work in progress, a book about the unexpected circumstances that make a battle go wrong. After our walk, he wanted me to read it, and while I sat hunched over the computer, he built a fire that roared loudly behind me. At one point I asked him a question, and he took the occasion to point out how big the fire was. The older, less exuberant Claus still needed to be admired.

I had told him that I wouldn't cook, but when he considerately asked what time I wanted to dine, adding: "Shall we have pasta or bread with the daub?", I put on the Italian pasta.

Claus apologized for wanting to keep tabs on the winter Olympics; I asked him if he still skied. "Yes, in fact I'm going tomorrow." We were standing in front of the fireplace, and he hugged me, just a bit shyly. I hadn't expected it and was moved, yet unsure of what I wanted. It had been four years since I had made love, and for the last two, surprisingly, I had ceased to mind. I enjoyed not having to think about make-up, and pushed my tendency to dress for comfort to the limit. Once in a while I had wondered how I would react if someone made a play, fearing alternately that it would disturb my equanimity or that my body would remain indifferent. On the way, I had decided I wouldn't make love with Claus just to please him.

Three and a half decades ago we had met at a check-in counter in Mexico and had a self-contained fling, two foreign journalists on a disputed island. Twenty-two years later we met again in Paris and had a more serious affair. I had appreciated Claus's maturity, and wondered why he was going through life with a sexual

handicap that could be overcome, concluding it was part of his need for stability. He had spoken of his mother, whom he visited regularly in Oslo; of his father, a general arrested in a conspiracy against Quisling; of the privations of war and his decision to emigrate at seventeen.

The phone rang stridently. It was one of Claus' daughters. At the end he said quietly: "Tell them I miss them. I miss all of you." Again I wondered at his new celibacy.

He suggested we eat by the fire and moved a table over. The fireplace was so big we could almost have sat inside. He lit three candles, but served from the pots. He'd made salad in the same bowl he'd apparently eaten from at lunch, the way I do.

After the fruit, Claus went hunting for chocolate, opening and shutting the doors of his antique painted cabinets. "I saw some in the kitchen", I volunteered, marveling for the umpteenth time how men never know where things are. We sat on the couch and munched our chocolate, and Claus drew me back against him. Again, it didn't register. But when his hands went under my cardigan, my body went into fourth gear.

I was elated that age had finally brought control to Claus' youthful vigor. He laughed, and I remembered how in Cuba he had claimed that love making was too serious for laughter. When we decided to sleep, sweetly, Claus rummaged through the house to find me an acceptable pillow, we giggled for a while, then turned out the light. Memories of a past life raced through my mind as Claus moved his leg off and on my hip, his arm on and off mine, as if to make sure I was there. The rest of the night was a series of mainly futile maneuvers to settle my body in an acceptable position, discovering that Claus was as much there when he slept as when he was awake. The bulk of the once lithe thirty year-old, its power accentuated by emphatic breathing and the assertive way he held me to him, belied the fragility I associated with sleep. Never had I experienced this sense of simultaneous abandon and authority.

At eight, Claus announced he would make tea and toast. After a breakfast punctuated by his usual journalist jokes, I went back to bed, thinking that once on the computer he wouldn't mind if

I slept. Less than two hours later, the dog started barking, and he came in to say it was almost eleven. I was reminded of a middle European housewife who, years earlier, as I slept beside my baby's crib, had announced with the same firmness: "acht und halb". Giving in to the weight of culture, I got up and announced I would shower.

"Then we can go for a walk," sentenced Claus.

In the shower, thinking about my four-thirty appointment at home and worrying about the two hour drive, I decided I had to leave immediately, hoping Claus would not feel slighted.

"I'll take you to the turn", he said matter-of-factly.

There he stopped, got out of his car, and repeated the directions through the first few villages. Waving my hand I remembered how Claus had always dashed out of my apartment in Paris with something urgent to do. I reflected that he was the only man with whom I'd slept at intervals over 36 years, and that it was a much better 'last time' than the one fate seemed to have reserved for me.

As I progressed along the near-empty road from the Vaucluse to the Var, the landscape became greener, matching my spirits. By the time I arrived home, I wondered whether, now that his stepdaughters were grown. Claus would continue on to a regretful old age. Or whether he would decide to make the most of a good thing, no matter how late it had come. No less, I wondered whether I would have the resolve not to make it my problem, content with the unexpected pleasure of a last fling. I decided those chances were fairly good, since I really didn't have any catching-up to do.

Chapter XXII - God, Otherness and Politics

During the next few years, as I savored a relatively uneventful life in a small town that was quiet enough to hear church bells on a distant hill, my bedside reading was Marcus Aurelius, Ludovico's favorite philosopher. I continued to follow world events closely, but was increasingly frustrated by the inadequacy of political theories to explain them. When a friend introduced me to the Chinese classic, *The Tao te Ching*, I discovered that Taoism shares much with the Roman Emperor's Stoicism, both of which were concerned with governance. Another friend's struggle with death reminded me that both these philosophies see death as part of life, and I began to wonder how Western religion, to which death is inextricably linked, influenced politics. In a sort of virtuous circle, I began to wonder how attitudes toward death and religion might affect the way people dealt with Otherness - and what that might mean for politics.

Around that time, in one of those serendipitous events that seem to punctuate my life, I was introduced to the French ethologist Boris Cyrulnik, whose work *Affective Nourishment* throws a crucial light on violence:

> *"Sometimes (civilization) is a fossil order structured by the immutable conviction that we must submit to a revealed truth written elsewhere, a long time ago, on a mysterious parchment, whose contents are transmitted by initiates. Those who cannot read the parchment, or refuse to submit, are considered as aggressors, to be aggressed in the most moral way so that order can reign. Creative violence, the cauldron of humanity had been born, the marvelous and the horrible had mated to produce civilization."*

Remembering how the ten-year old had been an agnostic without knowing the word, I decided to delve deeper into Cyrulnik's 'truth': how belief in God related to violence. I went back to Freud's last work, Moses, vaguely remembering it dealt with monotheism. Freud traced monotheism to Egypt, and saw it as the cause of intolerance. "With a remarkable intuition of future scientific thought Akhenaton," (who might have been Moses' contemporary) "declared solar energy to be the source of all living things, representing justice and truth... creating the first monotheistic religion."

I knew nothing about ancient Egyptian religion, but a work in the local library by the German Egyptologist Erik Hornung brought home to me the fact that worship always served power, the most important power being that over death. The Egyptian Pharaoh couldn't defeat death, but through his intermediary, the Gods saw to it that death imitated life. Even more exciting than its link to monotheism, was the fact that Egyptian religion saw evil as inherent in the nonexistent, making battle, confrontation and a questioning of the established order part of existence. There would have been no such thing as 'an evil Empire', to be defeated! Furthermore, four thousand years ago, the Egyptians knew that humans have a circular relationship to and a responsibility toward the cosmos; rigidly hierarchical Pharaonic society was all about sustainable development!

The central tenet of Egyptian life was the concept of Ma'at, which meant 'the rule', or justice. Ma'at stipulated that the Pharaoh was responsible for the well-being of his subjects, who in turn were responsible to maintain the Gods' gift of the life-giving Nile. Unlike his predecessors, Akhenaton was a logical thinker, and he decreed that because of Ma'at's centrality to life, it should be represented not by a host of idols, but by the sun, without which there was no life.

I wondered how things might have gone had it not taken more than three thousand years for science to confirm Akhenaton's insight that living things and matter are of the same essence. I mused that perhaps the reason why Western religions had not followed Akhenaton was that his successors, under pressure from the priests,

had ordered the Egyptians back to worshiping the old idols. Or perhaps it was because Akhenaton had unwittingly paved the way for Moses, then Christ, to place man and God outside of nature, separating God from man, and men from each other. It occured to me that men see themselves as created in God's image, yet the opposite is also true: like humans, God speaks, giving orders. Very differently, Akhenaton's sun was content to be, since it represented a concept, that of life, and it was the duty of the mortal Pharaoh to command the behaviors that ensured its continuity.

I then reasoned that the introduction of monotheism must have required a conceptual revolution, since worship of idols that were half-man half beast - or even worship of the sun - was unlikely to lead to the notion of supreme Otherness that we associate with God. Moses' God had first defined himself as 'He who is', which after all was not very different from 'the invisible' to which the Egyptians referred when they thought of God anthropomorphically. Maybe it was because the non-dualistic 'He who is' was two conceptual steps beyond idols (though invisible, God was a being in the image of man), that it was sacrificed to the dualistic idea that it was better to worship He who had power over the Whole, than the Whole itself. Not only was God 'other' as were idols; He, rather than a mortal pharaoh, was THE all powerful Other, and it was His ability to dominate nature that made Him so. (Although Pharaoh was the most powerful among men, he needed the intervention of the Gods to dominate nature.)

Surely, when told that they were fundamentally different from other animate beings, and that they must obey the One who, though made in their image, was the epitome of Otherness, men's relation to the universe must have changed. If God's supreme power makes Him the epitome of Otherness, should we not also fear human Others who have potential power over us?

Human others who stand in our way can be overcome by force, requiring that we entrust our fate to a powerful external authority. First God usurped the sacredness of the Whole, then the mantle of sacredness passed to God's surrogate, which no matter its form, represented external authority. With each successive

delegation of authority, each man's fear of each Other was magnified, providing what Cyrulnik described as the 'horrible' component in civilization.

Cyrulnik's point that the crucial difference between men and animals is that they are not in the same world of representation made things even more clear. A cat doesn't consider the orphans it makes when it pounces on a mouse. Similarly, God is not in the same world of representation as we are to ourselves. Western culture could have followed Akhenaton's insight about the sun, which belongs to our world of representation; instead, it separated itself from that Egyptian context, the immediacy of the Gods, and their inseparability from Nature.

A culture represents first and foremost that to which it answers, whether it be a person or an idea. And when our representation of all Others is shaped by our representation of God, our attitude toward them depends on the extent to which we feel obligated to answer to Him. A personalized God is also a way of rejecting responsibility: "It's God's will, not mine". "I'm only obeying Him".

By turning to signs, as Cyrulnik would say, instead of practicing rituals based on intuitive knowledge of the Whole, the world got dogmas and wars. Although most of today's conflicts are not about religion, the entire world is up in arms over God, thanks to films, radio and television that have spread the mindset derived from monotheism to its far corners. And what makes people feel so helpless is the instinctive knowledge that no one can win a war about God. There is an absoluteness about God that no amount of love - or power - can vanquish.

The invention of God seems to have turned awe of the Whole into fear of the superior being whose power made Him, rather than the Whole, sacred. When the Enlightenment replaced the notions of Awe and Responsibility taught by religion with those of Truth and Principles inspired by new scientific discoveries, it devalued Being in favor of Having, while failing to assuage our fear of death. No wonder the industrial revolution inspired a much quoted view of the cosmos as bleak and indifferent!

As the religious wars of the nineties raged in the former Yugoslavia, I wondered, like those around me, how the escapades of the American president could monopolize Congress. The land of my birth was ever foreign to me, and I expected to end my days in exile, as I had lived most of my life.

As the millennium drew to a close, that assurance was unexpectedly shattered. My mother found herself alone with a broken hip. My three week stay in Philadelphia was the longest since I had gone abroad at age fourteen, interrupted only by a trip to New York, where my father's second wife, Bette, had asked to see me. She had remained a friend to Howard's successive families, and I was genuinely fond of this woman who was very much her own person even as she came to terms with a final illness. Although Bette dealt in public relations, her living room on the lower East side, organized around several valuable paintings, was one of subdued elegance. As we chatted over fruit juice, she stunned me by asking my forgiveness. No one had ever done that, and nothing in our relations over the years, as I faded in and out of my father's life, had led me to imagine that his second wife could be haunted by her denunciation of my sexual initiation that had led to an absurd marriage at a time when I should have been going to school.

When I returned to Philadelphia, serendipitously, the prequel to Bette's gesture was revealed to me by my father's sister Shirley. Apparently, my parents' attempt at reconciliation in Atlantic City had been dictated by Regina's insistence that they get back together. Thus the scene on the train that had haunted me all my life had been caused unintentionally by the person I held most dear. Regina's oft-repeated assurance that she treated my mother "as though she were still married to your father" took on new meaning, and I understood why Bette had associated me with a past that was hostile to her.

I suggested that May come to live with me in France, but she could not part with her lifelong environment. Finally, not wanting to end up in a nursing home, she suggested that if I moved back to Philadelphia, I would be closer to my children, who had reclaimed their childhood. Ready to say a final adieu to France, I disposed of what was not worth transporting yet again across the Atlantic, and

three weeks later moved my mother out of a depressing retirement home. I had always told May that I would be there for her when she needed me, considering filial duty to be independent of feelings. She had not believed it, yet as soon as we moved in together, she cancelled the long-term care insurance she had been paying into for the last twenty-five years, and which she referred to vulgarly as her 'ace in the hole'.

Even as May neared death she manifested no genuine feelings for me, however much she enjoyed telling friends that I did everything for her. Her determination not to die played itself out for another six months as not going to bed until she woke up, in the wee hours, on the couch where she'd fallen asleep over the newspaper. She had degenerative heart disease, and we were told that an infection she preferred not to identify would cause her to gradually weaken until she drifted off. As a newly minted member of the Hemlock Society, I agreed with her wish not to be treated or hospitalized, and ultimately to be cremated. With the help of hospice personnel during the week she was bedridden, I was able to care for her as she'd always wanted me to since I was three years old, and her passing was as gentle as she had been brutal.

April 20, 2001

At the end of a day spent reading May's old journals, as she requested, I realize there was another meaning to the incident that followed her separation from Howard: not only was I denied my grief, but a person I loved was defined as someone who has a problem that I am expected to solve. My passion for trying to understand the world's problems and seek solutions probably owed a great deal to childhood affective problems that resulted in an ability to be at home in different cultures and to see things from different perspectives.

Last night I slept for six hours straight. Today I had another epiphany: it had never occurred to me that the three year-old actually experienced love for her mother. I had always remembered feeling sad when she came home late, but had not been in touch with the fact that I must have loved her. Perhaps because she didn't love me back, I was only aware of the hurt.

As usual, an emotion is rapidly succeeded by a thought: without the strength I had to develop to flourish without maternal love, I would not have considered it perfectly normal to be on my own at age fourteen, in a foreign land. I feel close to tears over this breakthrough, vulnerable for perhaps the first time in my life.

Chapter XXIII - God, the New Science and Politics

Calculating that by continuing to live frugally, I could manage for as long as my health allowed me a productive and relatively pain-free life, I wrote full-time to complete the book begun in France. Unlike most contributions to the religion vs. science debate that was developing in the United States in the early two thousands, the work eventually published under the title *A Taoist Politics: The Case for Sacredness* leads to a different way of thinking about politics. I worked on this manuscript longer than any other, but the unfamiliar material was incredibly exciting, starting with my discovery of the eminent biologist, Lynn Margulis, who in *What is Life?*, written with her son Dorian Sagan, paid tribute to Akhenaton:

> *"Ancient religious intuitions that considered terrestrial creatures, especially man, to be children of the sun were far nearer the truth than is thought by those who see earthly beings as simply ephemeral creations arising from the blind and accidental interplay of matter and forces..."*

Like the cherry on the cake for me, Margulis and Sagan also drew attention to the man who, in the sixteenth century, revived Akhenaton's vision of the Cosmos. The Italian monk Giordano Bruno displeased the Inquisition as much as Akhenaton had his own priests, and the Church burned him at the stake for insisting that life comes from the sun:

> *"Espousing a Pantheistic perspective in which God, life and mind were part of an ever-changing universe, Bruno even thought distant worlds might harbor intelligent beings.*

The same Christian view that Bruno defied holds firm today: God is as superior to the universe as mind is to matter, or soul is to body. Flesh, a necessary evil, is unclean; only spirit is pure....Bruno blended matter with energy, finite with infinite, world with God."

Margulis and Sagan also wrote: "Life is not merely matter, but matter energized, matter organized...." What was 'matter organized'? I had been scientifically challenged from the time I encountered algebra, but I was determined to understand this term. Had not the physicist Fritjof Capra written a book called *The Tao of Physics?*

Though I had not been captivated by Capra's book in the seventies, I resolutely confronted Gary Zukav's *Dancing Wu Li Masters*, which also deals with the commonalities between the new physics and Taoism. Luckily, Zukav made the laws of physics so amusing that it almost didn't matter how complex they were. These laws show that in a circular, counterbalancing world, there is no life without death, no pleasure without pain - and no final victory, and to me, these laws suggested a new way to think about politics.

Bruno had anticipated the discovery by modern physics that all living things are systems, and by now it is an accepted notion that just about anything humans create is a system: a motor is a system, families are systems, and so are governments and their relationships. The systemic relationship between heat, energy and work is elucidated by the science of thermodynamics, and because all systems operate on the basis of energy, its laws are ubiquitous in modern science. In closed systems (such as an engine), as energy is consumed, the amount available for work diminishes until the system reaches a point of entropy, also known as equilibrium, disorder, or death. When you hook up the gas pump, you turn the closed system that is your automobile into one which is 'open' to its environment, enabling it to import new supplies of energy, (and less

desirably, export its waste), thus creating a new state of order and work.

Systems show that we cannot possibly control events, since each interaction spawns a host of other interactions. And just as Werner Heisenberg's law of uncertainty says we cannot both predict where a moving body is headed and at what velocity, we cannot predict when a system is going to bifurcate, or what will happen when it does. When we call on the Judeo-Christian God, we are assuming He is part of a closed system, in which, in defiance of the second law of thermodynamics, things continue on instead of inevitably running down, providing certainty in defiance of Heisenberg's uncertainty principle. Whether we see God as part of our system, fixing everything, or of another system that provides our energy, we are positing a hierarchical relationship that leads to more separation and domination, rather than circular interactions that engender peaceful change.

In physics, 'order' and 'disorder' do not have the colloquial meaning we associate with these words. Also counterintuitively, it is 'chaos' (or rather its edge), that can lead open systems to bifurcate to a higher level of order. Two crucial elements in this process are feedback, in which the effects of inputs 'feed' back to modify the original situation, and catalysts, which speed up that process. Change occurs when a catalyst accelerates the flow of energy through a system until it reaches a tipping point, or bifurcation, that will create a new system, order, or life.

I had used the concept of systems to imagine a new kind of relationship between the Soviet Union and the entities that surrounded it, including Europe. The laws of the new physics suggest that problems between nations could best be addressed within the context of their circular, interdependent relationships than by linear, tit for tat exchanges that are the first steps toward armed conflict. (Another law of physics states that the direction of time is always forward, and this is probably why hopes of avoiding a full-blown conflict, as presently in Syria, are invariably illusory: once the energy in a system begins to accelerate, nothing can stop it.)

Sovietologists were unable to predict the end of the Cold War, not because they lacked information, but because they did not see discrete events as part of a systemic process. Mistaking a steady state for an immutable one, the West believed that the Soviet system would last forever. In desperation, it increased exchange programs, radio broadcasts, rock concerts, etc. These 'energy' inputs from outside the system gradually modified elements within the system via feedback - some, such as coca-cola and blue jeans, even acting as catalysts. As a result, the Soviet Union and its satellites in Eastern Europe eventually reached a tipping point (epitomized by the fall of the Berlin Wall), whence they bifurcated to a more ordered, complex society that gradually settled into a steady state.

In the late nineteen-nineties, Prime Minister Sharon's visit to the Al Aqsa mosque was the catalyst that rapidly increased the flow of negative energy into the Israeli/Palestinian system of relations, causing the relatively steady state that had existed for some time to accelerate to a tipping point that eventually burst into the second intifada. Similarly, the increased flow of energy introduced into Iraq by the U.S. invasion upset the fluctuating but relatively steady state of relationships among Sunnis and Shi'as. The ensuing violence can be expected to subside either when, through feedback, either the positive effects of the occupation,or the U.S. pullout, give rise to a locally directed process toward a functioning civil society.

The war in Syria is the ultimate example of a catalyst - American involvement in the Middle East - driving a system toward a bifurcation whose outcome no one can predict. Syria is the only secular Arab country, and although it has long been a dictatorship, unlike those which the United States supports, it is not a capitalist dictatorship. The ruling Ba'ath Party is a socialist party that promotes a modern role for women and a secular education system modeled on that of France, which previously had ruled Syria as a protectorate. Not surprisingly, the ruling family's Alawite form of Shi'ism is the most modern version of Islam, involving a personal form of worship that incorporates rituals from other religions. These facts go far toward explaining Syria's alliance with Hezbollah in neighboring Lebanon, of which more later. Unfortunately for

Syrians, their country also borders on Israel, which is now committed to global financial capitalism. While I do not doubt the relevance of Syria's alliance with Iran in Western meddling, I believe the campaign against Iran's nuclear program itself is also strongly related to the socialist orientation of that regime, however much its original ethos may have been compromised since it came to power more than thirty years ago. A book called *Democracy in Iran* by Vali Nasr and Ai Gheissari provides a history of left-wing movements in Iran that takes even well informed Americans by surprise.

American ignorance of the historical presence of socialist and communist parties in the Arab world is similar to its ignorance of the pervasiveness of socialist thought in Europe, Russia and China, and accounts for its inability to sort out the Arab Spring. During the Cold War it was widely believed that the Third World was in a state of political backwardness, flirting with socialism only to obtain Soviet support. We had and still have no inkling of the ideological ferment that continued uninterrupted during the twentieth century everywhere but in the United States.

Our economy and form of government have consistently been at the service of Having, while the socialist ethos comes closer to the pursuit of Being. For socialists, the outcomes of political processes are either altruistic or egotistical, corresponding to Taoism's Yin/Yang. When outcomes favor the Yang components of human nature - power, greed, selfishness, as opposed to its Yin components - non-differentiation of the Other, generosity, altruism - having for healthy survival becomes Having for having's sake, and instead of a natural, open-system process of alternation between the two political tendencies, we get a wasteful, closed-system process of increasing accumulation that, as the biologist Lynn Margulis says, must end in entropy and thermodynamic death.

The physicist Carl Bohm's statement that order/disorder 'is the way things are' is, for me, as irrefutable as the Hindu *tat tvam asi,* that art thou - or Ram Dass's 'what can't be said can't be whispered either'. Although I was unaware of all this when as a young mother living in Eastern Europe I thought about remaining connected to the world, I was in fact intuiting thermodynamics. I

condemned a desire for the kind of stability that means immobility. Now I know that healthy stability implies a 'steady state', one 'just-far-enough-from equilibrium' to avoid both entropy (death), and the bifurcations that can result from an uncontrollable flow of energy through the system. My desire to find a place to bring up my child while remaining linked to the world was an aspiration for "the magic moment in the vibrant regime of order/disorder, which is poised far from equilibrium at the edge of chaos.... where cognition and autopoiesis take place", as I would later write in *A Taoist Politics*. Capitalist systems tend to favor immobility, while leftwing ideologies are interested in change. (And yet, the fact that order/disorder is the way things are explains the failings of both 'real socialism' and unregulated capitalism.)

The Egyptian belief that evil existed even before the Gods is another way of saying that disorder - or death - is a permanent feature of life, which we can only try to manage. I believe a shift toward this world-view that could gradually replace religion with the realization of the sacredness of the Whole is already under way. Awareness of the basic laws of physics and biology can contribute to this shift. They prove that mass and energy are one, that waves and particles are one. And in the same way that Yin and Yang are one, science comes ever closer to proving that mind and matter are one. When these findings become common knowledge, reasonably intelligent believers of all religions could realize that they foreclose the likelihood of God, and begin to focus on preserving what God supposedly created. Instead of wasting energy fighting creationism, secularists could point out that God is simply another word for order/disorder. After all, He is both good and evil; He has created a wondrous world for us to enjoy - and ethnic cleansing; and he rewards dishonesty, scorning the righteous. As I suspected long ago, prayer really is useless because power over order and disorder is an illusion.

What is significant is not that politics is a dirty business, or even that power corrupts; it's that life proceeds via both competition and cooperation. And while political systems may be physically open systems that undergo change, they tend to be psychologically closed,

exclusionary systems, based on the double internal/external, us/them dichotomy, which does not favor equity. For a political system to remain just far enough from equilibrium to flourish, wealth has to be distributed relatively fairly, keeping oligarchy in check. When political systems fail to implement necessary change through peaceful alternations, catalysts arise to move things along, and bifurcations take the shape of revolt by those who produce the wealth that maintains the oligarchs.

Bt what about self-organization? In the seventies, the biologists Francisco Varela and Umberto Maturana had concluded that life consists not of things, as we had always thought, but of processes, in particular the process of self-making, for which they coined the word autopoiesis. In Fritjof Capra's sculptured definition, autopoiesis is: "a network pattern in which the function of each component is to participate in the production or transformation of other components". The phenomenon of network patterns processing information to further self-organization, or autopoiesis, is also known as cognition. And lo, cognition takes places when a system is in the magic realm of the steady state! How could anyone not find this is more exciting than religion?

As I was working these ideas through, *The Economist's* review of biologist Stuart Kauffman's *At Home in the Universe* made me suspect that this work also contained something my scientifically-challenged mind had to know. Kauffman's writing was so skillful that I managed to understand his message: the new biology reveals that human life was not an accident: we are part of the universe. (This may sound trite, but for some reason, that information eliminated a life-long tendency to experience anxiety.)

In the eighties, the new physics and biology persuaded the British cosmobiologist James Lovelock that the biosphere itself is a living entity. He named it Gaia, and his book *The Practical Science of Planetary Medicine* is a stunning pictorial illustration of how the biosphere works. Just as there is a symbiotic relationship between an organism's operating system and its environment, there is also one between humans and the biosphere. Lovelock's fear is not that human activity will destroy the earth, but that it will render it

inhospitable to human life. The planet will endure, but humans may not. While governments appear oblivious to Lovelock's warning, unpublicized programs exploring the possibility of space colonization show they are aware of the outcome he fears. As I finish this book, a planet that could perhaps support life has been identified.

But is this really our only hope? Will we have to abandon the planet? In humans, as opposed to other living things, the process of self-making is partly conscious, and that means that uniquely among all living entities, we are responsible for our fate. As the Egyptians knew instinctively, we have an existential obligation to preserve the Whole of which we are a part. Western hustle and bustle, the multi-tasking that drive us to aloneness or superficial relationships as we overrun everything in our path, may never allow us to reach the next evolutionary stage, when we acknowledge the needs of other living beings, including the biosphere.

Margulis wrote that "life as matter with needs inseparable from its history must maintain and perpetuate itself, swim or sink," echoing Lovelock's warning that we must devise a form of economic life less likely to render the planet inhospitable to us. Part of that effort would be to promote the concept of the sacredness of Being as opposed to the sacredness of God. Just because religions are an amalgam of beautiful ideas and absurd beliefs is no reason to deny people's need for a sense of the sacred. The sacred is defined as something worthy of absolute respect, an absolute value. As elucidated by modern science, the grandeur of the cosmos commands awe and absolute respect, and thus can rightly be called sacred. When I felt at one with the summer storm on Regina's porch, I was experiencing the sacred. When I pondered over the possible meaning of prayers in Regina's synagogue, I was not.

The sacredness of the Wholeis related to the concept of Oneness, and the Tao te Ching is its canon:

> *"The Tao gives birth to One*
> *One gives birth to Two*

two gives birth to Three
All things have their backs to the female
and Stand facing the male.
When male and female combine
All things achieve harmony
But the Master makes use of it
Embracing his aloneness, realizing
He is one with the universe."

The idea of Oneness has been around since men began reflecting on the nature of the universe and their place in it, and I believe it is more compatible with the modern ethos than the Judeo-Christian injunction to conquer nature. As expressed by modern science, Oneness could help us move away from the notion of Supreme Other incarnated in God, and thus from our inherent fear of all Others. Oneness can lead each person wherever he chooses, allowing non believers to find delight - and thereby serenity - in the existence of an all-embracing Cosmos that requires neither guru nor trimmings, and believers to realize that all religions are founded on the same basic insight, mysticism, which involves an individual's internal authority.

Our internal authority constitutes our only true freedom, and is intrinsic to consciousness, cognition and autopoiesis, which are the essence of both Man and the Cosmos. Unlike consciousness, through which each individual partakes of the Whole and of each Other, conscience is that which differentiates one individual from another. When conscience is seen as part of a mind/body dualism, it removes the individual ever further from the Whole. But when it is part of an all-embracing Consciousness, it replaces Otherness by Oneness.

The idea of internal freedom or authority, often expressed as the belief that neither prison nor dictatorship can take away our thoughts and beliefs, has been held by many rebels, but in modern times it has become associated with God and country, (Gott mit uns, In God we Trust.) The more direct the link between our rulers and

God, the more absolute the rulers' power. Louis XIVth was merely a ruler by divine right, compared to Akhenaton, who was the earthly incarnation of the sun. Today's rulers have convinced us that after a century of ideological confrontation, we must now accept a century of religious strife. Embodied in the notion of sovereignty as well as in religion, Otherness has become a permanent cause of violence. The fact that freedom of conscience is the basis of the secular state fails to prevent men from hating each other because they see God differently. We need to allow ancient intuitions, reflected by modern science, to confirm the link between religion and politics, and halt our rush to annihilation.

Once people became aware of their internal authority, they should be able to accept the fact that their lives consist of order/ disorder relieved by bifurcations, without having to subject themselves to God-inspired external authorities and their inevitable abuses. Through education to Otherness, we could transform closed systems into open systems, where cognition, or the processing of information, would restore individual authority and allow us to steer the world toward preferred outcomes, all the while knowing that no outcome will be permanent. The Occupiers and the 99% are already reclaiming the individual internal authority that fosters decentralization and a lessening of the ultimate external authority, that of the state.

Undeniably, when individuals are fortified by a religious idea, they feel invincible. But the fact that each individual is consciousness, and therefore linked to the Whole, is a stronger idea than the fact that each individual has two eyes and warm blood. And knowing that God (the Buddha, Shiva, the Atman), is in each of us, we would neither hate nor fear the Other. With Otherness attenuated, the freedom that is inside each of us would flourish. Each of us would be 'grounded', or reassured, in the knowledge that he is part of an infinite Whole. My internal freedom would be my ground, the Other's internal freedom his ground, and both could sit as lilies on a pond.

Chapter XXIV - America Revisited

[Photo by Fred Rose, 2010]

Since my return I have been drawing on my life experience to try to understand how the notion of freedom became distorted, as conscience and consciousness drifted apart. I had seen from other vantage points how two oceans kept America isolated from the centuries of give and take between neighbors on other continents. How we remained alone and proud of it, interacting with the rest of the world only to ensure that it served our needs, bought our products and agreed with our definition of freedom. Now we are more alone than we realize, as the rest of the world coalesces around the urgent tasks of the 21st century.

Reading various works on American history, my favorite being Howard Zinn's *People's History of the United States,* I realized that in the course of our 400 year history, the stunning wealth available from our natural environment had transformed the

United States from a society concerned with equal opportunity to one in which the notion of equity is anathema. In the U.S., the subject of equity is avoided, while religion colors many conversations. In Europe religion is never talked about, but questions of equity are the focus of serious discourse. I believe that both the global religious revival and the proliferation of conflicts are partly a consequence of America's failure to move from all-out competition to equity.

As revolutionaries, we were 'patriots'; in the nineteenth century, the egalitarian autonomy required on the frontier fostered entrepreneurship, while the less daring became 'wage earners'. By the time we became 'citizens', the heritage of self-reliance had transformed government into a tool of capital. Instead of solidarity among our citizens, nationalism in the face of an imagined Soviet threat brought us the Reagan Revolution and neo-conservatism, which anointed us as 'consumers'. Finally we got Wall Street Wizards who turned us into debt-ridden 'taxpayers'.

As the latest elections have shown, we are only 'citizens' when we vote, and if services are not profitable, 'we' don't get them, because they cost 'taxpayers' too much. We tout individual well-being, yet the notion of each person's intrinsic worth, based on his internal authority or conscience, is ignored. Not only have we eliminated the individual's say in how our money is spent, we have accepted that we cannot afford solidarity to ourselves. After more than fifty years of leftwing systems in Europe, Americans are still told that only market capitalism is compatible with individual freedom. So we rely on volunteers for services that should be the responsibility of government, while right wing propaganda fosters a lazy attitude among government employees, reinforcing the impression that it is wasteful. Our two hundred year old constitution, amended only twenty-seven times, has been rendered almost moot, beginning with a 19th century Supreme Court clerk's stroke of the pen that granted corporations the advantages of personhood. Money and perks are used the world over to make government responsive to certain interests, but in no other country has this practice been legalized.

In the 19th century journalists still spoke their minds, but under the notion 'All the News that's Fit to Print' the press was tamed, and a clever feedback loop was created: things foreign were branded as either inferior or threatening, and questions about the lack of international news were answered with finality that 'the American public is not interested in foreign affairs'. Enchanted by cinematography, which makes the most unlikely fantasies seem real, Americans have abandoned most of their internal authority to the daily spin devised to save them from the big bad world of solidarity. The fairy tale of exceptionalism that has kept us behind the rest of the developed world in terms of solidarity is to Americans what seventy-four Virgins are to Islamists. Still evoking its civilizing mission after dozens of wars, America can neither recognize the new constellations abroad, nor implement urgent reforms at home.

Legislation that deprives children of illegal immigrants born in the United States of citizenship is dictated by the fear of Others inscribed in our country's genes: Not only did the Pilgrims exile religious dissidents from their colonies, suspicion of sympathy for a foreign power became the object of legislation as early as 1798, with the four *Aliens and Seditions Acts*. In 1917, Congress passed another *Sedition Act*, and in 1918 it passed the *Espionage and Aliens Act*. In 1938, even before McCarthy's time, these documents led to the creation of the infamous *House un-American Activities Committee*, known as HUAC which he exploited so well.

The progressive movement that came into its own with the fight against slavery was a victim of that trajectory. President Franklin Roosevelt was a member of the upper class, but like Lenin, Mao and later, the Castro brothers, he knew that robber baron capitalism was leaving too many people out in the cold. In response, a corporate-owned press conflated his *New Deal* with socialism, and socialism with 'foreign', strengthening right-wing resistance to all things progressive. During the Second World War, Europeans knew that communists and socialists were in the forefront of the fight against fascism, while in America these ideologies were viewed as scarcely lesser evils than Nazi Germany.

After the defeat of fascism abroad, the United States was forced by the military-industrial complex to rev up for the Cold War, laying the groundwork for a new kind of fascism at home. The paranoia that defines the United States could have faded during the rebellious sixties, but the flamboyant raiments of the counter-culture's political message only succeeded in fanning the flames until it was 'born again' under the neo-conservatives. Although the rest of the world has always known that fascism unabashedly serves the few, while socialism is at least intended to serve the many, the American press continues to deliberately confound the two, favoring the corporate takeover of the American government that accelerated after 9/11. Communism imposed itself in Russia because the moderates failed to act when the industrial revolution brought intolerable living conditions to the Russian people. Fascism was a lethal reaction to non-democratic socialism, putting the industrial oligarchs in charge. The current weakness of America's moderates could lead to the same succession of tragedies that followed that of the Russian moderates a century ago.

Instead of saying that September 11th was God's punishment for our sins, we could see this catastrophe as a major bifurcation that capped decades of American intrusion into the Muslim world. Since its founding, Israel's refusal to grant the Palestinians a state has stoked Middle Eastern opposition to America as successor to Britain's imperial presence and cultural ikon. After the fall of the Soviet bloc, with the Israeli-Palestinian conflict unresolved, it was inevitable that there would be a full-blown conflict with Islam. Our focus on Bin Laden prevented us from seeing that he was merely a catalyst, as the flow of energy accelerated toward a tipping point that became an excuse for a 'war on terror', which in reality is a war over oil and equity.

We need to find ways to constantly counterbalance the competing claims of our societies. Stuart Kauffman describes three possible states that they can be in: one of equilibrium, one of near equilibrium - both of these being closed systems - and a far-from-equilibrium, open state that takes energy from outside and evolves toward a new dynamic regime, and this would apply as well to the

world system. Paraphrasing Kauffman's formula, from the seemingly haphazard 'edge of chaos' created by energy flows, an open system can bifurcate to a new, ordered regime, where poor compromises are found quickly (totalitarianism), or a chaotic regime where no compromise is found (revolution). In the periods during which counterbalancing enables the system to maintain a steady state, relatively good compromises can be achieved, and this is democracy. Liberal market democracy is a constant oscillation between the rigidity of oligarchy and the lack of cohesion that plagues a multiparty system. But while it ensures peaceful alternations of power, it does not solve the problem of equity, because those alternations are between competing interest groups that exclude the majority of citizens. And a world dominated by global financial capitalism is a disaster waiting to happen.

Sixty years after Israel's founding, inspired by its refusal to grant the Palestinians a state, Muslims, who constitute one fourth of the world's population, are demanding a fair deal for all peoples. Few Americans seem to know that Muslims include Sunni, Shi'a, Baa'thists, nationalists, and secular socialists. Or that both the Sunni Hamas and the Shi'a Hezbollah have gained popular support by doing the same things that Cuba's guerrillas did, helping the poor in their daily lives, while struggling for independence from other countries. The fact that the Arab Spring has led to increasing cooperation on the world stage by these armed groups belonging to the to main antagonistic forms of Islam tells us that equity is indeed beginning to supersede religious differences.

Alastair Crooke's account of current Shi'a thinking in *Resistance: The Essence of the Islamist Revolution*, shows that its leaders are surprisingly conversant with Western political ideas, and that Shi'ism is as much about equity as is the socialist tradition. Why condemn Muslims for believing that it is God's will that they treat each other with equity, justice and compassion? (And who can say where the American Black community would be today were it not for its churches?)

Unlike traditional Marxists, Hezbollah's leader Nasrallah calls for the same 'flat systems and independent minds' later

espoused by the Occupy Movement, claiming they enabled his troops to defeat Israel in 2006. Increasingly, Arab youth reject the marginal status of women, are anti-consumerist and anti-elite. No less significantly, China's support for Iran is not only about oil: There are similarities between the Confucian tradition of virtuous leaders and Shi'a defense of the underdog, and it is the social democratic version of liberal democracy that is most compatible with Confucian China, as well as with the Muslim ideal of an egalitarian umma. But Americans are told none of this.

Some American CEOs do realize that their profits are obscene, and that they must find innovative ways to spread the wealth. But meanwhile, climate change is catching up with us, and even in a second and last term, Obama will not be able to put Humpty-Dumpty together unless he is allowed to tell us that we must scale back 'growth', making products that can be fixed instead of junked in order to achieve a fairer distribution of wealth worldwide.

For progressive change to happen, the left must be sufficiently united to increase the flow of energy through the system that leads to bifurcations. Because the outcome of a bifurcation cannot be known in advance, the not unreasonable fear that we could end up with either fascism or anarchy largely discouraged united action until the fall of 2011 when the Occupy Movement was born, spanning the arc from liberals to anarchists.

Rebecca Solnit correctly identifies anarchy with direct democracy, but few Americans are taught that both socialism and anarchy are about individual responsibility (which I call internal authority). What American leaders disparagingly call 'mob rule', is in reality a coming together of many individual authorities. Mobs can be manipulated by dictators, but they can also oust them. And what else are efforts in favor of decentralization and local decision making, if not recognition of the need for individual responsibility, and hence the crucial role of internal authority? President Bush's 2006 evisceration of the Posse Comitatus Act of 1878 that prohibits use of the military in domestic law enforcement paved the way for military weapons such as drones to be used by police to disrupt

constitutionally guaranteed demonstrations, while the FBI, also in contradiction to the law, helps local police spy on citizens. The 99% are overcoming the fear that has kept them paralyzed for decades.

Perhaps the most significant change to have occured since I first returned from France twelve years ago is that torture, spying and police brutality are increasingly routine tools for dealing with bigger and denser populations, tailored to what each polity will tolerate. And this reveals another, little recognized reality: international leaders are in fact members of the same club. Though they may threaten one other, they agree on the need to keep their respective subjects in line. Jared Diamond's *Guns, Germs and Steel* brought the word kleptocracy into our vocabulary with a definition for all times: "The difference between a kleptocrat and a wise statesman...is merely one of degree: a matter of just how large a percentage of the tribute extracted from producers is retained by the elite, and how much the commoners like the public uses to which the redistributed tribute is put." I would add that kleptocracy is an inherent manifestation of closed systems, and that nationalism increases its abuse to the limit that the collective manifestation individual authorities permits.

I'm convinced that fundamental change will not occur in the United States thanks to the reelection of a supremely intelligent and when necessary ruthless president. It will come only if a solid majority of voters overcome a carefully nurtured, long-standing prevention against the state. Rather than a pariah that feeds off its citizens, government must be viewed as the means by which the solidarity of the community toward the individual is implemented. Creativity is capitalism's greatest claim to superiority, but no country has achieved a fair distribution of wealth without government involvement.

A few years ago, Thom Geohagan detailed the German blueprint for social democracy, the best redistributive system humans have so far known, in *Were You Born on the Wrong Continent*, and recently Richard D. Wolffe penned the book I had been waiting for, a modern Marxist critique of capitalism that recognizes the crucial role of the Occupy Movement. Both these

contributions to the national debate were ignored by the mainstream media. And yet, on the ruins of the Second World War, our foremost ally the British monarchy, adopted 'The Welfare State', with the other countries of Western Europe following suit, their governments alternating between the owners of capital and the defenders of workers. While all this was going on, the Scandinavian countries extended the Protestant notion of responsibility to the political sphere, transforming themselves into social democracies that make room for the both the creativity of capitalism, and the equality sought by communism. Unsurprisingly, they provide a number of envoys to strife-torn regions all out of proportion to their population.

As increasing numbers of Americans realize that both America's mainstream parties obey the same masters, it will not suffice for the Progressive Caucus to present an alternative 'People's Budget' inspired by the Occupy Movement. Its members need to leave the Democratic Party for the long dormant Social Democratic Party, just as the Tea Partiers, for all intents and purposes, split from the Republican Party. A 'really existing' Social Democratic Party standing up to the Tea Party would enable the United States to rein in the financial sector that created the present crisis and allow Americans to finally enjoy the system of government under which the majority of developed nations flourish. A twenty-first century Social Democratic Party would also foster decentralized, do-it-yourself solutions, such as those initiated by the Occupy Movement.

Our confrontation with militant Islam is nothing compared to the unintended consequences of travel and climate change. We are in a race against the clock, nearing what may be the planet's tolerance for our bungling. The new voters of the world want to save it from a climate catastrophe, but captive of the military/corporate complex, Obama is no more able to hear their pleas than those of financially burdened students or workers.

Our President is perhaps not weak, but supremely cognizant of the price others have paid for challenging America's carved-in-stone impediments to change. A Social Democratic majority would push for adoption of the program to limit carbon emission to 350 parts per million, as leading environmentalists recommend, before it

is too late to save the planet. Recognizing that governments will have to relinquish a part of their sovereignty to a supranational organization that can act quickly and effectively on a host of issues, America could begin to grant the United Nations the powers of an incipient world government whose need is recognized by many. For that power to enhance equity while saving the planet, a reconstructed U.N. will have to become the modern equivalent of a universal umma, where decisions are made among equals.

But other actors, too, are now required, to discipline the financial sector, as the economies of the developed world teeter, with worldwide repercussions. The scary truth is that we seem to have no more control over the financial crisis than we have over the climate. As extraordinary rains killed hundreds in southern Russia and Beijing, the American Midwest suffered its worst drought in fifty years, and wild fires ravaged the West. On the eve of the Presidential election, New York city and its surrounding area were ravaged by a hurricane rendered more deadly than ever by a warming Atlantic Ocean. As parts of the Big Apple lost power for a week and the subway system was flooded, rating agencies downgraded Germany's powerhouse economy, and the people of twenty European countries staged demonstrations and strikes on the same day.

It would have been unthinkable ten years ago, when Europeans began to share a common currency after so many wars among themselves, that the Eurasian peninsula could again be plunged into conflict. And yet, as anti-immigrant Nazi parties gain voters, the financially devastated 99% of southern Europe compare Germany's reluctance to help with Hitler's attempt to rule the continent by force, in a sinister replay of the early twentieth century events that led to the Second World War.

At least these unprecedented events have paved the way for the right question to be asked: What kind of economy and society could we build on the ruins of the old that would preserve the planet as fit for human habitation? While neither Amy Goodman on *Democracy Now* nor the well-intentioned anchors at *MSNBC* can bring themselves to pronounce the words social democracy, braver left-wing writers such as Chris Hedges and Thom Hartmann have

taken refuge on *Russia Today's* English channel, available on public television. Known discretely as 'RT', it broadcasts news ignored by most American media while exposing our flaws to the five continents.

I can't help thinking that the Russian government is at least partly inspired to fund this venture by memories of *The Voice of America* and *Radio Free Europe* beaming America's view of the world to the Soviet Union and its satellite countries in Eastern Europe for decades. Another explanation for RT's left-leaning political line is that although both Russia and China have espoused entrepreneurship, they retain the socialist peace ethos, as evidenced in their opposition to America's Middle East wars and their support for Iran's obstreperous Ahmedinejad, who laces his interviews with calls for world government.

I hope that some day progressives the world over will repocgnize that the ground of morality and hence of political responsibility, lies in Being with the Whole – our planet. While striving for peace, they would know that peace is always threatened, since it consists in the balancing of a steady state between disorder and death, and the unpredictable order that emerges from bifurcations. Then they would realize that the job of politics, rather than to substitute one group of rulers for another, is to enable citizens to select the least corruptible leaders, and for political activists to fulfill the role of watchdog.

Fear of Others creates the conflict over Having that imperils Being. But the belief in God that encourages that fear can be transformed into recognition of the on-going phenomenon of order/disorder that humans can influence, though not determine. Maybe it's because politics grew out of religion and philosophy that activists still tend to think exclusively in ideological terms, instead of analyzing power and its processes in systemic terms. The Tea Party's reinterpretation of our founding documents harks back to the victory of the moderate Enlightenment that defended church and monarchy over the radical Enlightenment that called for people's power and solidarity. Two hundred years later it is the radical Enlightenment espoused by the French Revolution that inspires people across the

world rather than the moderate one that inspired the American system.

Since my return I have experienced Americans as the most generous people on earth, yet tragically, fairy tales prevent our leaders from adapting an equitable form of government. As the conflict between the few and the many becomes global, lack of information allows Americans to believe that they can 'get the job (of foreign regime change) done', in the face of near-global opposition. The question is whether America will continue to view the world as a closed system destined to experience ever-increasing violence, or join the emerging players to foster an open system that will permit civilization to reach the higher level of organization that corresponds to equitable development.

Chapter XXV - Our Lives in the World

[First school]

Soon after my return to Philadelphia, I had driven by the house in Oak Lane where May and I had lived with Jake and Rose when I was a child. One day on a hunch, I followed Chelten Avenue, where I lived with May until her death, sensing that it would eventually lead to 19th and Ogontz. My stomach tightened when in the distance I saw the water tower on my first school, just across the street from Jake and Rose's house. Realizing that for the past year my childhood had lain in wait at the other end of the street reminded me of visits to Paris after moving to Italy, when I was unable to situate well-known places with respect to each other, although Paris is literally studded with landmarks.

Howard's desertion was also associated with these streets where May and I had lived with Jake and Rose, and now I realized

why the sight of Philadelphia's row houses was no longer distasteful, as it had been on the visits that punctuated my exile. It had to do with the fact that the words 'my country' are about childhood. Emigrants return to their place of birth to die, not for love of country, but for love of their childhood, which ultimately forms the core of their being. The ugly streets of Oak Lane and Overbrook, where I spent an unhappy childhood, revealed themselves as the oldest in a succession of sites discovered, lost and refound.

Contrasting those places with the myriad of those that followed, I suddenly understood that it is because of childhood's powerful hold that nationalism is so difficult to eradicate. Having witnessed anti-Americanism almost everywhere I lived, when George Bush was 'elected', I was frustrated at not being able to convince my compatriots how badly we looked to the rest of the world. When September 11th came, I was not surprised. The intelligence sophistication I had observed in the seventies had failed to reach larger swathes of Americans, as neo-conservatism increasingly restricted their horizons. I returned to my old school with a large Norman Rockwell poster that had belonged to May, showing people of all faiths and colors. I hoped my gift would contribute to an acceptance of Otherness that could make Americans less unpopular in the world.

Americans are only now being told that their country is seen by others as a threat, but I know from a lifetime of living abroad that this is not a passing fad. Since the end of the Second World War, anti-Americanism has never been far below a surface admiration, as we bungy-jumped our way around the world after saving it, failing to realize that the world includes a multitude of others who do not want the complete package we've created.

When I left the United States at fourteen, I held the common sense conviction that Americans didn't have all the answers. Half a century later, I found a country fighting yesterday's battles with tomorrow's weapons which, in the hands of unscrupulous leaders, have become today's catastrophes. My personal rug has not been pulled out from under me, as I once feared, but my country is driving the world toward a perilous bifurcation which no one can control. At

this pivotal moment I can only hope that more Americans will reclaim their inner freedom and take on responsibilities too long left to God and presidents.

Moving from domination to self-making will require us to see the world in terms of processes amenable solely to counter-balancing, understanding, like the Taoists, that acceptance of otherness means practicing an inclusive, open politics that replaces combat with tending-toward outcomes. At the end of this long journey, I worry that as we continue to prize Having, in a linear, tit for tat mindset that provokes conflict with the Other, we will not experience the circle that allows us to Be with the Whole, tending toward order but recognizing, like the Egyptians, that it is inseparable from disorder.

To create a political framework capable of moving the world toward desired outcomes, we would need to merge the physicists arrow of time that represents the forward direction of events, and the circular alternation of order/disorder. Because insufficiently counter-balanced forward motion results in bifurcations whose results cannot be predicted, we need to create decision-making systems that reflect individual internal authority, using technology to translate ancient tribal modes into modern forms.

Americans are increasingly hearing that progress is not a right/left issue. I disagree, because understanding that the absolute nature of Being applies to life in all its forms, and situating Being above the excessive Having that sooner or later leads to non-Being, requires cooperation rather than competition. A middle way between the Western impetus to solve problems, and what is seen as Eastern passivity, is the awareness that opposites grow out of each other. Knowing that we can only do our best to steer our lives toward preferred outcomes, individuals can make choices that tend toward the moral imperative of maintaining all of life.

Fidel used to say that when the revolution was won, men would find other challenges. But nothing is ever won for good, and when the human need for challenge is combined with the conviction that the Other is evil, we get war or terrorism, depending on the context.

Perhaps it's just a pipe-dream to think that this way of looking at Otherness, Being and Having can make a difference in a world undergoing so much change. Maybe I'm just rationalizing, yet when I become mesmerized by the dramatic parade of events on my TV screen, I remind myself that these challenges are merely manifestations of order/disorder. The essence of power is the same always and everywhere, humans are fundamentally the same everywhere, and so is the human condition, which is why similar actions take place under all latitudes, provoking similar counteractions.

September, 2009

> *I dreamt that I was at the Saudi court, which was undergoing some kind of attack, and somehow I was telling Prince Abdullah that it would bring great glory on Islam if the leader of the country in which the Holy shrine of Mecca was located would declare to the world that the only way for humanity to survive would be to change its lifestyle, starting with its use of oil and its relationship to the environment.*

Finally, I've come to believe that the problem of survival is linked to the way we understand happiness. In Budapest, I blamed schools for putting an end to childhood. Now I know that happiness can only be momentary, since it is part of the order/disorder of life. Because we are part of a Whole that is both 'this' and 'that', nothing can enable us to 'be' happy, that is, to experience a steady state of happiness.

Irresistibly attracted, men and women can rarely enjoy durable relationships. Men thrust themselves into the cosmic tempest, wishing for a haven; women, having overcome their biological limits, aspire to control their lives, and jump into the same maelstrom. But because the world consists of the order/disorder

dyad, as women become stronger, men become weaker, and osmosis can only be fugitive. The relationship movement is about teaching couples to maintain for as long as possible a relatively steady state through counter-balancing. But it wrongly implies that relationships can be permanent. If love and pain partake of the endless movement that is life, how can most relationships be forever?

The biological need to have children, who may eventually hurt us, is also part of the order/disorder of the Whole. At present, we are in the midst of a phase transition in the way society deals with that need. Whether or not women work, couples are likely to be no more permanent than revolutions, so society needs to organize around the principle that children belong to everyone. Children need male and female role models, challenges and nurturing, and tribes probably do that better than nuclear families. The campaign of the *Madres de Mayo* for the *desaparecidos* of the Chilean dictatorship seemed to recognize that.

Both love and suffering are part of the Whole which is. And because relationships are rendered more complex by the interactions of time, history and nature, we can neither do away with evil, nor retain happiness. They are one and eternal, but they are not outside ourselves. They are life, as are we. Pain is like a low cloud, the clap of thunder; but between storms, sun and stars enchant us. Great happiness is brief, but pleasures (which we are wrong to call small), occur every day. Most of the time we experience the indeterminate movement of the reed that bends with the wind, what Eastern wisdom calls calls the in-between. Recognizing this may be a question of education to the Self, not in opposition to the Other, but as part of the Whole. The ability to taste fully all the pleasures of the spirit and the senses and to share those pleasures in various circumstances and in various ways, is part of being with the Whole, making hedonism qualitatively different from the vulgarity that pervades the modern world. Hedonism is the opposite of the ugly commercial license that pervades the Western world, and it has a place in our lives.

If cognition consists in the processing of information, then authority and meaning are within ourselves. When we seek Buddha -

or God - outside ourselves, we place the meaning of life outside ourselves, and give external authority power over our lives. I think the mistake of Buddhists is to deny that the Ego is part of the order/ disorder of the universe, believing that we can separate it from the world through self-help. Gautama Buddha lived at a time when, for most people, life may hardly have been worth living. In our times, in our part of the world, unhappiness is more related to Having than to Being. Sickness is cured almost perfectly; there remain unrequited love and the desire for power. But one love will be followed by another, and the results of a struggle are never final. Only the loss of a loved one cannot be reasoned - the pain is as deep as the joy of his or her presence, because life and death are one.

For me, the ascendancy of Being over Having began with Regina. And when at seventeen I withheld judgment of Bette, whose denunciation changed the course of my life, it was because I sensed there were things I did not know, and that aggression is rarely a will to harm. Now I know that aggression results from interactions and repercussions that are part of the disorder of life. I know that the other shoe always drops, that it always happens to us, and that this is the only way life can be. Life is movement, because disorder must have a slight upper hand for change to occur. Education in hope rather than in reason as a moment in the process of order/disorder, hides Being, leaving us open to the promises of external authority and its deceptions.

Creationism tells us that someone put us here for a purpose, hence we must Do and Have. To this end, internal authority must bow to a myriad of external authorities who step in to regulate the Doing and the Having, placing codified law and the public morality upon which it rests, outside ourselves. But only internal freedom is absolute, therefore our need is for inner morality and public compromise to trace the limits of our external freedom.

Anthropology, the wonderful tale of how we got to be who we are, shows that humans are capable of interacting with the world in a non-dogmatic, non-ideological way. Evolution, through which Being unfolds, takes place through feedback and counter-balancing, and is part of the ongoing reconciliation of seeming opposites that is

life. Serendipitously, when Doing is part of Being, we catch a glimpse of a circular system that hums along from one bifurcation to another.

As a polity, rather than reliving the sixties, I think we need to weigh on the endless process of life, bearing in mind that disorder has neither party, sex, nor territory, and that when we muddle through, it's a question of attitudes rather than rules or laws, wars or treaties. 'Salvation', I think, lies in seeking knowledge, aware that it is never permanent.

If my life shows anything, it is that that one can overcome obstacles without religion, and without external authority. When my mother denied my grief for a lost father, she created a confusion in my mind over what I could control and what I could not. To compensate for my inability to have my needs met by my immediate environment, I thrust myself into a series of external environments. This made it difficult for significant others in my life. My children, in particular, were not served by my failure to make standard choices, as I tried to reconcile my need for involvement in the world with my desire to be present for them.

Had I not been the person I was originally, epitomized first by the enthusiastic child on the sled, then by the girl whose anxiety was masked by a monkey smile, I could never have become the one Ludovico urged me to be. Only an energetic person for whom everything takes on a sense of urgency is likely to wrap her mind around problems. There has probably never been a laid-back philosopher.

Yet had I remained longer with the man who most influenced my life, Raul and Michael would not exist. Other children would probably have been born, and perhaps they would have led happier lives; but these two beings whom I love so deeply, would not have existed.

Having loved Ludovico the Stoic, it was inevitable that I be attracted to Taoism, but it took a lifetime for me to experience the serenity it brings. That process began with an early awareness that no one could take away my freedom, because it was something I carried inside. Ultimately I realized that life has the meaning we give

it, and that we do not so much have to achieve, as to figure out what it's all about. For decades, like Raul and Michael, I was only capable of seeing and feeling what I saw and felt, of wanting what I wanted. I turn, they too have yet to understand that their very existence shows there is no absolute good or bad.

The letters I exchanged with Ludovico reveal a relationship that was profound for each of us in different ways. And ultimately, it was of such good quality that it lasted beyond his death. Many years after we broke up, Ludovico confessed that he had been jealous of the men I had loved after him. But although I mourned his rejection at the time, ultimately I would merely keep a tender corner of my heart for him - its primary place occupied by my children, the world, and other men.

Though he could not imagine the cost, Ludovico hinted that to accept what I could not change, I had to look at things from the outside. That day in Piazza Santa Maria, I could not understand what he was trying to tell me about seeing everything objectively, as in a play. But ultimately, being everywhere an outsider proved an advantage. Starting with Fellini, I was on the inside but could observe as an outsider. In Cuba and Eastern Europe, I was a sympathetic observer, but did not buy into the dogma. Not until twenty years after Ludovico's death did I become an insider, when I developed a non-dogmatic approach to political affairs.

When my peregrinations led me away from him, Ludovico complained that I was becoming someone else, someone who wore different kinds of clothes, suited to other climates and occupations. In a letter written in 1962, he evoked "the last time we made love, about five months ago, and we were disturbed by the arrival in your apartment of that horrible great desk, with its huge drawers, which, I immediately sensed, was going to swallow up what remained of our intimacy. And I was right. Since then, you have taken off to a series of other worlds."

So many worlds, starting with the one Regina evoked for my childhood, and so many tides! With May and Howard gone I can at last own her adopted land. And at a crucial time in the play I've been living and witnessing, I have this to say: order springs from disorder,

that is life, and we can only do our best, with beauty as our consolation for its inevitable chaos.